SHOWME™ GUIDES
OpenCart 1.5 User Manual

NOTICES

ShowMe™ Guides OpenCart 1.5 User Manual

©2012 Kerry Watson
OSCManuals.com

Printed in the USA January 1012

REVISED MARCH 2012 TO VERSION 1.5.2

TRADEMARKS & INTELLECTUAL PROPERTY

All terms mentioned in this book that are known to be trademarks or service marks have been appropriately denoted as of date of publication. Pithy Productions cannot attest to the accuracy of the information, and the information may change. Use of a mark in this book should not be regarded as affecting the validity of any trademark or service mark. Pithy Productions and ShowMe Guides are trademarks of Pithy Productions, Inc.

WARNING AND DISCLAIMER

Notice to Consumers

About the ShowMe™ Guides Series: "Everything you need to know"

The **ShowMe™ Guide Series covers everything that a new, non-technical store owner needs to know to open an online store**. Each task is rated from easy to difficult. If a task should be handled by a programmer, we say that. If you can get it done for free somewhere, we tell you that too.

Every book in the series is based on an ACTUAL install & setup of a full ecommerce store. You see before-and-after shots with a screenshot of the ACTUAL settings that work for that screenshot.

The most valuable part is the HOT TIPS for non-intuitive steps. You could buy our book just for the tips and get your money's worth.

All our books have a 100% no questions asked, full money-back guarantee for any reason.

All books in this series are arranged as follows:

- Quick Install & 30-Minute Quick Setup Guide
- Guide to the Menus
- Advanced Task Information, and
- Helpful Resources.

WE KNOW YOU ARE BUSY!

Our books are NOT loaded with page after page of the history of the Internet or filler material. We cover everything you MUST know, and nothing you don't.

About the author

Kerry Watson joined the Open Source movement in 1996 as the Producer for the Netscape Navigator website. There her mission was to make the Netscape browser accessible to everyday users, not just technical users, and she wrote plain-language tutorials such as Netscape Navigator for Internet Explorer Users and Netscape Tips & Tricks. Previously she was a vice president of an e-commerce turnkey outsourcing company like PayPal, years ahead of its time.

In 1999 Kerry founded Pithy Productions, Inc., a web project management company that specializes in ecommerce websites. Today she is a full-time writer specializing in open source ecommerce topics, an ecommerce columnist for Practical Ecommerce (www.PracticalEcommerce.com) and author of well over a dozen books on various open source ecommerce programs.

 # Tips for using this book:

1. This book is for new OpenCart users who have NO graphics or programming skills. All you have is product photos and a store logo, and a willingness to try something new.
2. Have your first store installed for you for FREE by a web host that SPECIALIZES in OpenCart web hosting. We list these hosts in the Appendix.
3. Print a copy of the Admin Menus Cheatsheet to quickly find each menu.
4. Follow the 30 Minute Quick Start Guide chapter to quickly work through each feature that MUST be set up for your store to operate.
5. Then use the Table of Contents to find specific information by task or menu name, and the INDEX in the back to quickly find every place a menu is discussed.
6. This book explains the way that is easiest for new users. You may know other ways to finish a task; be creative. Even advanced users and programmers will find this book a handy shortcut to quickly find what you want to do.

Other helpful books in this series

These books will be especially useful to OpenCart store owners:

**Using Power Tools with
Open Source Commerce Programs**

You don't need special skills or tools to start an OpenCart store, but after you have some experience you may want to roll up your sleeves and get into the advanced stuff. The tools in this book sure make life easier! It's like using a power saw instead of a hand saw.

The Power Tools I teach you how to use are:

- **cPanel Control Panel** used by many web hosts
- **Dreamweaver** HTML Editor for backup and editing
- **Photosho**p **and PaintShop Pro** (the menus are almost identical, any differences are pointed out!)
- **FTP Program FileZilla** to quickly upload and download files and/or change file permissions, and
- The compression program **WinZip.**

You can spend many hours trying to learn this stuff yourself by feel. OR, you can simply get this book.

Managing an Online Business

If you've just been handed the keys -- err, password -- to a new online store and don't have the faintest idea what to do, this book is for you. This book is a NON-technical guide to the *business strategy of running an ongoing online store*. It has specific information for OpenCart users, including such topics as:

- Search Engine Strategy
- Website Project Management, Testing & Acceptance
- Growing and Getting Help: Fulfillment, Warehousing, and Shipping Services
- Executive Management Decisions: Dealing with complaints, FRAUD, Setting Policies, Reporting

Icons used in this book:

 TIME SAVING TIP: Like a menu or button that is hard to see, or has an unexpected name, or something else.

 CAUTION: Follow directions exactly, this is easy to mess up!

 ADD-ONS: This is bonus information about an add-on contribution that could make running your store MUCH easier.

Win a free ebook!

Are you a fan? Do you love our books? TELL THE WORLD and win a chance for a free ebook of your choice! One free ebook will be awarded daily! No purchase required. LIKE us on Facebook, TWEET about us, DIGG us, tell a friend about us by email, or give a nice review on AMAZON.COM.

SEE website for details: http://oscmanuals.com/p28/WIN-A-FREE-EBOOK!/pages.html

Feedback, please!

If you have puzzled over ANY part of this book, please help so others do not have to! I welcome your comments. Please send me a quick note to talkback@oscmanuals.com. Each reader who sends feedback is automatically entered into the FREE EBOOKS OFFER Contest.

Sincerely,
KERRY WATSON

Table of Contents

SEE ALSO the Index at the back of the book for an exhaustive keyword listing of topics.

1. OpenCart User Manual Introduction

What is OpenCart?

OpenCart is an easy to-use, powerful, Open Source* online store management program that can manage multiple online stores from a single back-end Administrative area simply by filling in forms and clicking "Save." There are many professionally-written extensions available to customize the store to your needs.

An OpenCart store can be ready to take orders soon after installation. All you have to do is have it installed for you (any web hosts do it for free), select a template from the many free or low-cost template sites, add your product descriptions and photos, click a few settings, and you are ready to begin accepting orders. Our free Installation & Quick Start chapters show you how.

The public side or "Storefront" of OpenCart looks very professional and ready to sell almost as soon as it is installed:

The store is managed by logging into a private Administration panel or "Admin" and filling in form boxes. The OpenCart Admin is intuitively organized and pleasing to use:

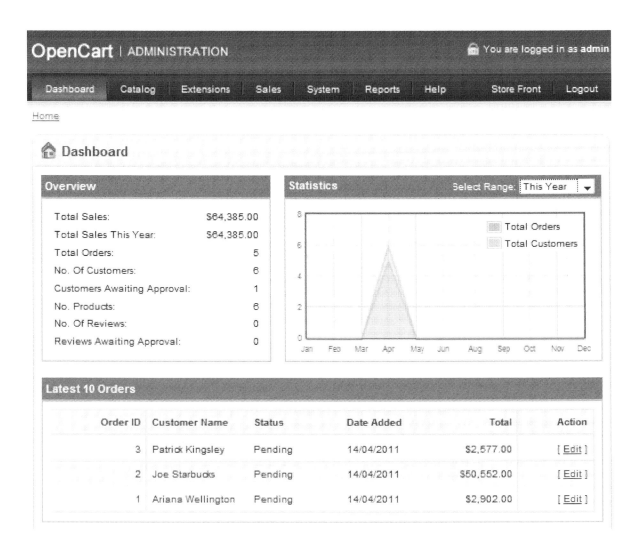

Admin Menu Cheatsheet

The next page is the Admin Menu Cheatsheet showing the above dashboard with all menus fully extended so you can find any item easily. Download a printable copy of this admin cheatsheet from http://OSCManuals.com/download/opencart/OpenCart-Admin-Menu-Cheatsheet.pdf

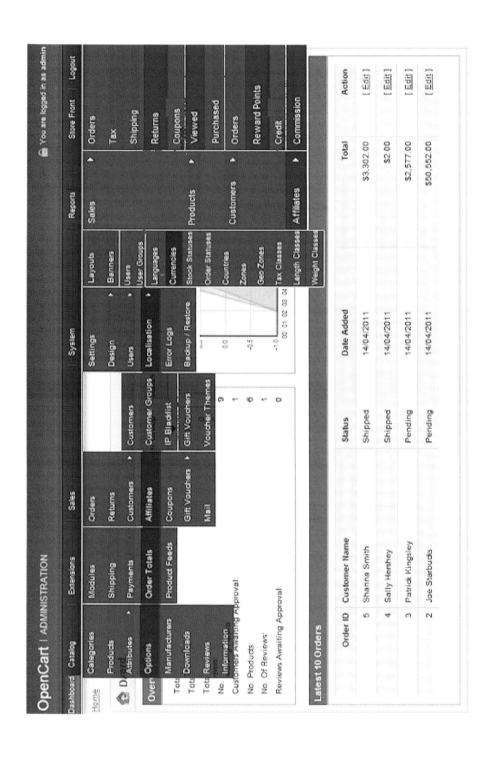

Features of OpenCart 1.5

- Very marketing-oriented, with features you can use right away to sell more products.
- User-friendly administration using your web browser and filling in forms
- Add/Edit/Remove categories, products, manufacturers, customers, and reviews
- Built-in payment gateways
- Unlimited Categories
- Unlimited Products
- Unlimited Manufacturers
- Templates
- Multi-Language
- Multi-Currency
- Product Reviews
- Product Ratings
- Downloadable Products
- Automatic Image Resizing
- Multiple Tax Rates
- Related Products
- Unlimited Information Pages
- Shipping Weight Calculation
- Discount Coupon System
- Search Engine Optimization (SEO)
- Module System
- Backup & Restore Tools
- Printable Invoices
- Sales Reports
- Fraud Control features Ban IP Address, MaxMind

B2B features

- Customer Groups (wholesale, employees, clubs)
- Quantity discounts
- Log in to display prices
- Guest checkout (no account required)

What's New in OpenCart?

Versions 1.5.1 through Version 1.5.2 have added the following advanced features:

- Reward Points System - award points for each product purchased, customers can redeem for additional merchandise.
- RMA System (Return Management Authorization) - manage customer returns and credits.
- Grid and List Product listings in store - customers can view products in list or grid.
- Gift Voucher System - customers can purchase gift certificates for another customer to use in your store.
- Google Analytics Integration – no need to install separate extension, now in SYSTEM – Settings – Server.
- Credit System - store credit that can be used during checkout.
- Reorder System - customers can quickly reorder a previous purchase.
- Wish List System - customers can add items to a wish list, move items to cart at any time.
- Affiliate System - allow other websites to refer customers to you for a commission.
- Optional Text Fields - customers can type instructions for customizing a product such as their initials or name.
- Banner Manager - easily change the slide show or large banner on the home page.
- One-Page Checkout - customers never leave the checkout screen; each section of the page slides open and shut.
- List View and Grid View – customers can change the view by clicking Display – List/Grid at top left of shopping page.
- Easy Reorder System – customers can log in, view order history, and hit REORDER.
- Wish List System - Items on Wish List can be moved to cart at any time.
- Order Editing System added in version 1.5.2 - EASY for store administrators to place an order for the customer using the Admin.
- MaxMind anti-fraud system added in version 1.5.2 - see maxmind.com. Located in menu System - Settings - new Fraud Tab.
- Ban customers by IP Address added in version 1.5.2 to help prevent fraud, located in menu Sales - Customers - IP Blacklist.
- Google Base availability tag added in version 1.5.2 - a behind-the-scenes improvement in the functioning of Google Product uploads, no menu changes.
- Mass mail system improvements added in version 1.5.2 - can now send emails unlimited by the program in Sales – Mail. No menu changes.
- Buttons are now images or links added in version 1.5.2 - so users can hit return to submit forms. No menu changes.

History of OpenCart

OpenCart is the brainchild of 35 year old Daniel Kerr, a talented developer from Blackpool, England who just couldn't find that perfect system, so he made his own. He had been involved in osCommerce development from 2003 to 2005, writing a number of contributions or add-on extensions to the program, but like many became frustrated with the slow rate of development. Today Kerr is an expat living with his family in Hong Kong.

Kerr's goals were to make the new OpenCart a lean, clean small ecommerce program that uses about 90% less code that other shopping carts, a template system, virtual or "search engine-friendly" URLs, valid XHTML and CSS. osCommerce was none of these things.

OpenCart was under development from late 2005 until January 2009, when the first public version 1.0 was released. Since then approximately 50 full and partial or "patch" versions have been released, with 1.5.2.1 the current version released in March, 2012.

*"Open Source" software is software whose code is available for users to *look at and modify freely.* It does not mean free cost! Many popular Internet programs in widespread use today are open source, including Linux, PHP, MySQL and Apache servers.

2

2. OpenCart Quick Install Guide

Installing a web-based program is not as easy as auto-installing a program on your Windows or Apple computer. You don't just pop in a DVD and click "Install." You need the skills or patience to create a database, set file security permissions, and to work with files with long path names.

Thankfully, there are many web hosts who can install your OpenCart store for you, either when you sign up for hosting or with a one-click installer called Softaculous, or a "semi-manual" install using a web host's cPanel Control Panel.

Method 1: FREE installation by your web host

Some web hosts will install your program for free, such as Arvixe the official OpenCart web host. They are specifically set up for easy OpenCart hosting!

TIP: Arvixe web hosting *offers everything an OpenCart store needs: 24/7 great tech support, unlimited space, free domain name, free SSL install, only $4.00 per month for secure ecommerce hosting! SEE APPENDIX for details on how to get the exact right account setup you need.*

OR see the full list of recommended OpenCart web hosts in Appendix A.

That's it! They do it all for you! But if that's too easy for you, then continue below.

Method 2: One Click Install with Softaculous Premium

OpenCart is included in the semi-automated installer program called Softaculous Premium (it currently is included only in the premium version). Find a web host that offers Softaculous Premium (See the list in Appendix A) and install as follows:

Log onto your cPanel control panel using the login information from your web host's Welcome email. Contact your web host if you need help finding this.

Find the box named Software/Services and double-click the icon named "Softaculous" to start. Note that the box and icons may look different on your web host, and be in a different order:

From the list of program types, click E-COMMERCE, then click the link OPENCART:

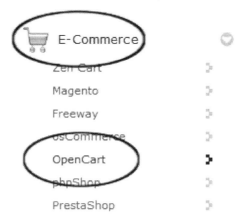

Now you see a long form named "Software Setup." See the detail below this screenshot for instructions:

Software Setup

Choose Protocol
If your site has SSL, then please choose the HTTPS protocol.

`http://`

Choose Domain
Please choose the domain to install the software.

`smithantiquesllc.com`

In Directory
The directory is relative to your domain and **should not exist.** e.g. To install at http://mydomain/dir/ just type **dir.** To install only in http://mydomain/ leave this empty.

Database Name
Type the name of the database to be created for the installation

`opencart`

Store Settings

Store Name `Smith Antiques`

Store Description `Unrestored treasures from the 18th century`

Store Owner `Smith Antiques, LLC`

Store Address `123 45th Street My City, OH 12345`

Database Settings

Table Prefix `store_`

Admin Account

Admin Username `Robin`

Admin Password `A long random password`

Admin Email `robin@gmail.com`

First Name `Robin`

Last Name `Smith`

[Install]

SOFTWARE SETUP

Choose Protocol:
Choose Domain:
In Directory:
Database Name:

Your web host should have installed https for security. If not, ask them to do it now.
Select your domain name from the drop-down box.
If you want to install several programs (such as a blog) choose a folder name like "store" or "shop," otherwise leave blank.
Give your database a name that helps you identify it, such as "opencart" or "store."

STORE SETTINGS

Store Name:
Store Description:
Store Owner:
Store Address:

This information displays on your CONTACT US page and/or for search engines, see example below.
The name you want to display on the Contact Us page.
A description that search engines will use to help people find you.
Name of store owner or company for Contact Us page.
Address customers can use to send mail to you.

DATABASE SETTINGS

Table Prefix:

In case you have a shared server or more than one database, a prefix is required to help identify it. Choose a prefix of your choice; if your host requires it, the prefix will already be filled in for you.

ADMIN ACCOUNT

Admin Username:
Admin Password:
Admin Email:
First Name:
Last Name:

The username you will use to log into your store.
The password you will use to log into your store. A long phrase that is easily remembered by only you, with numbers, capitalization, and punctuation, is best.
The email address you wish to use if you forget your password, also to receive store notices that will automatically be sent to you.
Your first and last names, for store notices that will automatically be sent to you.

Store Settings displayed on the Contact Us page:

After you finish filling in the long form, at the bottom of the page, click the INSTALL Button. After a minute, you will see a "Success screen" like the following:

Congratulations, the software was installed successfully

OpenCart has been successfully installed at : http://www.smithantiquesllc.com/

Administrative URL : https://www.smithantiquesllc.com/admin/

We hope the installation process was easy.

NOTE: Softaculous is just an automatic software installer and does not provide any support for the individual software packages. Please visit the software vendor's web site for support!

Regards,
Softaculous Auto Installer

Return to Overview

TIP: For help with a Softaculous installation, search the Softaculous support forum at http://www.softaculous.com/board/

Method 3: Do-It-Yourself (DIY) with a cPanel web host

Before you begin, check with your prospective web host to be sure OpenCart will work on their servers. If they are not familiar with OpenCart technical specs, tell your host you need the following:

- Apache Web Server
- PHP 5.2 or higher
- MySQL
- Curl
- Fsock

You will also need to have purchased a domain name from a domain name registrar. For help in domain name strategy, see our book "How to Manage an Online Business with Open Source eCommerce."

Check off each item as you complete it.

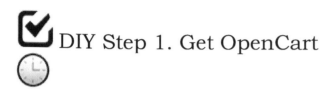

DIY Step 1. Get OpenCart

Get your FREE copy of OpenCart from the OpenCart.com website at http://www.opencart.com/index.php?route=download/download.

Download the most recent full version (the highest release number, example 1.5.2).

Click the DOWNLOAD link and save the file where you can easily remember - to your downloads directory or to your desktop.

TIP: Write down where you put the zip file, as you will need it for the next step.

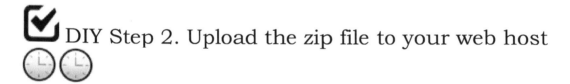

DIY Step 2. Upload the zip file to your web host

Log onto your web host's cPanel Home page, and click the FILE MANAGER link.

TIP: If you have difficulty locating cPanel's File Manager on cPanel's very long Home page, you can also click CTRL-F and type "File Manager" or use the "FIND" box in the top left of the cPanel Home screen.

In cPanel's File Manager, click the UPLOAD Button. This brings you to the Upload Files screen:

⬆ Upload files

Maximum file size allowed for upload: 500 MB

Please select files to upload to **/home/public_html/myopencartstore**

C:\Users\Kerry\Downloads\opencart_v1.4.9.4.zip	Browse_
	Browse_
	Browse_

Overwrite existing files: ☐

⊕ Add Another Upload Box

Back to /home/public_html/myopencartstore

Click the BROWSE Button to find where you saved the zip file. It will automatically begin uploading to your web host.

When it has finished uploading, click the link **Back to /home/public_html*** to return to the File Manager.

*Your web host's path may be slightly different - example, /www/ or /default/ or /home/. Just click the "BACK TO" link.

☑ DIY Step 3. Create your database

In order for the OpenCart installer to set up your database, you must make an empty database for it to fill. You will use cPanel's Database Wizard to:

- Create an empty database
- Create a database user, and
- Assign a user and permissions to the database.

In your web host's cPanel Home page, scroll down to the "DATABASES" section and click the MySQL Database Wizard:

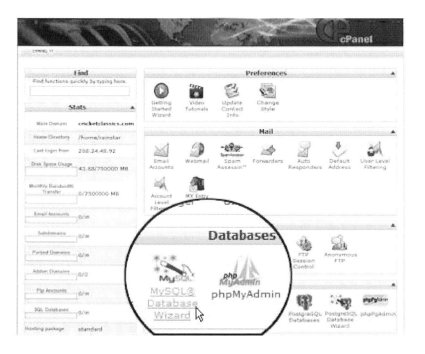

This easy Wizard will help you create the database.

Create Database Step 1: Make up a name for your database. Don't worry; the Wizard will tell you if you have used an incorrect character, or if the name you chose is too long or short. Then click the Next Step button:

TIP: The database name is not going to be exactly this name - the Wizard will assign an account prefix based on your web host's setup. For example, my account name is myopencartstore, so the database in this example will actually be named myopencartstore_mydatabase.

Create Database Step 2: Create a username, any name seven characters or less, and a password, then click the Next Step button:

TIP: Click the "Generate Password" Button to have the Wizard create a very secure, random password for you.

Step 2: Create Database Users:

Username:	AnyName	*Seven characters max
Password:	•••••••••••	
	Password Strength:	
	OK	
Password (Again):	•••••••••••	
	Next Step	

Create Database Step 3: Specify what privileges this user will have. You want this database user to have ALL PRIVILEGES, so be sure to check the ALL PRIVILEGES box, then click the Next Step button:

Step 3: Add User to the Database

User: **AnyName**
Database: **mystore_mydatabase**

☑ ALL PRIVILEGES	
☑ SELECT	☑ CREATE
☑ INSERT	☑ ALTER
☑ UPDATE	☑ DROP
☑ DELETE	☑ LOCK TABLES
☑ INDEX	☑ REFERENCES
☑ CREATE TEMPORARY TABLES	☐ CREATE ROUTINE

Next Step

Create Database Step 4: Print the MySQL Database Summary page:

 TIP: Notice the extra pieces of vital database information circled above - you did not enter this, it is your web host's SERVERNAME. You will need all four circled pieces of information for the next step!

 TIP: By default the server name is commonly named localhost, so if you do not see the circled message in your cPanel MySQL Database Wizard, try using localhost for the server name before contacting your web host for more help.

 Leave this window open to copy and paste the information directly, being careful to not copy any spaces before or after.

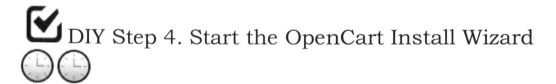 DIY Step 4. Start the OpenCart Install Wizard

Using your web browser, go to the following address:
http://www.yourdomainname.com/install/

If you have any problems finding the install folder, please check your web host's "Welcome Email" and then with your web host.

 TIP: If your domain name is new, it may not be active yet – it can take up to 72 hours. Instead, you can use your "IP Address" to install the program. If your website's IP Address is not listed in your web host's Welcome email, contact your web host's support department for your site's exact IP address.

 If you are copying and pasting information into your install screens and have trouble, check to be sure you are not pasting extra SPACES at the beginning or end of the words.

 If you see an error message instead of the Welcome screen, then your web host's server is not set up correctly for installing OpenCart. Contact your web host to see if they can change anything for you. If not, you will need to install at a different web host.

OpenCart Install Wizard Screens

Install Wizard Step 1 - License

Read the license, check the box "I agree to the license" and click the CONTINUE Button:

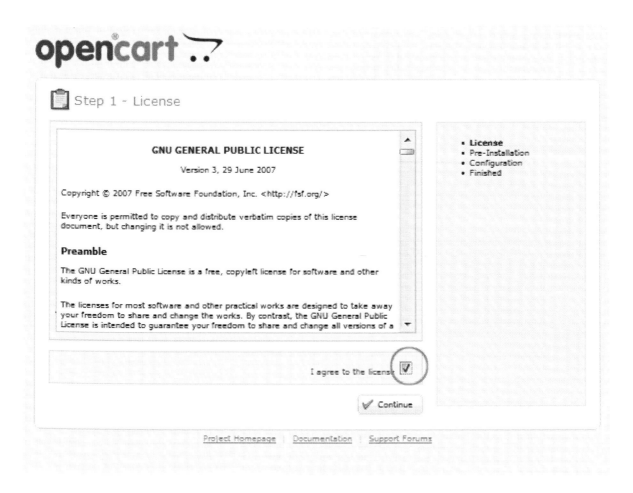

Install Wizard Step 2 - Pre-installation Check

The Wizard checks to see if your web server has everything needed to proceed so you won't have difficulty during installation.

Every item should have a green checkmark in the "STATUS" column:

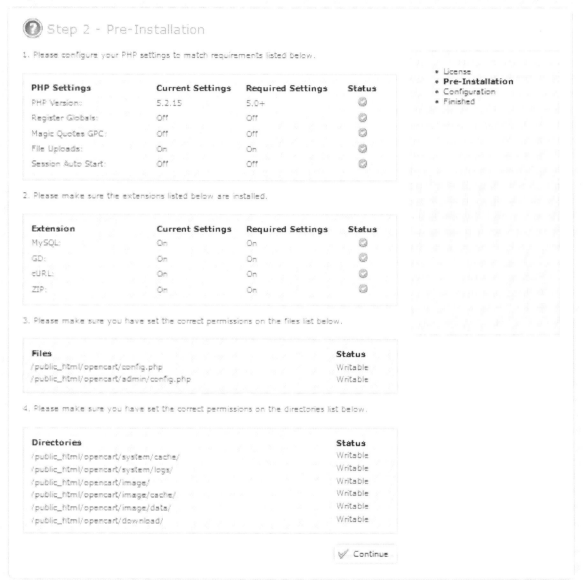

opencart

Step 2 - Pre-Installation

1. Please configure your PHP settings to match requirements listed below.

- License
- **Pre-Installation**
- Configuration
- Finished

PHP Settings	Current Settings	Required Settings	Status
PHP Version:	5.2.15	5.0+	✓
Register Globals:	Off	Off	✓
Magic Quotes GPC:	Off	Off	✓
File Uploads:	On	On	✓
Session Auto Start:	Off	Off	✓

2. Please make sure the extensions listed below are installed.

Extension	Current Settings	Required Settings	Status
MySQL:	On	On	✓
GD:	On	On	✓
cURL:	On	On	✓
ZIP:	On	On	✓

3. Please make sure you have set the correct permissions on the files list below.

Files	Status
/public_html/opencart/config.php	Writable
/public_html/opencart/admin/config.php	Writable

4. Please make sure you have set the correct permissions on the directories list below.

Directories	Status
/public_html/opencart/system/cache/	Writable
/public_html/opencart/system/logs/	Writable
/public_html/opencart/image/	Writable
/public_html/opencart/image/cache/	Writable
/public_html/opencart/image/data/	Writable
/public_html/opencart/download/	Writable

✓ Continue

TIP: If any Required Extensions or Required Settings are not enabled, then contact your web host to see if they can be changed for you. If they say they cannot, you will need to stop here and find a new web host. ALL hosts in Appendix A are set up correctly for OpenCart web hosting.

If any files or directories on Step 2 – Pre-Installation do not show a status of "Writeable," go back to the cPanel File Manager, click to the folder name, and in the "Perms" (Permissions) column change the setting to 755 and click the SAVE Button:

	Name	Size	Type	Perms
📁	cache	4 KB	httpd/unix-directory	0755
📁	config	4 KB	httpd/unix-directory	Save
📁	database	4 KB	httpd/unix-directory	Cancel
📁	engine	4 KB	httpd/unix-directory	0755
📁	helper	4 KB	httpd/unix-directory	0755
📁	library	4 KB	httpd/unix-directory	0755
📁	logs	4 KB	httpd/unix-directory	0755
PHP	startup.php	2.61 KB	application/x-httpd-php	0644

Install Wizard Step 3 - Configuration

Enter the database information exactly as you entered it in the Database Wizard.

 TIP: Don't close this window! Simply minimize your browser and hit the REFRESH button each time you make a change, to check your progress.

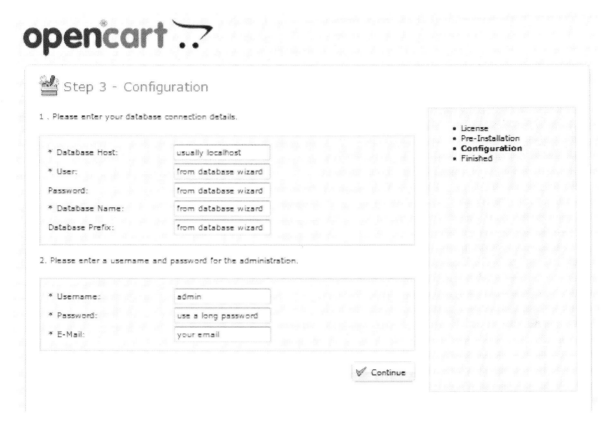

Choose a username and password you want to use when you administer your store, and enter the email address where you want to receive confirmations or password reminders. Click the CONTINUE Button.

Install Wizard Step 4 - Finished!

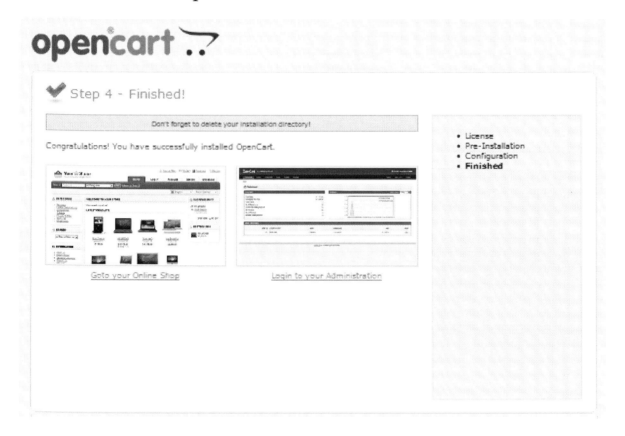

Click the GO TO YOUR ONLINE SHOP Link to see your new store in your browser, and immediately BOOKMARK it or add it to your Favorites list.

To begin setting up your new store, click the LOGIN TO YOUR ADMINISTRATION Link and log on with the info you entered in Step 3.

 CAUTION: If you do not delete the install directory and you later get hacked, they may be able to change your username and password, among other horrible, horrible things!

Install Step 5. Reset Security and Permissions

Using cPanel's File Manager for the three items in this section, you MUST do the following.

SECURITY WARNING: You MUST delete the Install folder AND change the permissions on your configuration files as instructed below, or your store will be a security risk.

Do this:	To folder:
A **For security,** DELETE the Install folder. In cPanel's File Manager, RIGHT-click the file name, then select DELETE from the drop-down menu.	**install**
B **For security,** change configuration file permissions **to 444** (0444) so only you, the owner, can read and write, and all others can read-only:	**config.php**
C **For security,** change ADMIN configuration file permissions **to 444** (0444) so only you, the owner, can read and write, and all others can read-only:	**admin/config.php**

Install Step 6. Installation Problem-Solving

If you've had any difficulty with your installation, and have no typos, check again to be sure that you have set the appropriate file permissions for each folder or directory that requires it. That usually fixes 99% of installation problems.

Installation Help

1. Read your Manual.
2. Ask your OpenCart web host.
3. Go to the technical forum at http://forum.opencart.com/ and SEARCH for a similar problem.
4. When all else fails, pay for technical support. See Appendix A for recommended technical pros.

3

3. OpenCart 30-Minute QuickStart Guide

After you have installed your store OR had your store installed for you, you are ready to do a Quick Start! This covers everything you absolutely MUST do to get an OpenCart store up and running. Get your product photos and store logo, and let's begin.

If you have any difficulty, contact your installer.

Log onto your new OpenCart "Admin" for the first time

Using your web browser such as Internet Explorer, go to the following address: http://www.yourdomainname.com/admin.

This brings you to your new Administration Login Panel:

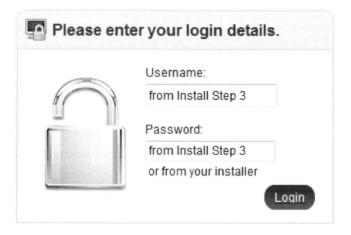

ENTER the email address and password you selected during installation Step 3, or from your installer.

TIP: If you forget the password, click "Password forgotten?" and look for a message at the email address you gave during installation.

If you haven't already, BOOKMARK your new Admin page or add it to your browser's "FAVORITES" List NOW! You will be going there every day from now on.

This brings you to your new **Administration Home Page:**

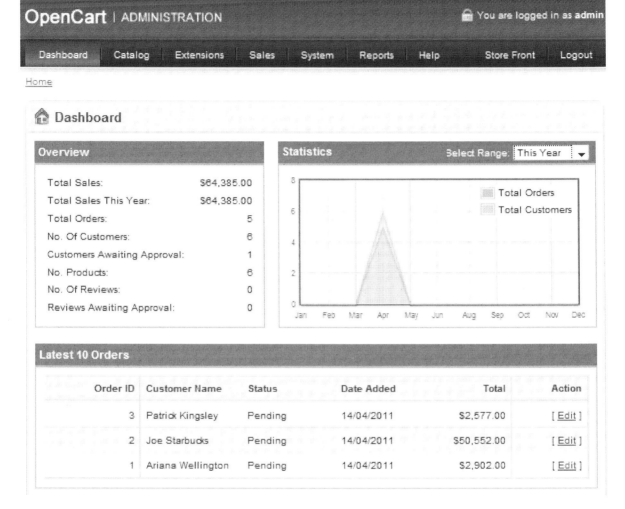

 TIP: The instructions in this book just use the address "yourstorename.com/admin" but if your store admin uses "store" "shop" or something similar, just substitute the correct address each time.

 TIP: It's easiest to open TWO browser windows - one on your Admin, and the other displaying your "Store Front" so you can quickly view the changes you make and see what your customers will see.

How to use your new Administration Panel or "Admin"

To make changes to your store in OpenCart, after logging in you will use the top navigation bar to select the menu you want to change. Example: product categories.

The menu generally brings you to a LIST of all existing items. Example: "Categories" brings you to a list of all existing (sample) categories.

To add a new item to the list, you will click a button labeled "INSERT" in the top right corner of the List. This brings you to a blank form.

You simply fill in the form following the screenshots in this book, and click the SAVE Button. Voila! The Admin does all the programming for you.

TIP: There is ALWAYS a SAVE Button that you must click when you finish a form!

Quick Start Checklist:

The following menus MUST be edited when you first set up your store, and are covered here in this Quick Start Guide:

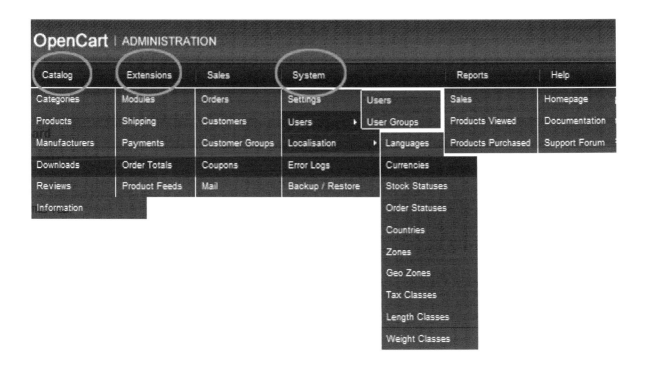

1. **CATALOG menu:** You will fill in forms about at least one product to display in your store; you will add or edit Information for the Information InfoBox such as About Us, Privacy, and Terms & Conditions as easily as typing an email. Delete the sample products and categories.
2. **EXTENSIONS menu:** Fill in forms about optional home page Welcome, shipping and payments vendors you will use; select screens that will display to customers during checkout.
3. **SYSTEM menu:** Fill in forms about important settings, upload your own store logo, set the store location (localization), and set other important options.

There are also many *optional* forms that are covered in later, detailed chapters of this book. For now, we just want to get you up and operating as quickly and easily as possible.

 1. CATALOG menu: Enter your product and category information

Before your product categories will appear in the top navigation bar in your store, you must first create the categories.

The **Category** Name is the link that will display to customers in the Categories box of your store. It is like a department in a non-online store. The sample categories are included with your store to help you see how to fill in the forms. Look around them to get ideas for your own store.

 Do you have dozens or hundreds of products, categories, and images to enter? If so, download the Export/Import Tool extension to add your products and images in one batch. Ask your installer to set it up for you. http://www.opencart.com/index.php?route=extension/ extension/info&extension_id=17.

To enter your product and category information, in your store's Admin, from the Top Bar Navigation Menu, select CATALOG - Categories.

In this example below, we have already inserted a sample category, Chairs:

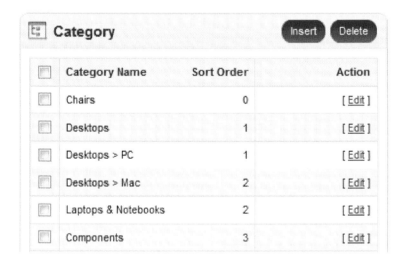

☑ Add your first category:

At the top right of the CATALOG - Categories page, click the INSERT Button (circled above), and fill in information in the GENERAL Tab as shown in the example below:

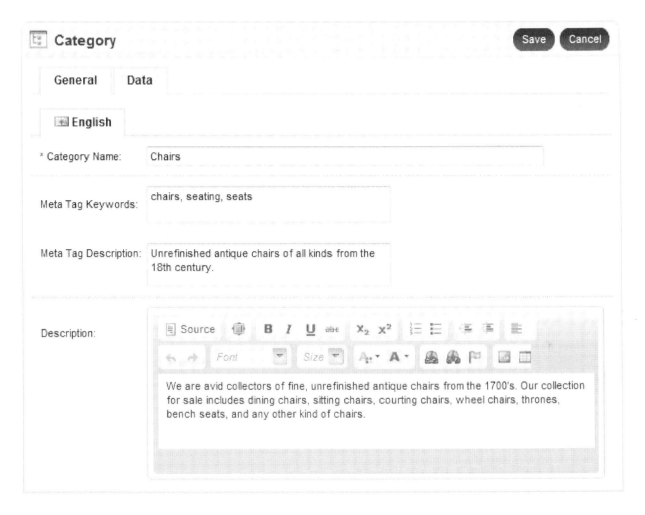

Next, near the top left, click the DATA Tab to select and/or upload a product image. OPTIONAL: Edit as shown below if you wish to make this category a sub-category; display in more than one online store at this web host; add search engine keywords; upload a category image from your computer OR select a category image from the web server; hide the category by selecting DISABLED; or move it up or down in the CATEGORIES InfoBox by changing the SORT ORDER:

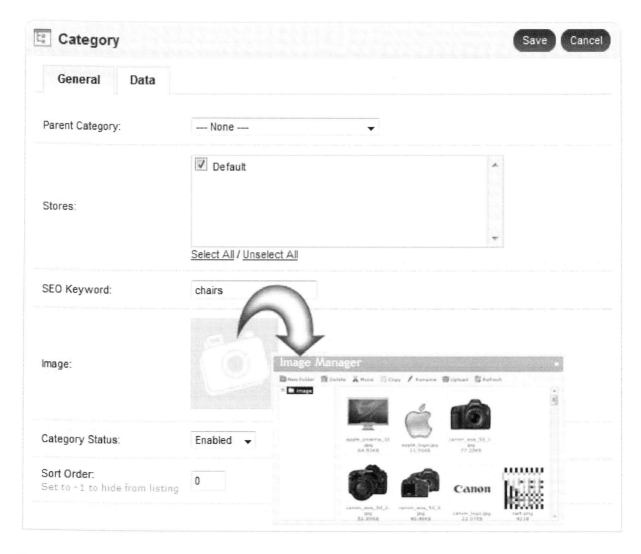

Be sure to SAVE your new category: at the top right, click the SAVE Button.

Look at your new category in your store - what your customer sees - before continuing. To look at your new category, open ANOTHER window in your browser like Internet Explorer by using the command CTRL-N, type the address of your store, then click the new category link you see in the Category InfoBox.

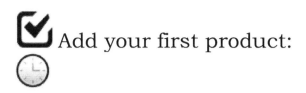

Add your first product:

In your store Admin's CATALOG - Products page, near the top right, click the INSERT Button. Note that many tabs are OPTIONAL. For a **Quick Start,** follow this example for the GENERAL Tab:

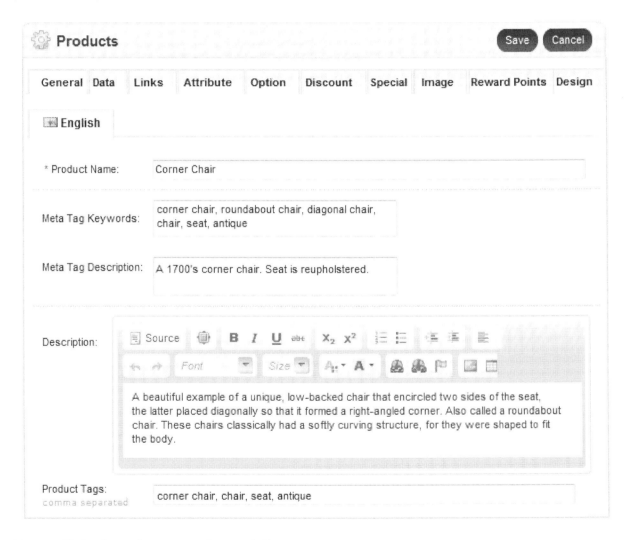

Next, click the other top tabs as follows:

DATA Tab: at a minimum enter product price, if taxable select TAXABLE GOODS, and you must enter the product's weight and weight class (pounds or kilos) for shipping calculations, and upload or select an image.

LINKS Tab: Put a check mark in the category where you want it to appear.

OTHER Tabs: Optional for a Quick Start, see PRODUCTS chapter for detailed info. You can always come back and modify!

IMPORTANT! IF you fail to specify a product weight, or if you enter a weight of zero, the program thinks it is a downloadable product and will NOT charge shipping!

For detailed assistance, and lots more pictures, or if you need to set up product OPTIONS such as sizes or colors, turn to the PRODUCT MANAGEMENT chapter or contact your installer for help.

 Add or edit your information pages

Next, add or edit information for the Information box such as About Us, Privacy, and Terms & Conditions as easily as typing an email.

Your Home Page "Welcome Message" is edited in the EXTENSIONS - MODULES Menu in the next step. Only the Information pages are edited here.

These boxes are surprisingly similar to the Product Information pages, so refer to that section above for more instructions:

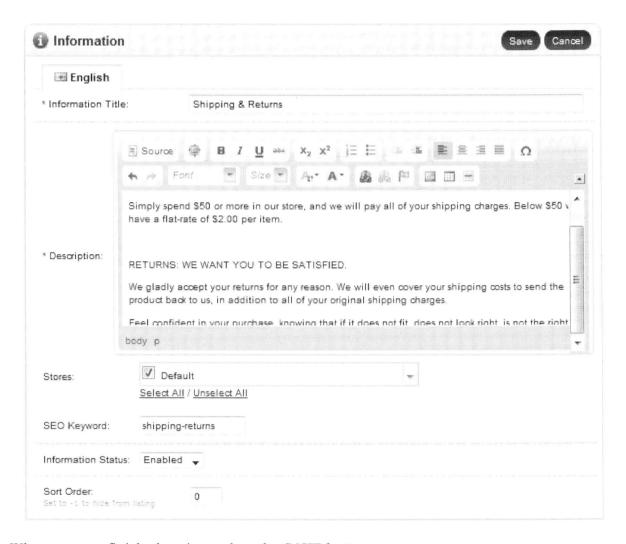

When you are finished typing, select the **SAVE button.**

Last item in step 1, delete the sample products and categories when you are finished referring to them OR before you launch your store. From the Admin's Top Navigation Bar, select CATALOG - CATEGORIES. Put a CHECK next to all categories you wish to delete, then near the top right click the DELETE Button. It asks you if you are sure, because it cannot be undone. If you are sure, click YES.

Don't forget to test, test, test! Pretend you are a customer shopping on your store, register as a new customer and navigate to your new category and product.

2. EXTENSIONS menu: Welcome, Shipping, Payments, and Order Totals

Fill in forms about the shipping and payments vendors you will use; select screens that will display during checkout in the Order Totals menu. Your store is set to charge a flat-rate per order for shipping, and "Cash on Delivery" for payment.

Extensions - Modules - Welcome Module

Insert or edit Home page welcome text, "Welcome to my store!" This text is optional and does not need to be installed unless you want it.

From the main Admin menu, select **EXTENSIONS – Modules.** Find the WELCOME Module in the list and click INSTALL, then EDIT. Type the information like you were typing an email. Click the SAVE Button when you are finished.

Take a look at the other modules, you can click INSTALL to view them (open a new window and look at your storefront) and then UNINSTALL to make them go away. The prompt that says "This cannot be undone!" means that the words you typed in the box will be deleted, NOT that the Welcome module part of the program will be deleted. You will have to re-type the words if you re-install.

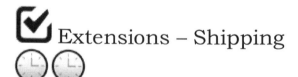Extensions – Shipping

For your customers' shipping charges to automatically be calculated online, you need to link to a shipping vendor.
If you do not yet have a shipping vendor, you can select, for example, a Flat Rate per Order of $5 or Per Item of $3 to charge fees you specify, and process your shipping offline using any shipper you wish. Here we show you how to change these easy shipping methods and to change the fees.

For product testing purposes, many store owners use the "Free Shipping" module, then disable it when they are finished testing.
See detailed instructions including rates and contact information in the detailed chapters.
From the main Admin menu, select **EXTENSIONS – Shipping**. "FLAT RATE" is enabled by default:

Shipping

Shipping Method	Status	Sort Order	Action
Citylink	Disabled		[Install]
Flat Rate	Enabled	1	[Edit] [Uninstall]
Free Shipping	Disabled		[Install]
Per Item	Disabled		[Install]
Parcelforce 48	Disabled		[Install]
Pickup From Store	Disabled		[Install]
Royal Mail	Disabled		[Install]
UPS	Disabled		[Install]
United States Postal Service	Disabled		[Install]
Weight Based Shipping	Disabled		[Install]

Click INSTALL and then EDIT for each method you wish to use (or examine) and follow the instructions, as shown in the Flat Rate example below. NOTE that "PER ITEM" shipping screen looks identical to this screenshot:

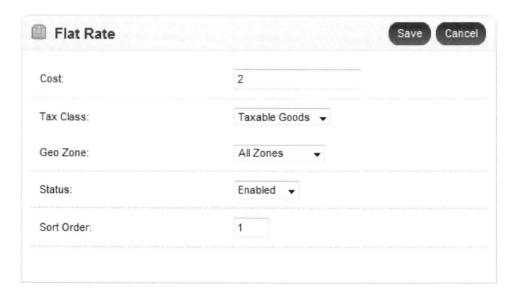

COST: This is the flat rate that will be charged for each customer ORDER. If your currency is in dollars, the Cost of "2" means $2. If your currency is other, it is 2 of your currency. NOTE: The currency unit will be set later in SYSTEM - LOCALIZATION.

TAX CLASS: If you are required to collect tax on SHIPPING in addition to product cost, select TAXABLE goods. Otherwise, select NONE from the drop-down box.

GEO ZONE: If you wish to charge a flat-rate only in certain shipping locations, select it here.

STATUS: If you want this shipping method to be active on your store, select ENABLED. To hide it, select DISABLED.

SORT ORDER: If you are offering customers multiple shipping methods from which to choose, and wish this method to be displayed first, enter a 1. To display second, enter a 2, and so forth.

Click the **SAVE Button** when you are finished setting up shipping vendor information.

Extensions - Payment

For your customers to pay online, you must link to a third-party online credit card processor. About twenty different methods are included with OpenCart, and over a hundred more extensions are available for a small fee on the OpenCart website Extensions Directory at http://www.opencart.com/index.php?route=extension/extension&path=3&sort=e.date_modified&order=DESC.

OpenCart can automatically link to many processors, including the popular and easy PayPal. If your online revenue is less than $1,000 per month, PayPal Standard is cheaper and easier because they only charge for each actual transaction. Over that, a payment gateway that uses monthly fees will be cheaper for you.

> *There are many strict security requirements for processing cards on your website (called PCI) which add cost and complexity. Start with an easy "off-site" processor such as PayPal or 2CheckOut, which meets most security requirements for you. See detailed instructions including rates and contact information in the detailed chapter.*

From the main Admin navigation menu bar, select **EXTENSIONS – Payment.** This brings you to the Payment screen:

🔒 Payment

Payment Method		Status	Sort Order	Action
AlertPay		Disabled		[Install]
Authorize.Net (AIM)		Disabled		[Install]
Bank Transfer		Disabled		[Install]
Cheque / Money Order		Disabled		[Install]
Cash On Delivery		Enabled	1	[Edit] [Uninstall]
Free Checkout		Disabled		[Install]
LIQPAY		Disabled		[Install]
Moneybookers	((((O	Disabled		[Install]
Paymate		Disabled		[Install]
PayPoint	PP PayPoint	Disabled		[Install]
Perpetual Payments		Disabled		[Install]
PayPal Website Payment Pro	PayPal	Disabled		[Install]
PayPal Website Payment Pro (UK)	PayPal	Disabled		[Install]
PayPal Standard	PayPal	Disabled		[Install]
SagePay	sagepay	Disabled		[Install]
SagePay Direct		Disabled		[Install]
SagePay (US)		Disabled		[Install]
2Checkout		Disabled		[Install]
WorldPay		Disabled		[Install]

Click INSTALL and then EDIT to look at each method. All information that needs to be entered in the form boxes such as Account Number, Transaction Key, MD5 Hash, etc. will be sent to you from the merchant bank after you are approved for an account. Ask the merchant processor for support if needed. In this Quick Start section, we will cover the most popular method, PayPal Standard.

PayPal Standard
http://www.paypal.com/

Setting up PayPal is done in three steps:

- **Open and set up your PayPal.com account for website payments as shown below.**
- **Fill in the OpenCart EXTENSIONS - PAYMENTS - PayPal Standard form as shown below.**
- **Test, test, test!**

PayPal Standard Step 1.

Open and verify your PayPal.com account, set up website payment preferences on the paypal.com website as shown below and copy the "Payment Data Transfer" (PDT) Identity Token from the PayPal website; and

| My Account | Send Money | Request Money | Merchant Services | Auction Tools | Products and Services |

Overview   Add Funds   Withdraw   History   Resolution Center   Reports   **Profile**

Website Payment Preferences

Back to My Profile

Auto Return for Website Payments

Auto Return: ⦿ On
　　　　　　　 ○ Off

Return URL: http://www.myopencartstore.com

Payment Data Transfer (optional)

COPY (CTRL-C) and PASTE (CTRL-V) into OpenCart's "PDT Token" box

Payment Data Transfer: ⦿ On
　　　　　　　　　　　　 ○ Off

Identity Token: 3TriHHKxQcpQ6C-zrYaRbTAs-O8QqpQxXHD31Gm0TriHHKxQcpQ6C-zrY9pG

Encrypted Website Payments

Block Non-encrypted Website Payment: ○ On　⦿ Off

PayPal Account Optional

PayPal Account Optional: ⦿ On
　　　　　　　　　　　　 ○ Off

Contact Telephone Number

Note: Selecting On **(Required Field)** could have a negative effect on buyer conversion.

Contact Telephone ○ On (Optional Field)
　　　　　　　　　 ○ On (Required Field)
　　　　　　　　　 ⦿ Off (PayPal recommends this option)

Express Checkout Settings

With this setting you determine if you technically support the German funding methods giropay Checkout implementation.

Support giropay and bank transfer payments: ○ Yes　⦿ No

[Save]　[Cancel]

PayPal Standard Step 2.

Fill in the OpenCart EXTENSIONS - PAYMENTS - PayPal Standard form, paste (CTRL-V) the PDT Identity Token from the PayPal website, and fill in each box as follows:

PayPal Standard   Save Cancel

* E-Mail:	me@MyPayPalAddress.com
PDT Token: (Payment Data Transfer Token is used for additional security and reliability. Find out how to enable PDT here)	COPY FROM PAYPAL
Sandbox Mode:	○ Yes ● No
Transaction Method:	Sale
Geo Zone:	All Zones
Status:	Enabled
Sort Order:	1
Debug Mode: (Logs additional information to the system log.)	Disabled
Order Status Completed: (This is the status set when the payment has been completed successfully.)	Complete
Order Status Pending:	Pending
Order Status Denied:	Denied
Order Status Failed:	Failed
Order Status Refunded:	Refunded
Order Status Canceled Reversal:	Pending
Order Status Reversed:	Reversed
Order Status Unspecified Error:	Failed

PayPal Standard Step 3.

Register several test accounts in your OpenCart store, and make several test transactions from different locations to be sure everything is set up properly.

TIP: PayPal not showing the correct shipping charges? Login to your Paypal account, and under MY ACCOUNT Tab click on PROFILE link. Under the Hosted payment settings heading, click the "Shipping Calculations" Link and make sure that it is turned OFF. Clear any custom shipping settings and click the SAVE Button.

Extensions - Order Total

There are 7 possible sections to show customers during checkout, and many of them are not necessary. Would you want to click SEVEN times before your order was placed? Select only the important ones now!

From the main Admin menu, select **EXTENSIONS – Order Total**. Choose the screens you want and in which order – the one with the smallest "Sort Order" number will be shown first, the highest "Sort Order" number will be shown last.

Click REMOVE or EDIT for each method and follow the easy instructions.

Order Totals

Order Totals	Status	Sort Order	Action
Coupon	Enabled	4	[Edit] [Uninstall]
Handling Fee	Disabled		[Install]
Low Order Fee	Disabled		[Install]
Shipping	Enabled	3	[Edit] [Uninstall]
Sub-Total	Enabled	1	[Edit] [Uninstall]
Taxes	Enabled	5	[Edit] [Uninstall]
Total	Enabled	6	[Edit] [Uninstall]

COUPON: Select only if you have previously set up optional coupons in your store. See detailed chapter for help.

HANDLING FEE: If you will charge a fee for handling your order, install and enable. Not recommended.

LOW ORDER FEE: If you will charge a fee for small orders, install and enable. Not recommended.

SHIPPING: If you want customers to select from multiple shipping methods, edit and enable. Recommended.

SUB-TOTAL: If you want customers to see and okay an extra screen showing the total of their cart before shipping charges, enable this screen. Optional.

TAXES: If you want customers to see and okay an extra screen showing the total of their cart with taxes, enable this screen. Optional.

TOTAL: Should always be the last screen. Required!

Don't forget to test, test, test! Pretend you are a customer shopping on your store, register as a new customer and actually purchase one of your products. Check your email box to see if you received the order receipt.

Before making a test purchase, change the product price to a very low price, $0.25 or $0.10, so you don't have to worry about getting a refund when the purchase is successful. Make adjustments as needed. Get your friends to help you test, but make sure they know they will not actually receive the goods!

3. SYSTEM menu: Settings Localization, and other important options

Fill in forms with information specific to your local area, including currencies, languages, wording for stock and order statuses, where you will sell, tax you will charge, whether to use inches, millimeters etc. in measurements and kilos or pounds in weights. Read each item below, optional menus are omitted.

Settings – General	Enter name of store, the "path" to the store such as myopencartstore.com/shop, and contact information that will appear on your Contact Us page and in system emails that the store will send to you, such as when you forget the Admin password.
Settings – Store	Name and description of your store, select a template if you have had one installed separately.
Settings – Local	Important: sets default information about your store. Select your country and state, and language. Select a default currency and, if you will accept multiple currencies, whether you want the store to automatically update the currency exchange rate daily. Select a default measurement length class (inches, centimeters or millimeters) and default weight class (Kilos, grams, pounds or ounces) which you will use to describe product sizes and weights. EXAMPLE: in a product description, if you enter "2" in the weight box, choose here whether the "2" means pounds, kilos, ounces. SEE ALSO SETTINGS - LOCALIZATION - LENGTH CLASS AND WEIGHT CLASS to add new units of measure or weight.
Settings – Image	UPLOAD or SELECT YOUR STORE LOGO - click the logo to bring up IMAGE MANAGER and select the new logo for your store; original is 210 pixels wide by 43 pixels high.
Settings –	USE SSL: AFTER YOUR WEB HOST INSTALLS YOUR SSL, SELECT YES for secure order processing.

Server

Localization - Languages	An advanced feature. For non-English speaking store owners, install a language pack by first downloading from OpenCart.com link below, use cPanel's File Manager to upload and then extract the zip file. Then in Admin go to SYSTEM - LOCALIZATION - Languages, click the INSERT Button, and enter the Language information from the file. Note that some languages are for the Admin only, others include the store. LANGUAGES EXTENSIONS: http://www.opencart.com/index.php?route=extension/extension&path=2&sort=e.date modified&order=DESC
Localization - Currencies	Display store prices in additional currencies that you specify. Default is British Pounds (CHANGE DEFAULT IN SYSTEM - SETTINGS - LOCAL).
Localization - Zones	For shipping and tax purposes, pre-defined areas of a country (example in US, Zones=states; in Canada Zones=provinces). You may refuse to ship or sell to a zone by locating the zone, then from the ZONE STATUS box select DISABLED and click the SAVE Button. TIP: to remove dozens or hundreds of Zones, ask your techie to do this with phpMyAdmin.
Localization - Geo Zones	For shipping and tax purposes, custom-defined groups or portions of a country. For example, create custom Geo Zones to charge local, state, and federal tax, OR charge less for shipping to your state + the states around you. EXAMPLE: Texas state tax, Houston city tax, South-Central US Shipping Zone. TIP: FIRST delete the existing tax classes. Click INSERT Button, give the Geo Zone a name and description, THEN Click ADD GEO ZONE Button, COUNTRY and select your country name and zone (state/province/etc.).
Localization - Tax Classes	TIP: Be sure you have first created a Geo Zone for each tax. On TAXABLE GOODS line, click the EDIT Link, select the first Geo Zone, enter a description and specify the exact Tax Rate you are required to charge. Enter priority number (1 for first, 2 for 2nd etc.). Click ADD TAX RATE Button for each tax you must charge, then in top right click the SAVE Button. Make test purchases with a fake customer account from each Geo Zone to be sure tax is set up correctly!!
Localization - Length Classes	Choose units of measure to use in product options and shipping by product dimensions OR add new lengths. SET DEFAULT in SYSTEM - SETTINGS - LOCAL.
Localization - Weight Classes	Choose units of weight to use in product options and shipping by weight OR add new weights. SET DEFAULT in SYSTEM - SETTINGS - LOCAL.

 CAUTION: Check with your accountant or lawyer so you know exactly what taxes to charge. This message is brought to you by: lawyers.

Don't forget to test, test, test! Pretend you are a customer shopping on your store, register as a new customer and actually purchase one of your products. Check your email box to see if you received the order receipt. Do you like what you see?

This completes your Quick Start!

Is there anything I could do to make this guide easier? Please let me know at talkback@oscmanuals.com – I take your messages very seriously. If you want detailed information on any of the subjects covered here, turn to the corresponding chapter in this book.

4. Catalog Menu

Catalog Menu Quick Checklist:

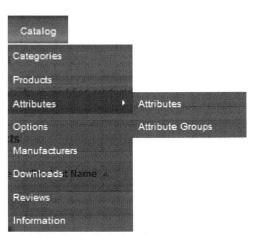

Step 1. Plan how to organize your categories, manufacturers, attributes and options.

Step 2. Create categories for a few test products.

Step 3. Create manufacturer or brand names.

Step 4. For downloadable products like music or ebooks, upload the file that customers will download after purchase.

Step 5. Create some attributes for the test products.

Step 6. Create some product options for the test products.

Step 7. Now create the test products, inserting images and search engine tags.

Step 8. Test, test, test and make any changes needed.

Step 9. Now add your remaining products.

TIP: To get started quickly entering simple products, turn to the Quick Start Guide at the beginning of this book.

 Do you have dozens or hundreds of products, categories, and images to enter? If so, download the Export/Import Tool extension to add your products and images in one batch. Ask your installer to set it up for you.

Step 1. Plan how to organize your categories, manufacturers, attributes and options like size, color, style

OpenCart is VERY flexible in how you list product options, so consider your decision carefully, and do some testing BEFORE you list all of your products. Flexible means it can get a little complex.

 TIP: Nearly everything you do can be EDITED if you change your mind. However, it can become a spaghetti-like mess if you have to edit dozens of products. Do a FEW, test, modify if needed, then continue.

There are many possible ways to describe each of a product's features. How you list product options is a *strategic decision* for your store. Should a feature of a product be a category, or an option?

- If a feature is REQUIRED - for example, the customer will consider only men's shoes - then it is likely to be a **Category.**
- If a feature will be COMPARED side by side by the customer - like computer memory, RAM, hard disk size in computers - it is an **Attribute.**
- If a feature is optional, and the customer will choose only one, it is likely to be a **Product option.**
- THERE IS NO ONE CORRECT WAY, only ways that are easier or harder for your customers to find what they want.
- Remember to Keep It Simple and be consistent from one product to another.

Categories

After you have decided on your store's organization, create your first product category.

Categories InfoBox

Categories
Chairs
Sofas
Tables

Before your products will appear in your store Categories, you must first create a product Category for it.

The **Category** Name is the link that will display to customers in the Categories Information box of your store, as shown to the left. It is like departments in a non-online store. Sample categories are included with your store to help you see how to fill in the forms. Look around them to get ideas for your own store.

To create a new product category, from the Admin's Top Bar Navigation Menu, click CATALOG - Categories. This brings you to the Category List:

	Category Name	Sort Order	Action
	Chairs	1	[Edit]
	Chairs > Dining Chairs	1	[Edit]
	Chairs > Sitting Chairs	2	[Edit]
	Sofas	2	[Edit]
	Tables	3	[Edit]
	Tables > Coffee Tables	1	[Edit]
	Tables > Kitchen Tables	2	[Edit]

Enter ONE category, its product attributes, manufacturer, and one product to test your store, THEN enter remaining products when you know you have done it properly.

From the Category List you may:

- **Insert a new category** by clicking the top right INSERT Button
- **Delete one or more categories** by checking the left checkbox and clicking the top right DELETE Button
- **Edit an individual category** by clicking the far right EDIT Link. From here you may also move them to a new parent category, change the category photo, and change the sort order (where the category displays in the Category InfoBox list).

CATALOG MENU

Category

Each product must be in a category, and you can also have sub-categories. In this example we will insert a category called Chairs, with sub-categories Dining Chairs and Sitting Chairs.

From the Admin's top nav bar, click CATALOG - Categories, then at the top right click the INSERT Button. This brings you to the New Category form. Notice at the top left that you start on the GENERAL Tab, but there is also a DATA Tab. Fill out the GENERAL Tab as shown below:

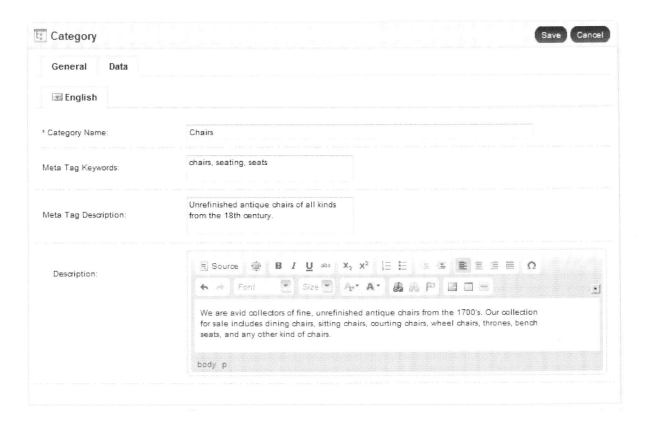

CATEGORY NAME: The name you want to display at the top of the category page (see image below) and in your store's Categories InfoBox.

META TAG KEYWORDS: Words your customers may use in search engines to try to find this category.

META TAG DESCRIPTION: The description that you want to display in the search engine when a customer has searched on the keywords above. Make it factual and informative, not sales-y.

DESCRIPTION: The words that will appear on the category page, see below.

Next, at the top left, click the DATA Tab and fill in the form boxes as shown in and explained below the image:

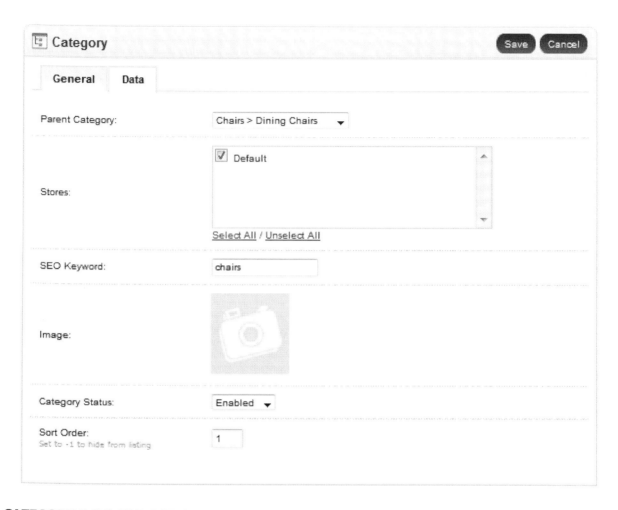

CATEGORY DATA TAB ACTIONS

PARENT CATEGORY: If you want this category to be listed as a sub-category, choose the parent category under which you want it to be listed.

STORES: If you run multiple stores from this Admin, they will be shown here. Select one or more.

SEO KEYWORD: This is for "SEO-Friendly-URLs" - another technique to help search engines find you. Enter the most important keyword here; if a key phrase, separate words with dashes (-) NOT spaces, like this: 17th-Century-Chairs. If SEO Friendly URLS is turned ON (ask your technical pro, it can be complex), you will see these words instead of numbers.

IMAGE: Upload an image to represent the category, see DINING CHAIRS. See the IMAGE MANAGER section after this table.

CATEGORY STATUS: Default is DISABLED or hidden. To allow your category to appear in your store, change to ENABLED.

SORT ORDER: 1 to appear first in the Category Box, 2 to appear second, etc.

When you have finished, be sure to click the top right SAVE Button.

Image Manager

Use Image Manager to upload or manage images. To start Image Manager, in the IMAGE box above, click the picture of the camera. This brings up IMAGE MANAGER:

From here, you may do the following:

IMAGE MANAGER ACTIONS

SELECT an image already on the server
Scroll down to the image you want and double-click it. The new picture replaces the picture of the camera.

CREATE a new folder or sub-folder for your category images
For example, if you have a large number of images. At the top left click NEW FOLDER and name the folder.

DELETE an image or folder from your web server
Single-click the image or folder to select it, then click the DELETE Link.

MOVE an image to a new folder you have already created.
Single-click the image to select it, then click the MOVE Link. A drop-down box comes up. From the drop-down box, select the folder where you want the image to go and click the SUBMIT Button.

COPY an image to a new folder you have already created.
Single-click the image to select it, then click the COPY Link. In Image Manager's left column click the file folders until you come to the folder where you want

RENAME an image.

the image to go, then click the SUBMIT Button. Single-click the image to select it, then click the RENAME Link. A text box comes up. In the text box, type the new name for the image and click the SUBMIT Button.

UPLOAD an image

A two-step process (the two links circled above). Click the UPLOAD Link, then find the image to upload on your computer and click the UPLOAD or OPEN Button. A SUCCESS box comes up, click the OKAY Button. Next click the circled REFRESH Link so your browser can SEE the new image. Double-click the image to select it, and the uploaded image replaces the picture of the camera.

Be sure to click the SAVE Button!

CATALOG MENU

Products

The product information you enter in the Products form is used in two main pages in your store - the CATEGORY Page, and the PRODUCT INFORMATION Page:

A Category page:

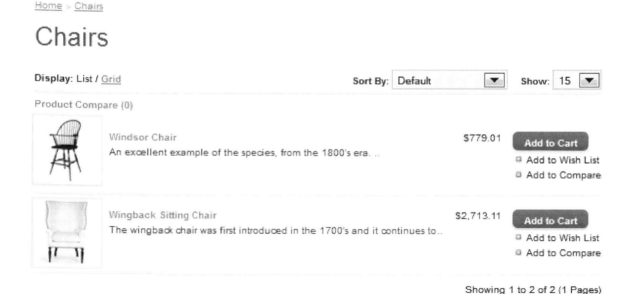

A Product Information page:

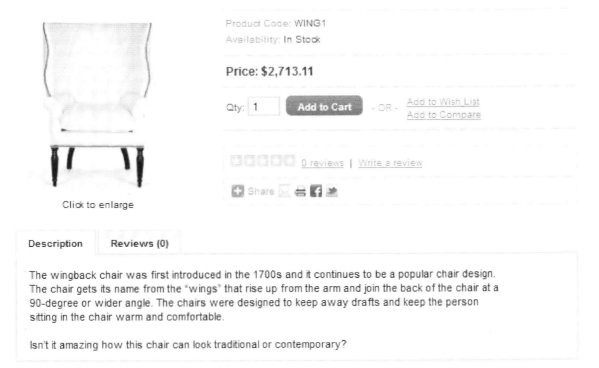

Wingback Sitting Chair

Product Code: WING1
Availability: In Stock

Price: $2,713.11

Qty: 1   Add to Cart   - OR -   Add to Wish List
Add to Compare

0 reviews | Write a review

Share

Click to enlarge

| Description | Reviews (0) |

The wingback chair was first introduced in the 1700s and it continues to be a popular chair design. The chair gets its name from the "wings" that rise up from the arm and join the back of the chair at a 90-degree or wider angle. The chairs were designed to keep away drafts and keep the person sitting in the chair warm and comfortable.

Isn't it amazing how this chair can look traditional or contemporary?

Tags: antique, chair, contemporary, traditional, wingback.

To begin entering your products, after you have set up your categories, manufacturers or brands, attributes and options, whew, from the Admin's Top Bar Navigation Menu, select CATALOG - Products.

This brings you to the PRODUCTS LIST:

	Image	Product Name ▲	Model	Price	Quantity	Status	Action
☐						▼	Filter
☐		English Regency Sofa	SOFAREG	17550.00	1	Enabled	[Edit]
☐		Gustavian Sofa	GUST-1	25275.00	2	Enabled	[Edit]
☐		Walnut Drop-Leaf Table	TABLEDL	2575.000	4	Enabled	[Edit]
☐		Windsor Chair	WIND-1	725.0000	10	Enabled	[Edit]

Products — Insert Copy Delete

The Products List is sorted by PRODUCT NAME (see the triangle after Product Name). To find a specific product, enter it in the top blank line, then click the FILTER Button.

At the top right of the Products List, click the INSERT Button.

This brings you to the Product Form, with seven tabs at the top: GENERAL, DATA, LINKS, ATTRIBUTE, OPTION, DISCOUNT, SPECIAL, IMAGE, REWARD POINTS and DESIGN:

See each section below for instructions for each tab:

Products - General Tab

Basic details about the product. Only the Product Name is required to get started; everything else can be added later.

You can jump from tab to tab without saving until you are finished. BUT I recommend that you save periodically. For security reasons, many servers will "Time Out" or force you to re-log on after a specific period of time, and you can lose your unsaved work.

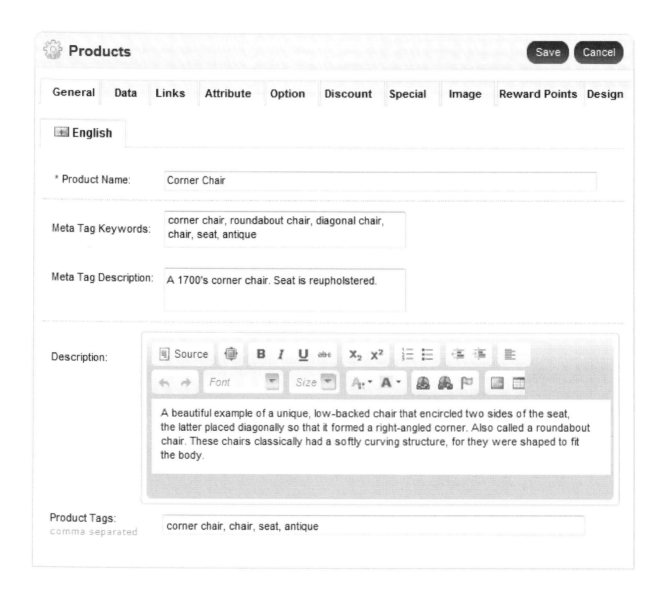

See next page for detailed instructions:

*PRODUCT NAME: The product name you want to appear under the product photo on the Category page, and on the product information page.

META TAG KEYWORDS: The words your customers will type into Google or other search engines when trying to find this product.

META TAG DESCRIPTION: Up to 25 words or 125 characters, after searching your customers will see this in the search engine's SEARCH RESULTS page.

DESCRIPTION: The long product description that will appear on the Product Information page's Description tab. See example above.

PRODUCT TAGS: The product tags that will appear at the bottom left on the Product Information page to aid visitors in searching. See example above.

Be sure to click the top right SAVE Button.

Products - Data Tab

Numerical and other data about the product.

Only a Model number or name is required to get started, but it may act unpredictably if you do not fill in other fields, for example:

- Price will appear as $0.00 unless you specify a price.
- The product will NOT appear at all in your store unless you set STATUS to "Enabled."
- Shipping will NOT be charged unless you enter a product WEIGHT.
- Read below to avoid other surprises.

⚙ Products

Save Cancel

| General | Data | Links | Attribute | Option | Discount | Special | Image | Reward Points | Design |

* Model: CH-CORNER1

Price: 2500.00

Tax Class: Taxable Goods ▾

Quantity: 2

Minimum Quantity:
Force a minimum ordered amount

Subtract Stock: Yes ▾

Out Of Stock Status:
Status shown when a product is out of stock Out Of Stock ▾

Requires Shipping: ⦿ Yes ○ No

SKU:

UPC:

Location:

SEO Keyword: corner chair

Image:

Date Available: 2011-05-04

Dimensions (L x W x H): 42   30   40

Length Class: Inch ▾

Weight: 65

Weight Class: Pound ▾

Status: Enabled ▾

Sort Order: 1

MODEL (REQUIRED):	Model name or number
STATUS:	Whether or not to show in store
PRICE:	The price you want the customer to see (not including tax). Appears on Category and Product pages.
TAX CLASS:	Select TAXABLE GOODS to charge tax or NONE. SEE ALSO chapter on Localization - TAX CLASSES.
QUANTITY:	If you wish to use the stock-tracking module, how many you have in stock.
MINIMUM QUANTITY:	If you wish to force a minimum number of items (example: if your price is per dozen, you put a "1" to force a minimum order of 1 dozen).
SUBTRACT STOCK:	Change to YES for the store to count down the stock each time an item is ordered.
OUT OF STOCK STATUS:	Set to IN STOCK or the product page will display warning "NOT IN STOCK"
REQUIRES SHIPPING:	If downloadable product (i.e. Ebook, Music) OR you allow customers to pick up in store only, select NO. Otherwise select YES for your store to add the shipping cost you specified in EXTENSIONS - SHIPPING.
SKU:	OPTIONAL Stock Keeping Unit, a unique identifying number you assign to track your products.
MISC. LOCATION:	OPTIONAL location or warehouse where the item is stored.
SEO KEYWORD:	Aids in search engines finding the page. Changes the product address FROM yourstorename.com/index.php?route=product/product&product_id=123 TO yourstorename.com/chairs/windsor-chair OR yourstorename.com/t-shirts/metallica. ADDITIONAL SETUP REQUIRED, see DETAILED CONFIGURATION Chapter.
IMAGE:	Click the image to upload a new product photo.
DATE AVAILABLE:	If the new product is not yet in stock, the store will begin to display it on the date you select.
SORT ORDER:	In the category or sub-category, put 1 to display first, 2 to display second, etc. You can skip numbers and it will continue to sort from smallest number to largest.
DIMENSIONS (L x W x H):	For dimension-based shipping and/or to inform the customer of the exact size. EXAMPLE: A picture frame 8 1/2 inches long x 10 inches wide x 1 inch thick. Enter 8.5 10.0 1.0.
LENGTH CLASS:	Are the numbers you put into the DIMENSIONS Box inches, feet, etc.? This overrides the default measurement. Set DEFAULT units of measure (inches, feet, cm, etc.) in SYSTEM - Settings - Local - Length Class. If the dimension you want is not there, add it in SYSTEM - Localization - Length Class.
WEIGHT:	For weight-based shipping and/or to inform the customer of the exact weight. EXAMPLE: A pound of fudge candy sold by the pound. Enter 1.0.
WEIGHT CLASS:	Are the numbers you put into the WEIGHT Box kilos, pounds, etc.? This overrides the default measurement. Set DEFAULT units of weight in SYSTEM - Settings - Local - Weight Class. If the dimension you want is not there, add it in SYSTEM - Localization - Weight Class.

Be sure to click the top right SAVE Button.

Products - Links

Simple - what category pages do you want linked to this product?
What other pages do you want linked to this product?

To select multiple categories, hold down the CTRL button and
mouse-click as many categories as desired.

To link this product to one or more categories, from the top navigation bar select
CATALOG – Products. Select the product name and click the EDIT Button. From the
product page top tabs, click the LINKS Tab and fill in as follows:

MANUFACTURER: Allow search by Manufacturer or Brand name by selecting it in the BRANDS InfoBox. If you have previously added manufacturer information in CATALOG - Manufacturers, from drop-down box select the manufacturer name.

CATEGORIES: Put a check in the box to the left of each category in which you want this product to appear. Only one category is required for product to display.

STORES: If you manage multiple stores, check all stores in which you want product to appear. Otherwise, leave at DEFAULT.

DOWNLOADS: If you have previously uploaded a downloadable file, check the box. The file will appear after the customer checks out.

RELATED PRODUCTS: To have another product appear in a RELATED PRODUCTS box on this product's Product Info page, select the product from the drop-down menu so it appears in the LEFT Box.
Choose to have THIS product appear on the OTHER product Information page: In the left box highlight the product name, then click the RIGHT ARROW.

Be sure to click the top right SAVE Button.

Products - Attribute Tab

Features that will be compared side by side by the customer when deciding on which item to choose. FIRST: Set up Attributes above in CATALOG – Attributes above.

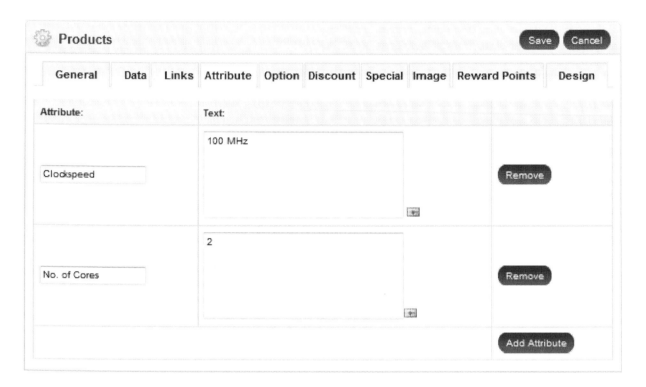

ATTRIBUTE: Click the ADD ATTRIBUTE Button, then begin typing the name in the Attribute box. A drop-down list will appear for you to select the correct Attribute Name.

TEXT: In the TEXT Box, type all the possible choices for this product. In this example for the Sony Vaio shown above, this product comes in 3 clockspeeds.

REPEAT steps 1 and 2 for each attribute. This example Sony Vaio above has two attributes.

When you have finished adding attributes, be sure to click the top right SAVE Button.

Products - Option Tab

Options that customers can choose to customize their product, such as size or color. FIRST: Set up Options in CATALOG – Options above.

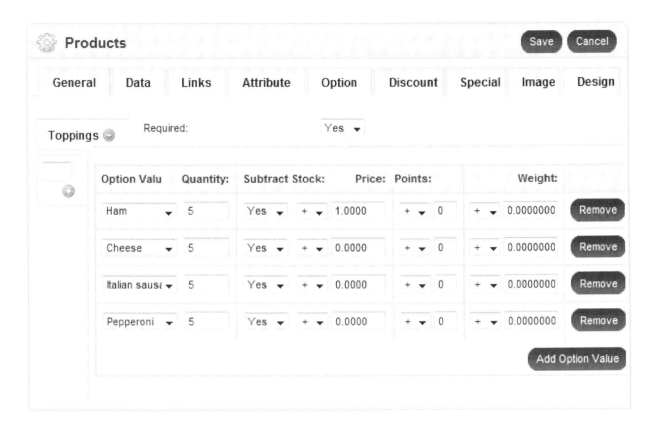

REQUIRED: Select YES if you want customer to be forced to select an option, or NO to let them check out without choosing.

OPTION VALUE: Example Small, Medium or Large. Try to be as descriptive as possible so customers do not have to look up many charts (example Small - fits child size 0-4)

QUANTITY: If you are tracking stock, how many of this option you have.

SUBTRACT STOCK: If you wish to track stock levels of this item, leave at YES. Otherwise select NO.

PRICE: If you wish to charge extra (or less) for this product, enter the amount here. EXAMPLE: Men's extra large t-shirts cost $2 more from the manufacturer. The "+$2.00" will appear in the option box of your store.

+/-: If you wish to ADD the extra amount, i.e. $2 MORE for this option, select "+" If you wish to DISCOUNT this option, select "-"

POINTS: If you wish to give Reward Points for purchasing this option, enter the number of points.

WEIGHT: Enter the weight of this option IF it is significantly heavier or lighter than the normal option to charge extra (or less) in shipping this option.

+/-: Specify whether the weight is more for this option (+) or less (-).

Products - Discount Tab

Give a discount to specific groups of customers such as Wholesale or Employees. Discount will not display UNTIL the customer has registered for an account and their group approved by you. The Customer MUST be logged in for the discount to display.

FIRST: ADD ADDITIONAL CUSTOMER GROUPS such as "Employees" in SALES - Customer Group - Insert.

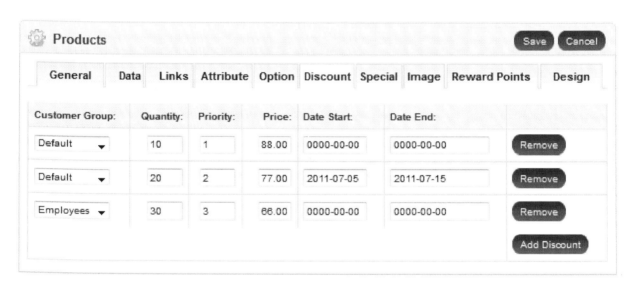

CUSTOMER GROUP:	To give employees a discount on THIS product, at the far right click the ADD DISCOUNT Button. From the far left drop-down box, select EMPLOYEES.
QUANTITY:	The minimum quantity the customer must order for the discount to apply.
PRIORITY:	If you will offer multiple discounts and specials, enter 1 for this discount to be applied first, 2 to be applied second, etc.
PRICE:	The discount price you want this customer group to receive.
DATE START:	Start date for the discount to automatically begin displaying in your store.
DATE END:	Stop date for the discount to automatically stop displaying in your store.
	Be sure to click the top right SAVE Button.

Products - Special Tab

Give a special price on THIS product to all customers, OR specific groups of customers such as Wholesale or Employees. If for a specific group, special price will not display UNTIL the customer has registered for an account and their group is approved by you. The Customer MUST be logged in for the special customer group price to display.

FIRST: ADD ADDITIONAL CUSTOMER GROUPS such as "Employees" in SALES - Customer Group - Insert.

In this example below, anybody who comes to the store can receive this discount (default). If they are eligible for another discount, this will be applied first (priority 1). The discounted price is $90.00. There is no start or end date - it is live now, and the store owner will turn it off manually.

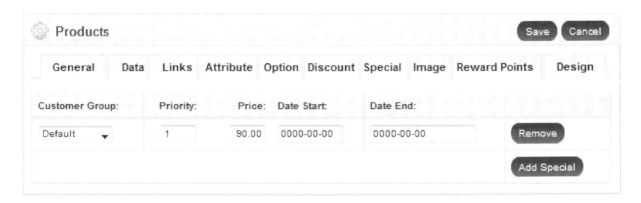

CUSTOMER GROUP: Leave at DEFAULT for all customers. To give employees a special price on THIS product, at the far right click the ADD SPECIAL Button. From the far left drop-down box, select EMPLOYEES.

PRIORITY: If you will offer multiple specials and discounts, enter 1 for this discount to be applied first, 2 to be applied second, etc.

PRICE: The special price you want this customer group to receive.

DATE START: Start date for the discount to automatically begin displaying in your store.

DATE END: Stop date for the discount to automatically stop displaying in your store.

Be sure to click the top right SAVE Button.

Products - Image Tab

Upload additional images or product views. OpenCart will automatically resize it for you.

At the far right, click the ADD IMAGE Button. OR to replace an image, CLICK THE IMAGE.

Follow instructions in previous section CATALOG – Categories for IMAGE MANAGER.

Repeat for as many additional images as desired.

Be sure to click the top right SAVE Button.

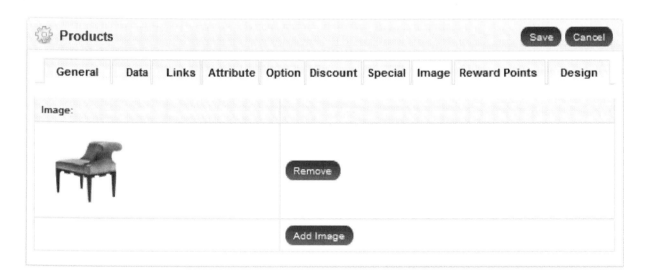

Products – Reward Points Tab

Customers can earn loyalty points for buying products from your store, then redeem them after they have accumulated sufficient points. Customers can check the number of points awarded in your store by logging onto My Account and clicking the REWARD POINTS Link. After a customer makes a purchase, activate that number of points in the customer order page SALES - Orders - order number.

Turn rewards points ON or OFF in EXTENSIONS - Order Totals - Reward Points - Uninstall.

Products   Save Cancel

| General | Data | Links | Attribute | Option | Discount | Special | Image | Reward Points | Design |

Points:
Number of points needed to buy this item. If you don't want this product to be purchased with points leave as 0.

1000

Customer Group:	Reward Points:
Default	100
Employees	50
Wholesale	10

POINTS: Specify the number of points this item will COST a customer who wants to purchase it using rewards points.

CUSTOMER GROUP: Set a different number of points a member of a customer group will EARN for purchasing this product.

Products - Design Tab

If you have created and uploaded separate page layouts, or the template you have installed has separate layouts, you can select the different layout that will override the main template for the following pages:

Account, Affiliate, Category, Checkout, Contact, Default, Home, Information, Manufacturer, Product, Sitemap.

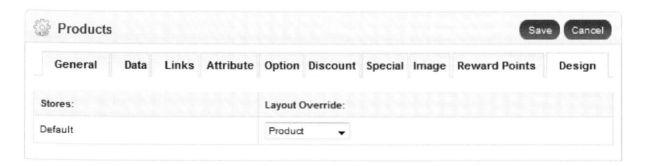

When you have finished filling in the above tabs, be sure to click the SAVE Button. Note that you can always come back and add information later on.

CATALOG

Attributes

Attributes are features that will be compared side by side by the customer when deciding on which item to choose. See the example below of both the Attributes listed in the product columns, and the Attribute GROUPS listed in the left column:

Product Comparison

Product Detail		
Product	MacBook	Sony VAIO
Image		
Price	$500.00	$1,000.00
Model	Product 16	Product 19
Brand	Apple	Sony
Availability	In Stock	In Stock
Rating	▭▭▭▭▭ Based on 1 reviews.	▭▭▭▭▭ Based on 1 reviews.
Summary	Intel Core 2 Duo processor Powered by an Intel Core 2 Duo processor at speeds up to 2.16GHz, the new MacBook is the fastest ever. 1GB memory, larger hard drives The new MacBoo..	Unprecedented power. The next generation of processing technology has arrived. Built into the newest VAIO notebooks lies Intel's latest, most powerful innovation yet: Intel® Centrino® 2..
Weight	0.00kg	0.00kg
Dimensions (L x W x H)	0.00mm x 0.00mm x 0.00mm	0.00mm x 0.00mm x 0.00mm
Speed	8gb	32G
Clockspeed	0.8	1.1 1.2 1.3
No. of Cores	1	2
	Add to Cart	Add to Cart
	Remove	Remove

Attribute GROUPS...

Memory

Processor

..and ATTRIBUTES

Continue

Attributes Summary

Attributes are created in three steps:

- **Attributes Step 1.** Create the Attribute GROUP.
- **Attributes Step 2.** Create the Attributes.

- **Attributes Step 3.** When you are ready to add attributes to a product, open the product information page and link the product to its attributes.

Attributes Step 1. Create the Attribute GROUP.

In your store Admin's top nav bar menu, select CATALOG - Attributes - Attribute Groups. This brings you to the Attributes Group List:

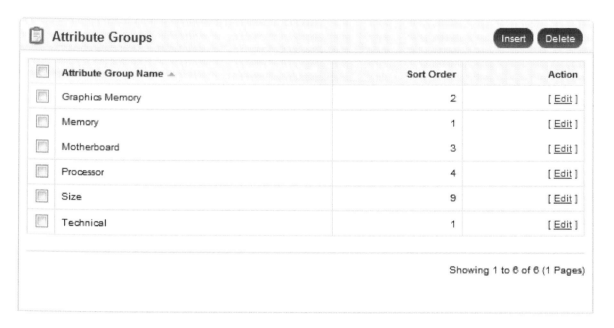

To insert a new Attribute Group, click the top right INSERT Button. This brings you to the Attribute Group Form:

Give your attribute group a name, and if you have multiple attributes for this product, give it a 1 to display this group first in the list, 2 to display second, and so forth.
When you have finished, click the top right SAVE Button.

Attributes Step 2. Create the Attributes.

Now that you have a created an attributes group, next create as many attributes as you like to go under that group.

In your store Admin's top nav bar menu, select CATALOG - Attributes - Attributes. This brings you to the Attributes List:

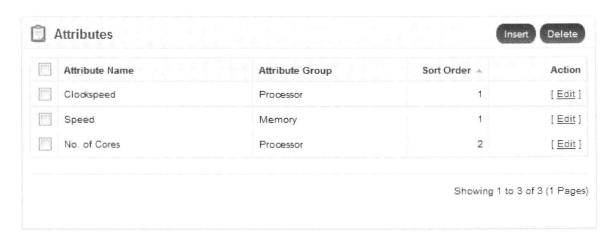

To insert a new Attribute, click the top right INSERT Button. This brings you to the Attribute Form:

Give your attribute a name, select the attribute group from the drop down box, and if you have multiple attributes for this product, give it a 1 to display this attribute first in the group, 2 to display second, and so forth.
When you have finished, click the top right SAVE Button.

Attributes Step 3. Link the attributes to the product.

When you are ready to add attributes to a product, open the product information page and link the product to its attributes.

From your store Admin's top nav bar menu, select CATALOG - Products, and select the product name to which you wish to add the attributes by clicking the EDIT Link (or click the top right INSERT Button to add a new product).

At the top tabs click the ATTRIBUTE Tab and fill in the form as follows:

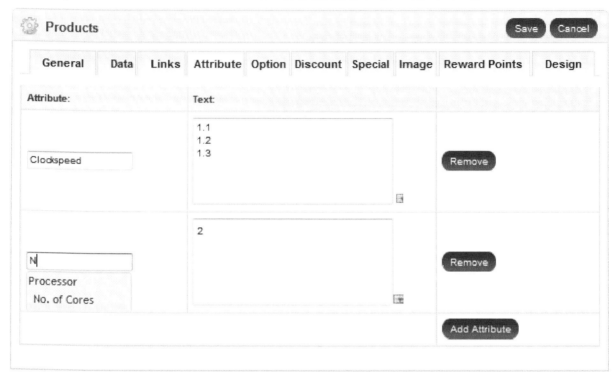

1. Click the ADD ATTRIBUTE Button, then begin typing the name in the Attribute box. A drop-down list will appear for you to select the correct Attribute Name.

2. In the TEXT Box, type all the possible choices for this product. In the example above for the Sony Vaio, this product comes in 3 clockspeeds.

3. REPEAT steps 1 and 2 for each attribute. The example above has two attributes.

When you have finished adding attributes, be sure to click the top right SAVE Button.

CATALOG MENU

Options

Options that customers can choose to customize their product, such as size or color.

Many people get confused between OPTIONS and OPTION VALUES, but it's easy if you take it step by step.

- Option is the group name (size, color, etc.).
- Option Values are the CHOICES that you want listed under the group:

STOREFRONT VIEW:
Available Options

* **Size:**
- Small
- Medium
- Large

Product Options Checklist:

Options Step 1. Write a list of all the options and option values you wish to use in your store.
Options Step 2. Create the options in CATALOG - Options.
Options Step 3. Now create or edit the product that will use the options in CATALOG - Products - Product Name, and specify the options and option types on the OPTIONS Tab as shown below.

Product Options Step 1. Write a list of all the options and option values you wish to use in your store.

If you already own or manage a physical "bricks and mortar" store and/or a product catalog, your options will most likely be organized in the same way as your existing store. Your product options will also be influenced by your existing product category names, model numbers, and/or SKU's.

If you are starting a new business and do not yet have your products organized into existing departments (categories), list options according to how your potential customers will search and buy. You may need to do some research to find the best method of organization. Test some competitors' stores and see if it is easy or difficult to find similar products to yours.

TIP: Write out a description of all product features your customers may consider about an item, then make the required items CATEGORIES and optional items PRODUCT OPTIONS. See the example below.

EXAMPLE: customers are very likely to search for rock band T-Shirts by the band name, and there is some flexibility in the sizes and colors they might buy. For example, they may select an extra-large if large is not available, or a black if red is not available. Men will not select a women's T-shirt, so sex is required as a category.

Now draw a table to sort out all attributes of the product. In this table below, the store owner is selling T-Shirts for the rock band Metallica. The shirts come in men's and women's styles and sizes, and the manufacturer charges extra for the men's extra-large shirt. That gives the following:

TABLE OF ALL FEATURES ABOUT A PRODUCT, 'METALLICA ROCK BAND T-SHIRTS'

Category	Sub-Category	Sub-Category	Model #	Manufacturer or Brand*	Product Options	Option Values	Option Type	Sort Order**	Extra Cost?	SKU
Garment	Sex	Band Name	From existing store or mfr.	If customers are brand-loyal	Options to create		Radio OR Drop-down			Existing SKU
T-Shirts	Men's	Metallica	7952-1		Men's Red	Medium		1		75112
						Large		2		75113
						X-Large		3		75114
					Men's Black	Medium		4		75115
						Large		5		75116
						X-Large		6	+2.00	75117
	Women's	Metallica	7952-2		Women's Red	Small		1		76112
						Medium		2		76113
						Large		3		76114
					Women's Black	Small		4		76115
						Medium		5		76116
						Large		6		76117

*Manufacturer/Brand is a separate InfoBox.

**Sort order is how you want the DROP-DOWN BOX to appear. In the above example, Men's Red Medium will appear first in the list. Leave blank to sort alphabetically.

IMPORTANT: A product can be listed in multiple categories as well as in options, so note that Men's is both a category and repeated as an option above. There are many ways to do it. This allows easy product searching AND clarity when customers are selecting options.

Now draw a table like the above for a sampling of several of your products to see the best way to organize your store.

Another store or even your competitor may organize their product options quite differently. After you have decided on how to organize your site, continue below.

TIP: You can test your store organization--OR a competitor's! --quickly and inexpensively at http://www.usertesting.com.

Product Options Step 2. Create the options in CATALOG - Options.

You cannot CREATE options on a product's information page, even though it LOOKS like you can. You must FIRST create the options and option values in CATALOG - Options, THEN use them on the product information page.

CAUTION: If stock tracking is turned on, your option will not appear UNLESS you give it a quantity larger than zero! It will disappear when the stock has been sold.

To begin creating product options, in your store Admin's top nav bar menu, select CATALOG - Options. This brings you to the Options List:

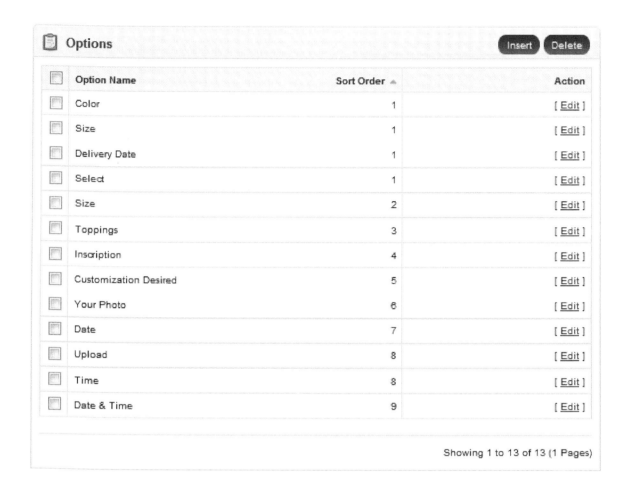

To add a new option, click the top right INSERT Button, then follow specific instructions with screen shots below for each type of option:

Option Type: Radio Button

Radio buttons allow only ONE choice from a list. They are similar to a drop-down box because they allow only one choice, but you can see ALL the choices without having to click the box.

Available Options

* Size:
  ○ Small
  ○ Medium
  ○ Large

Option Type: Radio Button Step 1. Create the options in CATALOG - Options. Fill in the form as follows:

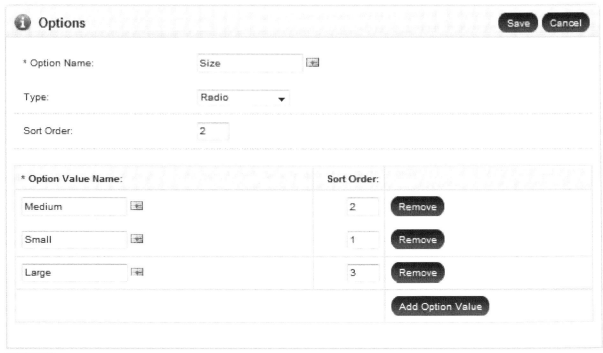

OPTION NAME:	Give the option a name that will appear as the heading of this option.
TYPE:	Select RADIO.
SORT ORDER:	If you will use multiple options, such as COLOR and SIZE, put a 1 for this option to appear first, 2 to appear second, etc.

NEXT to add the Option Value Names, you must click the bottom right ADD OPTION VALUE Button for EACH option you want to appear.

In the example above, ADD OPTION VALUE was clicked three times - once each for small, medium, and large.

OPTION VALUE NAME:	Give the option value a name that will appear next to the radio button.
SORT ORDER:	If you do not specify a sort order, the option values will be in ALPHABETICAL ORDER. To change it, put a 1 for the option value to appear first, 2 for the option value to appear second.

BE SURE TO CLICK THE TOP RIGHT "SAVE BUTTON" or your work will not be saved!

Option Type: Radio Button Step 2. Now create or edit the product that will use the options, and select the options on the OPTIONS Tab as shown below.

From your store Admin's top nav bar menu, select CATALOG - Products, and find the product name (or create the new product). Click the OPTION Tab. This brings you to an

almost blank page with only a box and green "+" button.
BEGIN TYPING the name of the option for this product, and a drop-down box will appear with all the options that match:

After you have selected the option name, in the bottom right click the ADD OPTION VALUE Button, once for each option this product will have, then fill in the form as shown:

Option Value:	Quantity:	Subtract Stock:		Price:			Points:			Weight:		
Small ▼	12	Yes ▼	+ ▼		+ ▼	50		+ ▼			Remove	
Medium ▼	7	Yes ▼	+ ▼		+ ▼	50		+ ▼			Remove	
Large ▼	2	Yes ▼	+ ▼	2.00	+ ▼			+ ▼	1.0		Remove	
											Add Option Value	

REQUIRED: Select YES if you want customer to be forced to select an option, or NO to let them check out without choosing.

OPTION VALUE: Example Small, Medium or Large. Try to be as descriptive as possible so customers do not have to look up many charts (example Small - fits child size 0-4)

QUANTITY: If you are tracking stock, how many of this option you have.

SUBTRACT STOCK: If you wish to track stock levels of this item, leave at YES. Otherwise select NO.

PRICE: If you wish to charge extra (or less) for this product, enter the amount here. EXAMPLE: Men's extra large t-shirts cost $2 more from the manufacturer. The "+$2.00" will appear in the option box of your store.

+/-: If you wish to ADD the extra amount, i.e. $2 MORE for this option, select "+" If you wish to DISCOUNT this option, select "-"

POINTS: If you wish to give Reward Points for purchasing this option, enter the number of points.

WEIGHT: Enter the weight of this option IF it is significantly heavier or lighter than the normal option to charge extra (or less) in shipping this option.

+/-:   Specify whether the weight is more for this option (+) or less (-).

BE SURE TO CLICK THE TOP RIGHT "SAVE BUTTON" or your work will not be saved!

Checkbox Options

Checkboxes allow MULTIPLE choices. Note that you can charge additional (or less) for certain options.

Option Type: Checkbox Step 1. To create the option checkbox, from your store Admin's top nav bar menu, select CATALOG - Options.
Click the top right INSERT Button and give the option a Option Name: (Toppings).
Type: "checkbox"

Available Options

* Toppings:
- [ ] Pepperoni
- [ ] Cheese
- [ ] Italian sausage
- [ ] Ham (+$1.00)

Sort Order: If this product will have multiple options, (i.e. CRUST: Deep Dish or Thin Crust; SAUCE: Marinara or Alfredo; TOPPINGS: shown below). This example is Toppings and we want it to display after Crust and Sauce, so we put a 3.
NEXT CLICK THE BOTTOM RIGHT "ADD OPTION VALUE" Button once for EACH OPTION VALUE and give each a Sort Order. Note in the example below Pepperoni will be listed first with Sort Order of 1, Cheese second, etc.
BE SURE TO CLICK THE TOP RIGHT "SAVE BUTTON" or your work will not be saved.

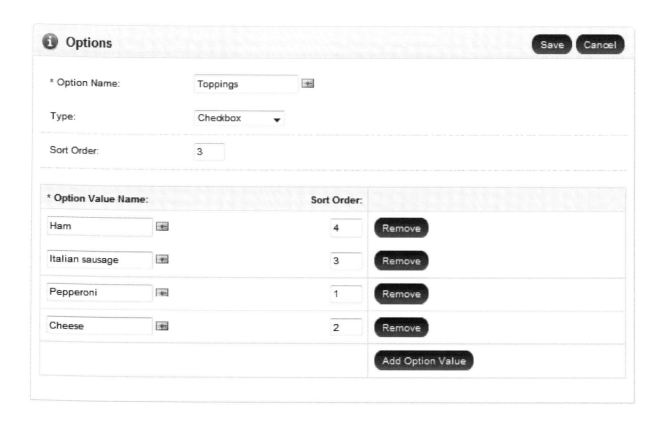

Option Type: Checkbox Step 2.

NEXT, open the Product Information Page that will use this option, and link the option to the product.

From your store Admin's top nav bar menu, select CATALOG - Products, and find the product name (or create the new product).

Click the OPTION Tab and enter information into the form as follows:

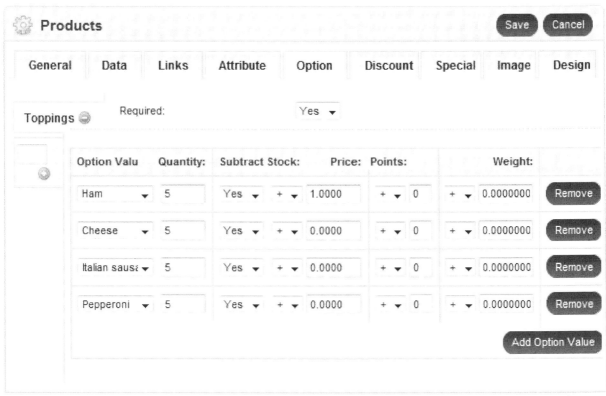

REQUIRED: Select YES if you want customer to be forced to select an option, or NO to let them check out without choosing.

OPTION VALUE: Example Small, Medium or Large. Try to be as descriptive as possible so customers do not have to look up many charts (example Small - fits child size 0-4)

QUANTITY: If you are tracking stock, how many of this option you have.

SUBTRACT STOCK: If you wish to track stock levels of this item, leave at YES. Otherwise select NO.

PRICE: If you wish to charge extra (or less) for this product, enter the amount here. EXAMPLE: Men's extra large t-shirts cost $2 more from the manufacturer. The "+$2.00" will appear in the option box of your store.

+/-: If you wish to ADD the extra amount, i.e. $2 MORE for this option, select "+" If you wish to DISCOUNT this option, select "-"

POINTS: If you wish to give Reward Points for purchasing this option, enter the number of points.

WEIGHT: Enter the weight of this option IF it is significantly heavier or lighter than the normal option to charge extra (or less) in shipping this option.

+/-: Specify whether the weight is more for this option (+) or less (-).

Option Type:
Optional Text Field

Optional Text field allows ONE line of text to be typed by the customer.

In this example, a customer can specify their initials to be inscribed on a ring or bracelet.

Available Options

* Inscription:

4 letters max

Option Type: Optional Text Field Step 1. Create the options in CATALOG - Options. Fill in the form as follows:

OPTION NAME: Give the option a name that will appear as the heading of this option.
TYPE: Select TEXT.
SORT ORDER: If you will use multiple options, such as COLOR and SIZE, put a 1 for this option to appear first, 2 to appear second, etc.

When you have finished, be sure to click the top right SAVE Button.

Option Type: Optional Text Field Step 2. Now create or edit the product that will use the options, and select the option on the OPTIONS Tab as shown below.

From your store Admin's top nav bar menu, select CATALOG - Products, and find the product name (or create the new product).

Click the OPTION Tab. This brings you to an almost blank page with only a box and green "+" button.

BEGIN TYPING the name of the option you created for this product, and a drop-down box will appear with all the options that match.

REQUIRED: Select YES if customer MUST fill in this line, or NO to let them skip it.

OPTION VALUE: Enter a message to the customer letting them know what you expect.

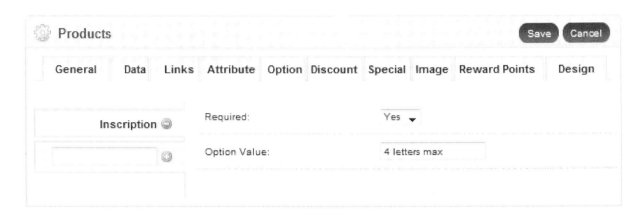

Option Type Textarea

Option Type Textarea is identical to text, but it is multiple lines instead of a single line.

Please follow **Option Type Text** above for instructions. The OPTION VALUE box is optional.

Available Options

* Customization Desired:

Option Type File

FILE allows the customer to upload a file from their own computer by clicking the UPLOAD FILE Button and selecting the image from their computer. For example, to have the image customized onto a T-Shirt or coffee cup.

Please follow **Option Type Text** above for instructions, but there is NO VALUE Box -- you only specify the option name

Available Options

and whether or not required.

Option Type: Date, Time, or Date & Time

DATE & TIME allows the customer to select a date and time from a drop-down box that appears when the customer clicks inside the box.

DATE is the same but without the TIME section.

TIME is the same but without the calendar DATE section.

Please follow **Option Type Text** above for instructions. Leave the OPTION VALUE box blank.

CATALOG MENU

Manufacturers or Brands

If your customers will shop by manufacturer or brand name only -- such as ONLY Hanes T-Shirts, or ONLY Apple Computers -- you can have them appear in the "Find Your Favorite Brand" linked from the "Brands" link in all footers only -- such as ONLY Hanes T-Shirts, or ONLY Apple Computers -- you can have them appear in the "Find Your Favorite Brand" linked from the "Brands" link in all footers in your store (see below).

If all of your products are by the same manufacturer or made by you or your own company, you can skip this step.

TIP: If you do not want to use it, the "BRANDS" Link in the footer cannot be automatically removed at this time. A techie will have to remove it from the code for you.

Find Your Favorite Brand

Brand Index: A B C H P S

A

AMD   Abbott Labs   Acer   Apple

B

B&B Brand   Blackberry   Bluebonnet   Bush's

C

Canon   Compaq   Computer Associates (CA)   Conway

Customer Service	Extras	Account
• Contact Us	• Brands	• Login
• Returns	• Gift Vouchers	• Order History
• Site Map	• Affiliates	• Wish List
	• Specials	• Newsletter

OpenCart Version 1.5.1.1 added an additional brand display called "Carousel." It displays a slideshow of brand logos. The slideshow can be in a side column, on your home page, or on another page that you specify. Individual carousel banners must be created from your existing images in **SYSTEM - Design - Banners** and linked together in a slideshow in **EXTENSIONS - Carousel**. See those chapters for detail.

From the Admin's Top Bar Navigation Menu, select CATALOG - Manufacturers. This brings you to the Manufacturer List:

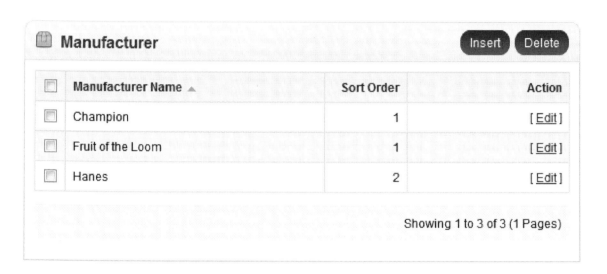

In the top right, click the INSERT Button and enter the desired information.

Click the IMAGE to upload the image. Follow instructions in Categories section above for **IMAGE MANAGER**.

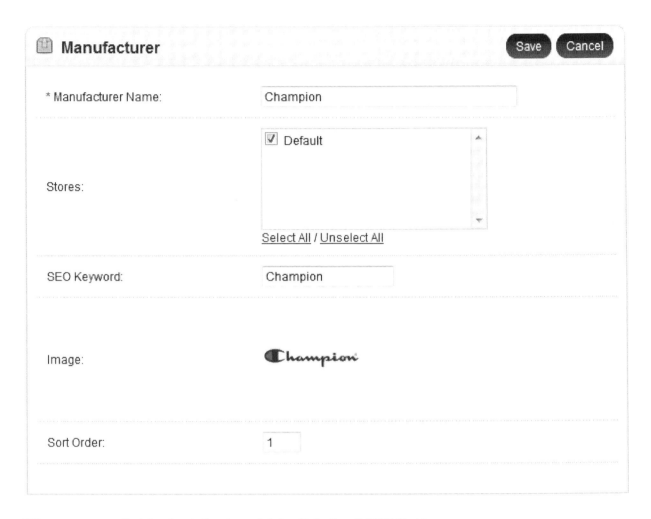

When you are finished, at the top right, click the SAVE Button.

Repeat for each manufacturer or brand, then continue to the next section.

CATALOG MENU

Downloads

If you are selling music, ebooks, any documents in PDF format, or any other downloadable product, you will upload that file, give it a name, and set a maximum number of downloads.

From the Admin's top navigation bar, click CATALOG - Downloads. This brings you to the Downloads form:

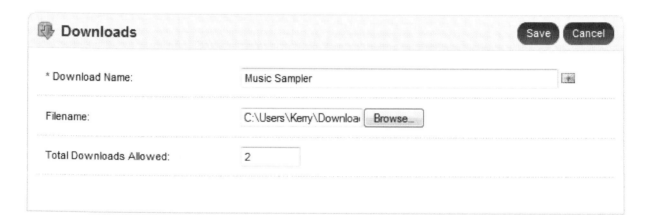

*DOWNLOAD NAME: A unique name that the customer will see upon downloading.

FILENAME: Click the BROWSE Button and select the file from your computer. After you hit Save, the file will be automatically uploaded to your website.

TOTAL DOWNLOADS ALLOWED: If you set it to 2, customers who get an error while downloading the first time will not have to contact you for help. The number is your choice. Set to 1 to be sure each customer can only get one copy.

After you finish, in the top right click the SAVE Button.

You can now see your new downloadable product in the DOWNLOADS List:

 This is only part of the DOWNLOADS Setup: You must also LINK the product to this download on the Product Information page's LINKS Tab (shown below) and set the product's weight to "0" so it knows the product is a download.

NEXT on CATALOG -Products - (then select the product name and click the EDIT Link), select the top left LINKS Tab, and check the name of the file for customers to download:

Be sure to test your downloadable product to be sure it is set up correctly.

CATALOG MENU

Reviews

Customers can write a review of merchandise they own and love or hate by navigating to that product's page and clicking the REVIEWS link. Reviews are automatically displayed in your store on the Product's REVIEWS Tab as shown below.

The review will not be visible to other customers until AFTER you go to CATALOG - Reviews and approve it.

To view and approve customer reviews, from your store Admin's top nav bar menu, select CATALOG - Reviews. This brings you to the Reviews List:

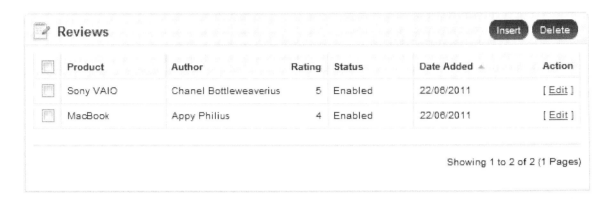

Click the EDIT Link of the review you want to approve. This brings you to the REVIEWS Form:

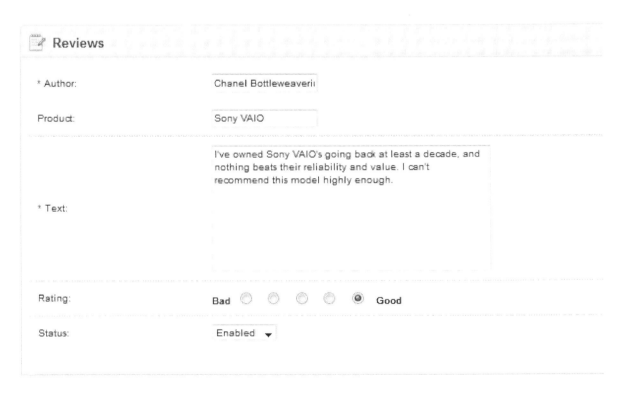

Fill in or edit the form as shown above.

When you have finished, be sure to click the top right SAVE Button.

CATALOG MENU

Information pages
(Content Management System or CMS):
About us, Privacy Policy, Terms & Conditions

The Information pages are linked into the footer of your new store. You can add any number of pages here, and even sort them into categories.

The new Information pages that you create automatically appear in this column, called a "dynamic footer":

To edit the Information Box pages, in your Admin's top nav bar select CATALOG - Information. This brings you to the Information List:

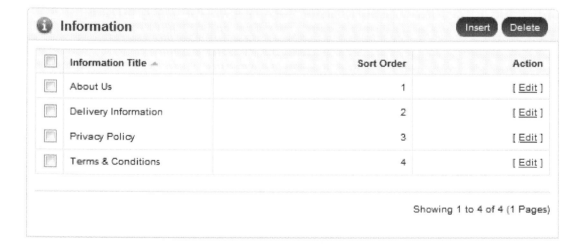

On the Information List page, you may:

- **Edit an existing page** - click in the far right column the page's EDIT Link. Note many other options are available on the edit page, see below.
- **Insert a new page** - click the top right INSERT Button and fill in the form boxes.
- **Delete a page** - put a check in the far left checkbox, then click the top right DELETE Button.

TIP: Don't delete a page unless you will NEVER need it again. We recommend that you DISABLE it (hide from visitors, but it remains in your Admin). To disable a page, in the Admin's CATALOG - Information List, click the EDIT Link of the page you want to hide, then in INFORMATION STATUS box change to DISABLED.

Insert new pages in the Information box

Many payment processors require you to have a page about "Shipping & Returns." It is also good business practice. Your customers may also need a SIZE CHART so they order the correct size the first time, a color chart, or any other information that will help you reduce returns. Create these new pages here.

To insert a new page in the Information box, from the Admin's top nav bar, select CATALOG - Information.

This brings you to the Information List. In the top right, click the INSERT Button to open the Insert Information page:

INFORMATION TITLE: The name you want to appear in the Information box and at the top of the new page.

DESCRIPTION: The words you want on the page. Edit like editing an email. TIP: Put your mouse over any button to see the button's name.

STORES:	If you manage multiple stores, check their names for this page to appear in more than one. Otherwise, just leave "Default" checked.
SEO KEYWORD:	IF you use the SEO URLs module, the name you want to display instead of http://myopencartstore.com/index.php?route=information/information&information_id=6. NO SPACES BETWEEN KEYWORDS; USE A DASH (-) INSTEAD.
INFORMATION STATUS:	To SHOW the page in the Information box and allow visitors to see the page, select ENABLED. To HIDE the page from the public but keep it in your Admin, select DISABLED.
SORT ORDER:	To list the page FIRST in the Information Box, enter the SMALLEST NUMBER (can be zero). To list the page LAST, enter the LARGEST NUMBER. TIP: numbers do NOT need to be in sequence. EXAMPLE: 10, 20, 25, 50, 99 will display the same as 1, 2, 3, 4, 5. Using larger numbers is easier to change sort order, because you do not need to change every page number. TIP: PREVENT a page from being listed in the Information box, BUT visible on your website so visitors CAN go directly to it, enter a sort order of -1. When you have finished, in the top right click the SAVE Button.

Step 8. Test, test, test and make any changes needed

After you have finished going through all items in the CATALOG menu, make some test purchases to be sure you have completed each step before adding your remaining products!

Some tips to make testing easier:

1 Register for an account in your store as if you were a real customer.

In your storefront, click the top right LOG IN Tab and in the box "I am a new customer" Click the CONTINUE Button and fill in the registration form.

2 Temporarily select the "FREE SHIPPING" Method

In EXTENSIONS - Shipping - Free Shipping, set up the form as shown below, then in the top right, click the SAVE Button.

3 Temporarily select the "FREE CHECKOUT" Method

In EXTENSIONS - Payment - Free Checkout, set up the form as shown below, then in the top right, click the SAVE Button.

4 Now purchase some products from your store, making modifications as needed.

Open TWO browser windows - one with your storefront and the other with your store Admin. In your browser, click CTRL-N to open a new window. Now you can quickly swap between your store and Admin, making and testing changes.

5 IMPORTANT LAST STEP - disable FREE CHECKOUT and FREE SHIPPING

You don't want real customers to think they can have your products for free! In EXTENSIONS - Payment - Free Checkout, change STATUS to DISABLED, then in the top right, click the SAVE Button. Go to EXTENSIONS - Shipping - Free Shipping, change STATUS to DISABLED, then in the top right, click the SAVE Button:

5

5. Extensions Menu

"Extensions" are add-on programs that improve your store and make it easier to make money. There are hundreds or thousands of extensions for sale or free for downloading, but these are pre-installed in your OpenCart store.

EXTENSIONS MENU

Modules

Before you start, some important information about extensions:

- Most modules require additional setup.
- This menu generally turns the extension ON or OFF.
- Some modules, even when set up correctly, will not appear until after a specific condition is met. Example, the Bestsellers box appears in your store until after one

customer has made a purchase in your store. SO to see and test it, you must first re-create the conditions of that box by making a test purchase in your store.

To begin using Modules, from your store Admin's top navigation bar, select EXTENSIONS - Modules. This brings you to the MODULES List:

Modules

Module Name	Action
Account	[Edit] [Uninstall]
Affiliate	[Edit] [Uninstall]
Banner	[Edit] [Uninstall]
Bestsellers	[Install]
Carousel	[Edit] [Uninstall]
Category	[Edit] [Uninstall]
Featured	[Edit] [Uninstall]
Google Talk	[Install]
Information	[Install]
Latest	[Install]
Slideshow	[Edit] [Uninstall]
Specials	[Install]
Store	[Install]
Welcome	[Install]

ACCOUNT:	Information box about the customer's account, including email address, password, street address for shipping and billing. Appears only after the customer has logged in.
AFFILIATE:	Information box about becoming an affiliate who receives commissions for referring customers to your store. Appears only if you have set up an affiliate program.
BANNER:	Ad or other banners that can be placed in left or right column, on home page above or below page content, or on a specific template. See also slideshow below.
BESTSELLERS:	Automatically tracks the most commonly purchased products in your store. Appears only after you have had a sale.
CAROUSEL:	A slideshow of manufacturer logos that appears on the home page in a new store, can be customized to manage any set of small images. Requires additional setup.
CATEGORY:	Product navigation box. May be in addition to, or in place of, the product top navigation bar.
GOOGLE TALK:	Chat with live customers. You must sign up for a Google Talk account.
INFORMATION:	A box of information customers need to buy from you. Also appears in the footer. Box of additional pages for shipping information, privacy policy, and any other purpose.
LATEST:	Automatically lists the newest products added to your store. You must add at least one new product for this box to appear.
SLIDESHOW:	Select different ad banners to display as a slideshow. See also banners above.
SPECIALS:	Display discounted products in a box. You must set up at least one special for this box to appear.
STORE:	If you have multiple stores, "Choose a Store" box allow customers to choose which store to browse. You must have at least two stores for this box to appear.
WELCOME:	Home page welcome message or other text to greet customers. Unlike most modules, this is also where you enter or edit the text. TIP: In earlier editions prior to OpenCart 1.5, this was in System Settings - General.

OpenCart Modules can be automatically installed and modified as you like. From the MODULES list you can do the following:

- Install or uninstall the module box in your store.
- Move the box into the left or right column. Some can also be moved to the home page bottom middle or to other page templates.
- Set the maximum number of items to display in the box.
- Move the position of the box up or down in its column.
- Show or hide the box.

Some modules have additional settings, and some require additional setup on another menu (for example, to create a special you must go to the Catalog - Product information page and click the SPECIAL Tab for the product to appear in the Specials box).

EXTENSIONS MENU - MODULES

Account module

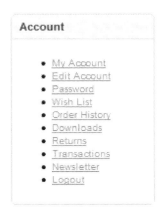

This is a handy navigation box for customers who are logged in. *It does not appear until after the customer logs in.*

Account module allows the customer to quickly get to the information they need about their account and their orders.

Account module is already turned ON in a newly-installed OpenCart store.

To use or modify the Account module, from your store Admin's top navigation bar, select EXTENSIONS - Modules and select Account from the Modules List. This brings you to the Account module:

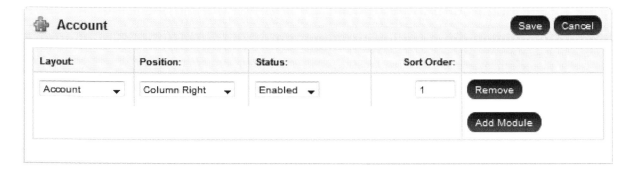

LAYOUT: What page layout (a sub-template) do you want to use for this module? Select from the drop-down list.

POSITION: Do you want the box to appear in the left column, right column, or in the middle of the home page top or home page bottom?

STATUS: Turn ON by selecting ENABLED; turn OFF by selecting DISABLED.

SORT ORDER: This box will display at the top with the sort order of "1." Set to two to display second in its column or position, three to display third, etc.

When finished, in the top right, click the top right SAVE Button.

EXTENSIONS MENU - MODULES

Affiliate module

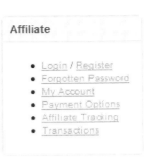

This is a handy navigation box for your affiliates (resellers) who are logged in. It does not appear until after the affiliate logs in. Affiliate module allows the affiliate to quickly get to the information they need about their account and their orders.

Affiliate module is already turned ON in a newly-installed OpenCart store.

IMPORTANT: Set up your Affiliate Program in SYSTEM – Settings – Option – Affiliate Terms AND Affiliate Commission, and create a new Affiliate Terms & Conditions page in CATALOG – Information.

To use or modify the Affiliate module, from your store Admin's top navigation bar, select EXTENSIONS - Modules and select Affiliate from the Modules List. This brings you to the Affiliate module:

LAYOUT: What page layout (a sub-template) do you want to use for this module? Select from the drop-down list.

POSITION: Do you want the box to appear in the left column, right column, or in the middle of the home page top or home page bottom?

STATUS: Turn ON by selecting ENABLED; turn OFF by selecting DISABLED.

SORT ORDER: This box will display at the top with the sort order of "1." Set to two to display second in its column or position, three to display third, etc.

When finished, in the top right, click the top right SAVE Button.

EXTENSIONS MENU - MODULES

Banners

Banners are many kinds of images that can appear in your store. Customers can click them to go to a link that you specify.

Here are some examples of banners:

- Advertising banners from other advertisers
- Special promotions for products in your store
- A slideshow on your home or other page to wow customers or demonstrate how a product works
- A special kind of slideshow called a "Carousel" that displays a strip of many small images such as logos.

Banners include the Home Page slideshow and Manufacturers logo carousel.

Unless you have special graphics skills, you normally must have the individual images created for you by a graphics artist, or the advertiser must provide the artwork to you according to specifications you give them. Graphic design is an advanced topic not covered by this user manual.

BANNER SPECIFICATIONS

Banner "specs" are necessary because artwork files can be too large and slow down your page load times. This can cause Google and other search engines to penalize you. Page load times are very important. Specs are also necessary so your store looks consistent and gives you a professional image.

You can Google "Advertising specification" for examples of specs used by big advertisers, and/or use these general guidelines:

- OpenCart will resize your images, but this can cause distortion if the original images are extremely large.
- Make all images for a slideshow, carousel or other banner the same height and width.
- Images must not be wider than the location they will go. Example: If a left or right column is 200 pixels wide, do not use an image 230 pixels wide. (Pixels can be estimated at 100 per inch).
- The more images in a slideshow, carousel or other banner, the smaller file size for each image.
- If your average customer has a large computer screen and fast Internet connection, you can use wider/taller images and greater file sizes.
- If your average customer has a small monitor, tablet or even mobile device, use the smallest images and file sizes possible.

To use or modify the Banner module, from your store Admin's top navigation bar, select EXTENSIONS - Modules and select Banner from the Modules List. This brings you to the Banner module. Fill in as follows:

EXTENSIONS MENU - MODULES

Bestsellers module

Your OpenCart store will automatically track the best-selling items in your store, and display them in this box.

Bestsellers appears in your store only after you have had a sale. So to test it, you must sign up as a customer and make at least one test purchase.

To modify Bestsellers, in your store Admin select EXTENSIONS - Modules, and from the Modules List far right column, click the INSTALL Link (if necessary), then click the EDIT Link.

This brings you to the Bestsellers form:

LIMIT: How many items do you want to appear in the box?

IMAGE (WxH): The small images in the example are 32 x 32 pixels.

LAYOUT: Select a template from the drop-down box.

POSITION: Do you want the box to appear in the left column, right column, or in the home page bottom middle (home)?

STATUS: Turn ON by selecting ENABLED; turn OFF by selecting DISABLED.

SORT ORDER: This box will display third from the top with the sort order of "3." Move up by decreasing the number; move down by increasing the number.

When finished, in the top right, click the SAVE Button.

EXTENSIONS MENU - MODULES

Carousel module

Carousel is a special kind of slideshow banner for manufacturers/brands. The customer can click the arrow to the right of the carousel to see additional brands. When the customer clicks a logo, your store displays all of the merchandise you sell for that manufacturer.

Example: if the customer clicks the SONY logo in the carousel, it takes them to a Sony page listing all of the Sony items you sell.

Carousel requires additional setup as follows:

1. Save all of the manufacturer or brand logos to your personal computer.
2. Upload them to your store in **SYSTEM - Design - Banners**.
3. Now you are ready to follow the instructions below to tell your store how to display these banners in a carousel.

To modify Carousel, in your store Admin select EXTENSIONS - Modules, and from the Modules List find Carousel. In the far right column, click the INSTALL Link (if necessary), then click the EDIT Link.

This brings you to the Carousel form:

BANNER: "Manufacturers" is the pre-installed manufacturer's logo banners, or select another banner if you have created a custom one.

LIMIT: How many logos do you want to appear on the screen at one time?

SCROLL: How many logos do you want to move left or right when a customer clicks the arrow?

IMAGE (WXH): The program will reduce your images to the same size. 80 is about 8/10's of an inch. Play around with different numbers here.

LAYOUT: Select the HOME layout (template) for the carousel to appear on the home page, or a custom layout you have made.

POSITION: Do you want the box to appear in the left column or right column?

STATUS: Turn ON by selecting ENABLED; turn OFF by selecting DISABLED.

SORT ORDER: This box will display at the top with the sort order of "1." Move up by decreasing the number; move down by increasing the number.

When finished, in the top right, click the SAVE Button.

EXTENSIONS MENU - MODULES

Category module

The Categories box is an easy way for your customers to find your products if you do not use top bar navigation.

If you set it to appear in a left or right column, it will appear only on pages that have that column.

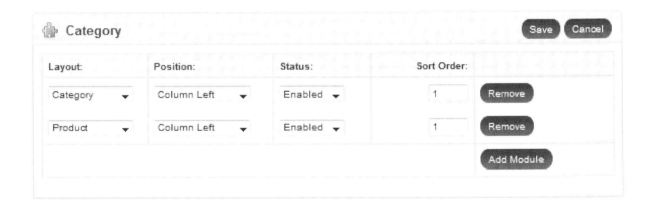

LAYOUT: Category and Product layouts (templates) are pre-selected for you. Or select a custom template you have made.

POSITION: Do you want the box to appear in the left column or right column?

STATUS: Turn ON by selecting ENABLED; turn OFF by selecting DISABLED.

SORT ORDER: This box will display at the top with the sort order of "1." Move up by decreasing the number; move down by increasing the number.

When finished, in the top right, click the SAVE Button.

EXTENSIONS MENU - MODULES

Featured products module

You may highlight products you especially want customers to see and buy -- like a store window display, or putting them on a display at the end of a store aisle.

This is different from a SPECIAL - the price is not reduced.

The Featured Products you select may be displayed in either the left OR right column, OR in the home page at the bottom middle.

To add the Featured Products module to your store, in your store Admin select EXTENSIONS - Modules, and from the Modules List find Featured. In the far right column, click the INSTALL Link (if necessary), then click the EDIT Link.

This brings you to the Featured Products form:

PRODUCTS: Type the FIRST letter of a product name, and select from the drop-down box of products appears.

IMAGE: Specify size and height you want the product image to appear in the Featured box. The program will reduce your images to the same size. 90 is about 9/10's of an inch. Play around with different numbers here.

LAYOUT: What page layout (a sub-template) do you want to use for this module? Select from the drop-down list.

POSITION: Do you want the box to appear in the left column, right column, OR in the home page bottom middle (home)?

STATUS: Turn ON by selecting ENABLED; turn OFF by selecting DISABLED.

SORT ORDER: This box will display second in the middle of the home page with the sort order of "2." If there are not 2 boxes in that position, it will be first. Move up by decreasing the number; move down by increasing the number.

When finished, in the top right, click the SAVE Button.

EXTENSIONS MENU - MODULES

Google Talk module

A Google Talk box lets your potential customers chat with you whenever you are logged in to Google Talk. If you are not logged in, the box will say "Unavailable."

On your computer, whenever you are logged in, you can chat with potential customers like the following example.

After a customer clicks the Chat Box above, it opens a window on both the customer and store owner/administrator computers as shown below:

Get Google Talk

To use Google Talk, you must have a Google Account. Go to http://google.com and at the top right, click the "SIGN IN" link. Click on the "Don't Have an Account?" and follow the instructions.

Next, still logged into your Google account, go to http://www.google.com/talk and then click on "DOWNLOAD GOOGLE TALK".

Save the file to your computer, then double-click it to install it.

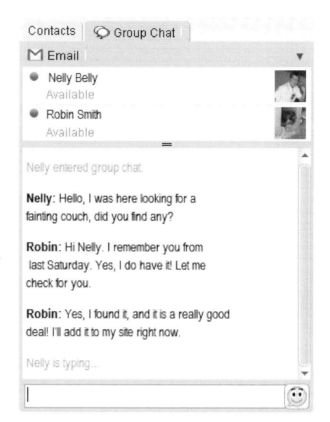

Get the Google Badge for your website

Still logged in to Google, go to http://www.google.com/talk/service/badge/New?pli=1 This brings you to the following Google page:

Sign out

Create a Google Talk chatback badge

A Google Talk chatback badge will let visitors to your web page chat with you. They'll be able to chat with you whenever you're signed in to Google Talk. For more information, visit the help center.

Each time you visit this page, we generate a new badge for you so you can use badges with different settings on different web pages. For example, you can share your status message on your personal blog and not on your public blog. To change a badge later, just return to this page and get a new one.

Here's your badge:

> ◔ **Chat with Robin Smith**
> Away

Edit ▼   Disable old badges

To use this badge, copy and paste the HTML code below into your web page. If the site that hosts your web page does not support direct HTML editing or embedded frames then click 'Edit' to select a style of badge that does not use frames. If you want to include your badge in an email message, you should use the 'Hyperlink only' or 'Url only' styles.

```
<iframe src="http://www.google.com/talk/service/badge/Show?
tk=z01q6amlqtin29b0t3cg9rs64rl8v6o4d28h2n5fdhp20e6jm2ctbl08v6pa0g8suko5j7u2a6lvifl52h6eud49v645n42gkmpimr8u2dt
76nvmpqgkcnha1752b7bjqgds5oo9mhglsirjqtn6894cjn4d76idnv5i7bev7&amp;w=200&amp;h=60" frameborder="0"
```

In the light blue box at the bottom of the page, copy everything in the box by highlighting it, then RIGHT-CLICK and from the menu that pops up, select COPY.

Now in your OpenCart store Admin, select EXTENSIONS - Modules, from the Modules List find GOOGLE TALK, and click the far right EDIT Link. This brings you to the Google Talk form:

In the GOOGLE TALK CODE Box, click inside the box and paste the code with a RIGHT-CLICK, then from the menu that pops up, select PASTE.

Move the position to the left or right box if desired.

Change the STATUS Box to ENABLED, move box up in SORT ORDER with a smaller number or down with a larger number, and at the top right click the SAVE Button.

EXTENSIONS MENU - MODULES

Information module

The Information Box contains links to information pages that you create in the **CATALOG - Information menu.** See that chapter for detailed help setting up the information pages.

NOTE That the links in the box are "Dynamic." This means that as you add or remove pages in Catalog - Information, the pages are automatically added or removed from this box.

This module simply turns the box off or on, and specifies the position of the box in the column:

To edit the Information box, from your store Admin's top nav bar, select EXTENSIONS - Modules. This brings you to the Modules List. In the INFORMATION Row, click the INSTALL Link if not installed, then click the EDIT Link.

This brings you to the INFORMATION form:

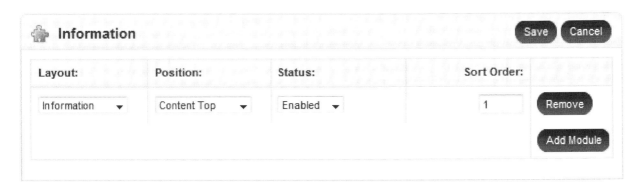

LAYOUT: Select the INFORMATION template from the drop-down box.

POSITION: Do you want the box to appear in the left column or right column?

STATUS: Turn ON by selecting ENABLED; turn OFF by selecting DISABLED.

SORT ORDER: This box will display third from the top with the sort order of "3." Move up by decreasing the number; move down by increasing the number.

When finished, in the top right, click the SAVE Button.

There is also a "dynamic link" to Information pages in the footer – that means as you add or remove pages in the Information menu, the pages are automatically added or removed from the footer. Awesome!

EXTENSIONS MENU - MODULES

Latest products module

The Latest Products automatically displays the products that you most recently added to your store.

It can display in the left or right column, and by default it is initially set up to display in your home page bottom middle.

The example to the right is a Latest Products Box as it appears in a left or right column.

To edit your Latest Products box, from your store Admin's top nav bar, select EXTENSIONS - Modules. From the Modules List that appears, find the LATEST row, click Install if needed, and at the far right click the EDIT Link.

This brings you to the LATEST PRODUCTS Form:

LIMIT: How many items do you want to appear in this box?

IMAGE (WxH): The program will reduce your images to the same size. 80 is about 8/10's of an inch. Play around with different numbers here.

LAYOUT: Select the LATEST template from the drop-down box.

POSITION: Home, left column or right column.

STATUS: Turn ON by selecting ENABLED; turn OFF by selecting DISABLED.

SORT ORDER: This box will display third from the top with the sort order of "3." Move up by decreasing the number; move down by increasing the number.

When finished, in the top right, click the SAVE Button.

EXTENSIONS MENU - MODULES

Slideshow module

OpenCart has a big fancy slideshow banner on the home page that changes from one picture to another using special effects called "AJAX" (for Asynchronous JavaScript - doesn't matter, it just means it's cool).

Each picture of the slideshow links to a different product.

The slideshow helps you sell more products.

Note that the banners in your slideshow must first be uploaded in the **SYSTEM - Design - Banners menu.**

This Slideshow Module form lets you change the dimensions and look of the slideshow.

To edit your slideshow, from your store Admin's top nav bar, select EXTENSIONS - Modules. From the Modules List that appears, find the SLIDESHOW row and at the far right click the EDIT Link.

This brings you to the SLIDESHOW Form:

BANNER: Leave at Manufacturer or change to another custom banner.

DIMENSION (WXH):   The program will reduce all your images to the same size. 980 by 280 is about 9.8 inches wide by 2.8 inches high. This size will fit nicely on nearly all computer screens. Play around with different numbers here.

LAYOUT: Leave at HOME to display the slideshow on the Home page.

POSITION: On top or bottom of page content, left column or right column.

STATUS: Turn ON by selecting ENABLED; turn OFF by selecting DISABLED.

SORT ORDER: If you have specified multiple boxes on the content bottom, this box will display first from the top with the sort order of "1." Move down by changing to a 2 or more.

When finished, in the top right, click the SAVE Button.

EXTENSIONS MENU - MODULES

Specials module

You can display special pricing in the Specials box that all customers can see OR only certain groups when logged in (example, wholesale only), and have the special price start and stop on certain dates.

SPECIALS

Windsor Chair
$725.00 $695.00

IMPORTANT: For Specials to appear in the Specials Box, you must also set the special prices in CATALOG - Products. See below for more info.

The special price also appears in your Admin's CATALOG - Product List:

☐		Walnut Drop-Leaf Table	TABLEDL	2575.0000	4	Enabled	[Edit]
☐		Windsor Chair	WIND-1	725.0000 695.0000	10	Enabled	[Edit]
☐		Wingback Sitting Chair	WING1	2525.0000	3	Enabled	[Edit]

Setting up the Specials module is done in two steps:

- **Step 1. First set up the special in the CATALOG – Products menu.**
- **Step 2. Then return to EXTENSIONS - Modules and turn on the Specials module.**

Specials Step 1. In your store Admin's CATALOG - Products menu, find the product you want to put on special, and at the far right, click the EDIT Link. At the top left, click the SPECIAL Tab and enter the information as follows:

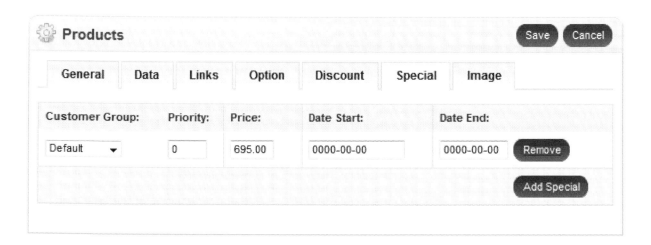

CUSTOMER GROUPS: Do you want only a certain group to see this special, for example, employees only? Select that group here. YOU MUST FIRST ADD ADDITIONAL CUSTOMER GROUPS such as "Employees" in SALES - Customer Group - Insert.

PRIORITY: You can have multiple specials on the same product - see the bottom right ADD SPECIAL Button. If so, do you want this special offered to the customer first, or the other special? EXAMPLE: a general special, and a special for wholesale customers. The Wholesale special will probably have the higher priority (1) and the general special (2).

PRICE: The special price you want the customer to see.

DATE START: Click in this box to set a start date. The special will NOT appear before then. Leave blank to start immediately.

DATE END: Click in this box to set an end date. The special will NOT appear after this. Leave blank to run until you manually turn the special OFF.

When finished, in the top right, click the SAVE Button.

Specials Step 2. Then return to EXTENSIONS - Modules and turn on the Specials module.

After creating one or more specials, in your Admin's top nav bar, select EXTENSIONS - Modules and from the Modules List far right click the EDIT Link. This brings you to the SPECIALS Form:

LIMIT: How many Specials you want to fit into the SPECIALS Box.

IMAGE (WXH): The program will reduce your images to the same size. 80 is about 8/10's of an inch. Play around with different numbers here.

LAYOUT: Select SPECIALS template or a custom template you have uploaded.

POSITION: Left column or right column, top or bottom of content.

STATUS: Turn ON by selecting ENABLED; turn OFF by selecting DISABLED.

SORT ORDER: This box will display 3rd from the top with the sort order of "3." Move up by decreasing the number; move down by increasing the number. If there are not 3 boxes, it will simply appear last in the column.

When finished, in the top right, click the SAVE Button.

EXTENSIONS MENU - MODULES

Store module

If you have several related stores, you can allow customers to quickly navigate from one to the next.

More commonly, if you have multiple stores and are logged in as an Admin, you can use this box to quickly navigate through the different stores when you make a change you need to see.

To set up the Store module, from your Admin top nav bar menu select EXTENSIONS - Modules and from the Modules List, select Store. This brings you to the Store form:

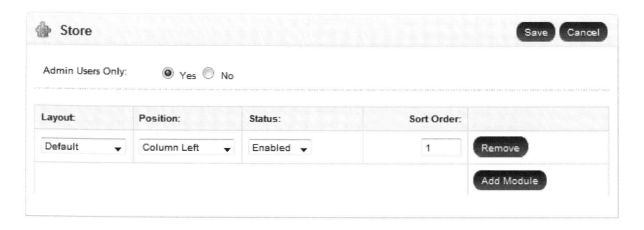

LAYOUT: Select DEFAULT template or a custom template you have uploaded.

POSITION: Left column or right column, top or bottom of content.

STATUS: Turn ON by selecting ENABLED; turn OFF by selecting DISABLED.

SORT ORDER: This box will display at the top of the left column with the sort order of "1." Move up by decreasing the number; move down by increasing the number.

When finished, in the top right, click the SAVE Button.

EXTENSIONS MENU - MODULES

Welcome module

When a new visitor comes to your store, they decide in the first few seconds whether or not to stay. This special Information Box lets you greet the customer and quickly tell them your qualifications. It is like a store owner standing in their own doorway, warmly greeting shoppers who enter the store.

If for some reason you do not want to display any products on your home page - i.e. Featured Products, Specials, etc. - you can turn the home page into a text page with this module. OR you can use it in addition to other home page modules, as shown here:

To edit your home page Welcome box, in your store Admin's top navigation bar select SYSTEM - Settings. At the top left tabs, click the STORE Tab:

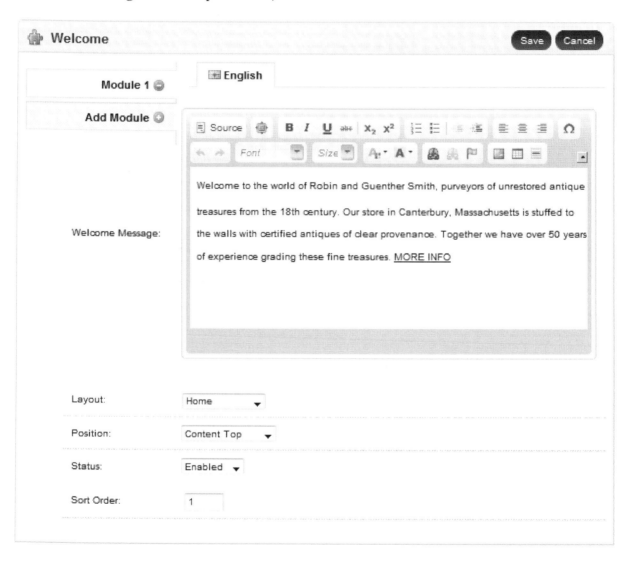

In the WELCOME MESSAGE Box, simply type your welcome message, then set up the rest as follows:

LAYOUT: Select HOME template or a custom template you have uploaded.

POSITION: Left column or right column, top or bottom of content.

STATUS: Turn ON by selecting ENABLED; turn OFF by selecting DISABLED.

SORT ORDER: This box will display at the top of the left column with the sort order of "1." Move up by decreasing the number; move down by increasing the number.

When finished, in the top right, click the SAVE Button.

TIP: The Home page Welcome message can be ANY LENGTH! There appears to be no limit, so make it as long as you like.

TIP: In versions 1.4.9 and earlier, the Home Page Welcome was located in SETTINGS – General.

EXTENSIONS MENU

Shipping

NOTE: If you don't see your shipper, many other shipper extensions are also available on the OpenCart.com website at http://www.opencart.com/index.php?route=extension/extension&path=4. These can be installed by your technical pro.

Selecting a shipping method is a business decision you need to make. You will be able to fine-tune your decision as you go, and make changes as you gain experience, so don't agonize about your choice now.

Remember you want to recoup the *average* cost of your shipping, boxes, labels, and packaging. Occasionally you will go over or under on an individual shipment. If it happens more than occasionally, examine your costs and consider changing shipping methods. Otherwise, don't worry about it.

The generic modules - Flat Rate, Per Item, Free Shipping and Weight Based Shipping - will work with a large variety of shippers. They are great for starting out.

TIP: Many of the shipping companies have strict requirements for opening an account, and it can take a couple of weeks to get the correct type of account open and finalized. Start early, or open your store with a simple method and then change the method later.

TIP: Which shipping module do I recommend? Start a store with a simple method such as Flat Rate, Per Item, or Weight-Based Shipping if you have entered product weights for each product. As you gain shipping experience, open an account with a shipper and change to a more accurate method.

Shipping

Shipping Method	Status	Sort Order	Action
Citylink	Disabled		[Install]
Flat Rate	Enabled	1	[Edit] [Uninstall]
Free Shipping	Disabled		[Edit] [Uninstall]
Per Item	Disabled		[Edit] [Uninstall]
Parcelforce 48	Disabled		[Install]
Pickup From Store	Enabled	2	[Edit] [Uninstall]
Royal Mail	Disabled		[Install]
UPS	Disabled		[Install]
United States Postal Service	Disabled		[Install]
Weight Based Shipping	Disabled		[Install]

Use the following comparison chart to compare the different methods available. Find the columns that describe your merchandise most closely, and select the method that is appropriate for you:

Comparison Chart of OpenCart Shipping Methods

	Method	Location	Heavy Items	Light Items	Large Items	Small Items	Variety	Similar	Inter-national	Easier to Install?
1	Citylink	United Kingdom		•		•	•	•		•
2	Flat Rate	Worldwide		•		•	•	•		•
3	Free Shipping	Worldwide		•		•		•		•
4	Per Item	Worldwide	•		•		•		•	•
5	Parcelforce 48	United Kingdom		•		•		•		
6	Pickup from Store	Worldwide	•		•		•			•
7	Royal Mail	United Kingdom		•		•		•	•	•
8	UPS United Parcel Service	Worldwide	•		•		•		•	
9	US Postal Service	USA		•		•	•	•	•	
10	Weight Based Shipping	Worldwide	•	•	•	•	•	•	•	•

After you have selected the method that is right for you, open up an account with that shipper if necessary. Information on setting up accounts is included below.

Shipping Extensions

To set up all new shippers, from the Admin's Top Bar Navigation Menu, select EXTENSIONS - Shipping. Here you find the above list of shipping companies that can be automatically installed.

Select the shipper you want, click the Install Button and fill in the information you received from the shipper when you set up the account.

CAUTION: Shipping methods can easily conflict with one another, especially if you install multiple methods. INSTALL ONLY ONE AT A TIME, AND BE SURE TO TEST THOROUGHLY BEFORE INSTALLING ANOTHER: Sign in as a customer and put a product in your cart. Does this shipping method appear in checkout? If not, go back and check the above settings.

EXTENSIONS - SHIPPING

1. Citylink
http://www.city-link.co.uk/

The UK's leading Premium Express Delivery Company providing high quality, flexible and innovative courier services across the UK, Ireland and Worldwide. You MUST send parcels on a regular basis, they do not offer one-time pickup service. Rates vary depending on volume.

Apply for service at http://www.city-link.co.uk/become-a-customer/online-form.html

After you receive your welcome package, log onto your store's Admin and from the top navigation bar, select EXTENSIONS - Shipping.

In the CITYLINK row click INSTALL if needed, then click the EDIT Link and edit as follows:

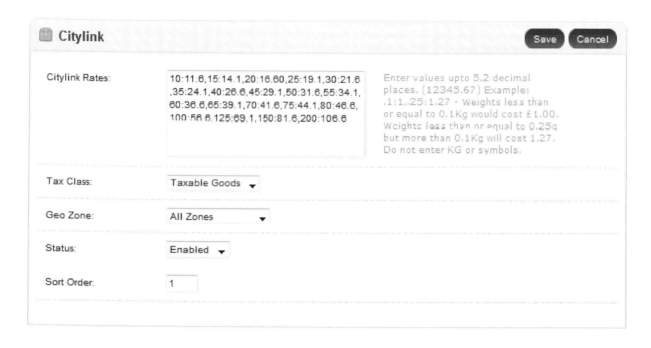

CITYLINK RATES: As instructed in your Welcome packet. In this example, the store owner has been given the following rates: Up to 10 Kg, £11.6; up to 15 Kg, £14.1; and so forth.

TAX CLASS: Are you required by your taxing authorities to charge tax on shipping costs? If so, select TAXABLE GOODS.

GEO ZONE: To what zones are you willing to ship using this method? This method will only appear in the zones you select.

STATUS: MUST be enabled for it to appear to customers.

SORT ORDER: If you offer multiple shipping methods, do you want this to appear first, second, etc.? The numbers do not need to be in exact order, the lowest number will appear first. Note that zero is the lowest number you can use.

When you are finished, be sure to click the top right SAVE Button.

Remember to test, test, test! Sign in as a customer and put a product in your cart. Does this shipping method appear in checkout? If not, go back and check the above settings.

EXTENSIONS - SHIPPING

2. Flat Rate Shipping

Select Flat Rate Shipping if you wish to charge a single per-order shipping fee to all customers, regardless of what product(s) they ordered or how many.

COST: How much do you wish to charge per order shipped? YOU MUST ALSO specify what currency this is (i.e. $2.00 US, or £2.0 UK, etc.) in SYSTEM - SETTINGS - LOCAL - Currency.

TAX CLASS: Are you required by your taxing authorities to charge tax on shipping costs? If so, select TAXABLE GOODS.

GEO ZONE: To what zones are you willing to ship using this method? This method will only appear in the zones you select.

STATUS: MUST be enabled for it to appear to customers.

SORT ORDER: If you offer multiple shipping methods, do you want this to appear first, second, etc.? The numbers do not need to be in exact order, the lowest number will appear first. Note that zero is the lowest number you can use.

When you are finished, be sure to click the top right SAVE Button.

Remember to test, test, test! Sign in as a customer and put a product in your cart. Does this shipping method appear in checkout? If not, go back and check the above settings.

EXTENSIONS - SHIPPING

3. Free Shipping

If you don't want to mess with separate shipping charges include a shipping price within the product price, OR if your products are downloads, you get to use this easy shipping module

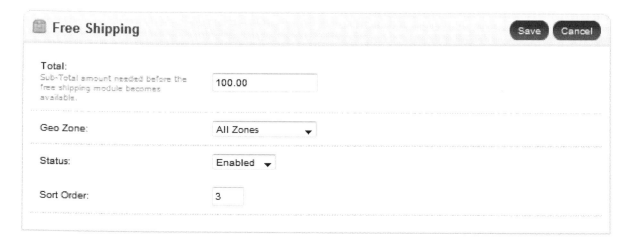

TOTAL: How much do you want customers to order before they get free shipping? YOU MUST ALSO specify what currency this is (i.e. $100 US, or £100 UK, etc.) in SYSTEM - SETTINGS - LOCAL - Currency.

GEO ZONE: To what zones are you willing to ship using this method? This method will only appear in the zones you select.

STATUS: MUST be enabled for it to appear to customers.

SORT ORDER: If you offer multiple shipping methods, do you want this to appear first, second, etc.? The numbers do not need to be in exact order, the lowest number will appear first. Note that zero is the lowest number you can use.

When you are finished, be sure to click the top right SAVE Button.

Remember to test, test, test! Sign in as a customer and put a product in your cart. Does this shipping method appear in checkout? If not, go back and check the above settings.

EXTENSIONS - SHIPPING

4. Per Item Shipping

Select Per Item Shipping if you wish to charge a separate shipping fee for each item. For example, shipping for one book is $5, 2 books is $10, and so on. Be careful if you choose this method and ship internationally... enable it only for your country's Geo Zone.

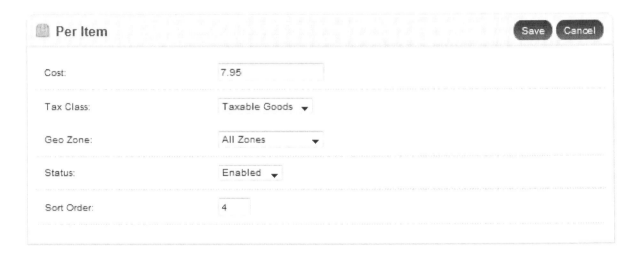

COST: How much do you wish to charge per order shipped? YOU MUST ALSO specify what currency this is (i.e. $7.95 US, or £7.95 UK, etc.) in SYSTEM - SETTINGS - LOCAL - Currency.

TAX CLASS: Are you required by your taxing authorities to charge tax on shipping costs? If so, select TAXABLE GOODS.

GEO ZONE: To what zones are you willing to ship using this method? This method will only appear in the zones you select.

STATUS: MUST be enabled for it to appear to customers.

SORT ORDER: If you offer multiple shipping methods, do you want this to appear first, second, etc.? The numbers do not need to be in exact order, the lowest number will appear first. Note that zero is the lowest number you can use.

When you are finished, be sure to click the top right SAVE Button.

Remember to test, test, test! Sign in as a customer and put a product in your cart. Does this shipping method appear in checkout? If not, go back and check the above settings.

EXTENSIONS - SHIPPING

5. Parcelforce 48

http://www.parcelforce.com/

UK shipper, part of the Royal Mail Group. Ships worldwide, specializes in 48 hour shipment of packages but also ships from small parcels to pallets. The Rates Box" on the next page is difficult to read, but it means as follows:

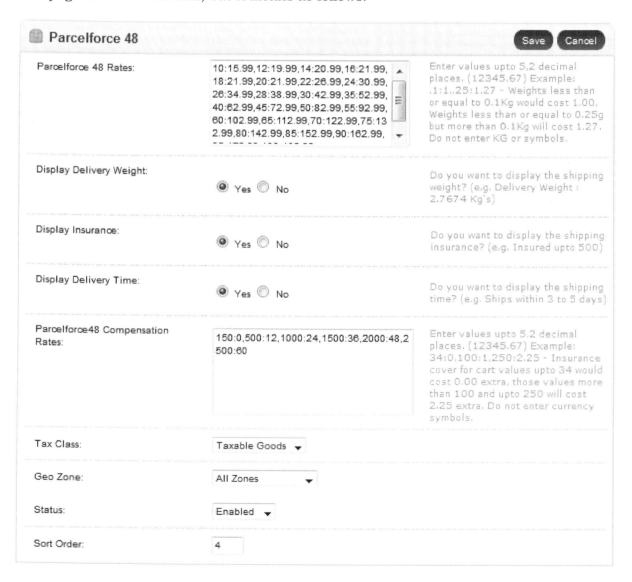

PARCELFORCE 48 RATES:	What rates do you wish to charge your customers?

Price you want to charge customer:	**Abbreviation:**
Up to 10 Kg costs £15.99	10:15.99;
10.00001 to 12 Kg costs £19.99	12:19.99;
12.00001 to 14 Kg costs £21.99	14:21.99;

DISPLAY DELIVERY WEIGHT:	Do you want customers to see the actual weight during checkout?
DISPLAY INSURANCE:	Do you want to display the insurance amount?
DISPLAY DELIVERY TIME:	Do you want to display the delivery time?
COMPENSATION RATES:	How much is the insurance compensation on packages shipped via this method?
GEO ZONE:	This method will only appear in the zones you select.
STATUS:	MUST be enabled for it to appear to customers.
SORT ORDER:	If you offer multiple shipping methods, do you want this to appear first, second, etc.? The numbers do not need to be in exact order, the lowest number will appear first. Note that zero is the lowest number you can use.
	When you are finished, be sure to click the top right SAVE Button.

Remember to test, test, test! Sign in as a customer and put a product in your cart. Does this shipping method appear in checkout? If not, go back and check the above settings.

EXTENSIONS - SHIPPING

6. Pickup from Store

Do you have local customers who want to pick up their goods in your retail store or other location? If so, this module is for you.

Pickup From Store		Save	Cancel
Geo Zone:	All Zones		
Status:	Enabled		
Sort Order:	2		

GEO ZONE: This method will only appear in the zones you select.

STATUS: MUST be enabled for it to appear to customers.

SORT ORDER: If you offer multiple shipping methods, do you want this to appear first, second, etc.? The numbers do not need to be in exact order, the lowest number will appear first. Note that zero is the lowest number you can use.

When you are finished, be sure to click the top right SAVE Button.

Remember to test, test, test! Sign in as a customer and put a product in your cart. Does this shipping method appear in checkout? If not, go back and check the above settings.

EXTENSIONS - SHIPPING

7. Royal Mail
http://www.royalmail.com

If you want to check on delivery within the UK, Royal Mail's Recorded Signed For™ fits the bill. With proof of posting, signature on arrival and online tracking, your delivery is easy to trace. Most First Class Recorded items arrive by the next working day. If you need Proof of

Delivery, you will also soon be able to see a Proof of Delivery online - a copy of the actual signature that was taken as receipt of delivery - by using their online Track & Trace application at http://www.royalmail.com/portal/rm/track?catId=500185&mediaId=22700601&keyname =track_home/link/rm/track?catId=500185&mediaId=22700601

It's great value too, at just 66p plus First or Second Class postage.

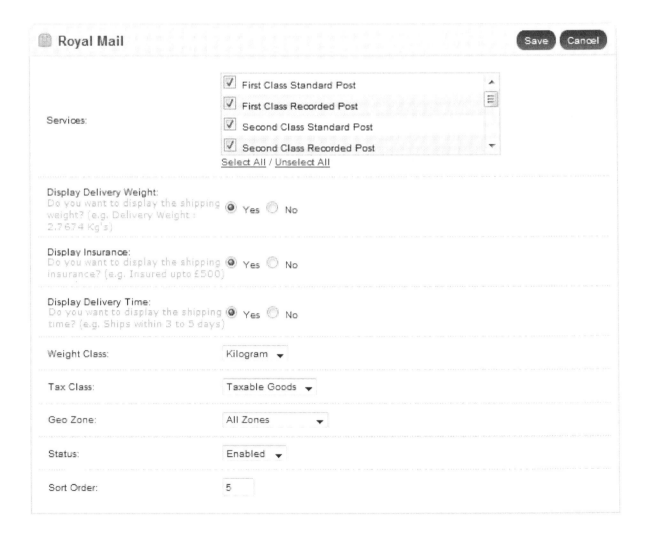

When you are finished, be sure to click the top right SAVE Button.

Remember to test, test, test! Sign in as a customer and put a product in your cart. Does this shipping method appear in checkout? If not, go back and check the above settings.

EXTENSIONS - SHIPPING

8. UPS Shipping
http://www.ups.com

It is difficult to get approved for a UPS United Parcel Service ecommerce account unless you are already shipping daily with them.

Note that you must have or open TWO accounts with UPS:

- **A Shipping Account, and**
- **A Developer Account.**

So first begin by opening a UPS Shipping account, ship daily, THEN open a Developer Account so you can add this method to your store.
OPEN UPS ACCOUNT:
https://www.ups.com/myups/login?returnto=https%3a//www.ups.com/account/us/start%3floc%3den_US%26WT.svl%3dFooter&reasonCode=-1&appid=OPENACCT

Before you can fill out your store's UPS Shipping form, you must do the following:

- **UPS Step 1:** Register for a Developer Account with My UPS at
  https://www.ups.com/one-to-one/register?sysid=myups&lang=en&langc=US&loc=en_US&returnto=https%3A%2F%2Fwww.ups.com%2Fupsdeveloperkit%3Floc%3Den_US%26rt1
- **UPS Step 2:** Log-in to your new account at
  https://www.ups.com/myups/login?returnto=https%3A%2F%2Fwww.ups.com%2Fupsdeveloperkit%3Floc%3Den_US%26rt1
- **UPS Step 3:** Request a UPS Access Key (or Developer's Key at
  https://www.ups.com/upsdeveloperkit?loc=en_US

Then see below screenshots for detailed explanation of how to fill out this long form:

* Origin State/Province:
Enter the two-letter code for your
origin state/province.

TX

* Origin Country:
Enter the two-letter code for your
origin country.

US

Origin Zip/Postal Code:
Enter your origin zip/postalcode.

12345

Test Mode:
Use this module in Test (YES) or
Production mode (NO)?

⚪ Yes 🔘 No

Quote Type:
Quote for Residential or
Commercial Delivery.

Commercial ▾

Services:
Select the UPS services to be
offered.

☑ UPS Next Day Air
☑ UPS Second Day Air
☑ UPS Ground
☑ UPS Worldwide Express

Select All / Unselect All

Display Delivery Weight:
Do you want to display the shipping
weight? (e.g. Delivery Weight :
2.7674 Kg's)

🔘 Yes ⚪ No

Weight Code:
Allowed kgs or lbs. Make sure you
match the weight class with the
UPS accepted weight code.

lbs

Weight Class:
Set to kilograms or pounds.

Pound ▾

Tax Class:

Taxable Goods ▾

Geo Zone:

All Zones ▾

Status:

Enabled ▾

Sort Order:

6

ACCESS KEY: From your Developer Account (NOT your shipping account, see above). May also be referred to as the XML rates access key.

USERNAME: From your Developer Account

PASSWORD: From your Developer Account

PICKUP METHOD: Do you have a daily pickup, bring packages to a UPS store, call for a one-time pickup, on call air pickup, bring to a letter center or air service center, or use suggested retail rates at a local UPS store. Ask UPS if you are not sure.

PACKAGING TYPE: What type of packaging will you use? You must standardize for this method.

CUSTOMER CLASSIFICATION CODE:
01 - Bill to a UPS account AND have daily UPS pickup
02 - Bill to a UPS account but no daily pickup
03 - NO UPS account OR NO daily pickup
04 - Shipping from a retail outlet - US origin only

SHIPPING ORIGIN CODE: Select US, Canada, EU, Puerto Rico, Mexico or All Others. Different shipping types are available in different locations, so this ensures your customers will see the correct shipping types for your area.

ORIGIN CITY: Name of your city

ORIGIN STATE OR PROVINCE: Name of your state

ORIGIN COUNTRY: Your TWO LETTER country code. See codes at
http://www.worldatlas.com/aatlas/ctycodes.htm

ORIGIN ZIP CODE: Your zip or regional code.

TEST MODE: Select TEST if you are just testing and do not want UPS to actually pick up and ship these packages. Change to PRODUCTION when you are ready for real pickups.

QUOTE TYPE: Is the pickup location residential or commercial? UPS charges more for residential pickup.

SERVICES: Select all services you want to offer to your customers.

DISPLAY DELIVERY WEIGHT: Do you want the customer to see the shipping weight? Yes or no.

WEIGHT CODE: Enter lbs or kgs.

WEIGHT CLASS: Set to kilos or pounds.

TAX CLASS: Are you required by your taxing authorities to charge tax on shipping costs? If so, select TAXABLE GOODS.

GEO ZONE: To what zones are you willing to ship using this method? This method will only appear to customers who are in the zones you select. Example, choose US if you only wish to ship via UPS to customers in the US.

STATUS: MUST be enabled for it to appear to customers.

SORT ORDER: If you offer multiple shipping methods, do you want this to appear first, second, etc.? The numbers do not need to be in exact order, the lowest number will appear first. Note that zero is the lowest number you can use.

When you are finished, be sure to click the top right SAVE Button.

Remember to test, test, test! Sign in as a customer and put a product in your cart. Does this shipping method appear in checkout? If not, go back and check the above settings.

EXTENSIONS - SHIPPING

9. US Postal Service Shipping

https://www.usps.com/

Available in USA only. Note that USPS will not ship packages over 70 pounds (1,120 ounces if you measure by ounces), and there are size restrictions as well. Typically the maximum or large package length + girth is between 84 and 108 inches. Ask your local Post Office if you have questions.

To use the USPS shipping method and have rates automatically calculated by your store and shown and billed to the customer, you must first register with the US Postal Service for their USPS Web Tools at https://secure.shippingapis.com/registration

Your new account will be set to TEST MODE by default. Test means that the USPS will not yet pick up and ship your packages.

 IMPORTANT: After you have finished testing, you must email the USPS at the address specified in your " Welcome Email" to request your server changed to PRODUCTION. THEY will change your service to production and begin picking up your packages.

After you have opened your USPS Web Tools Account, see below screenshots for detailed explanation of how to fill out this form:

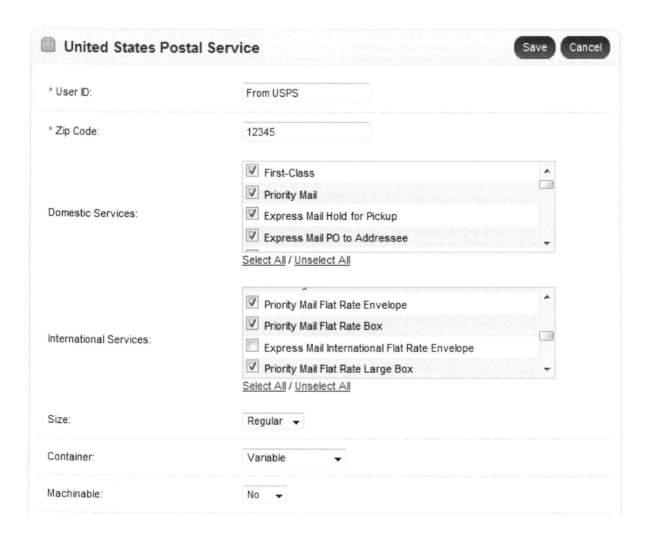

Dimensions (L x W x H):	Measure your boxes
Girth:	Measure
Display Delivery Time: Do you want to display the shipping time? (e.g. Ships within 3 to 5 days)	● Yes ○ No
Display Delivery Weight: Do you want to display the shipping weight? (e.g. Delivery Weight : 2.7674 Kg's)	● Yes ○ No
Weight Class: Set to pounds.	Pound ▼
Tax Class:	Taxable Goods ▼
Geo Zone:	All Zones ▼
Status:	Enabled ▼
Sort Order:	7

USER ID: From your USPS Web Tools Account's Welcome Email, or log onto your USPS Web Tools Account.

ZIP CODE: Shipping zip code.

DOMESTIC SERVICES: Check all services you wish to offer to your US customers. Only these services will appear in your store.

INTERNATIONAL SERVICES: Check all services you wish to offer to your customers in other countries. Only these services will appear in your store.

SIZE: Your typical shipping box size.
REGULAR: Package length + girth is UNDER 84 inches.
LARGE: Package length + girth is between 84 and 108 inches.
OVERSIZE: Package length + girth is between 108 and 130 inches.

CONTAINER: Rectangular, non-rectangular, or variable.

MACHINABLE: Machinable is required if you select shipping type FIRST CLASS FLAT LETTERS, OR PARCEL POST.

DIMENSIONS: Length, width, and height of your boxes.

GIRTH Measure all the way around the box, all four sides.

DISPLAY DELIVERY TIME: Do you want customers to see the shipping time?

DISPLAY DELIVERY WEIGHT: Do you want customers to see the shipping weight?

WEIGHT CLASS: POUNDS OR OUNCES ONLY. USPS does not ship by kilos.

TAX CLASS: Are you required by your taxing authorities to charge tax on shipping costs? If so, select TAXABLE GOODS.

GEO ZONE: To what zones are you willing to ship using this method? This method will only appear to customers who are in the zones you select. Example, choose US if you only wish to ship via UPS to customers in the US.

STATUS: MUST be enabled for it to appear to customers.

SORT ORDER: If you offer multiple shipping methods, do you want this to appear first, second, etc.? The numbers do not need to be in exact order, the lowest number will appear first. Note that zero is the lowest number you can use.

When you are finished, be sure to click the top right SAVE Button.

Remember to test, test, test! Sign in as a customer and put a product in your cart. Does this shipping method appear in checkout? If not, go back and check the above settings.

EXTENSIONS - SHIPPING

10. Weight-Based Shipping

Very handy extension! Select Weight Based Shipping if you wish to charge the shipping cost based on weight of your items. It is your choice which carrier to use, and you can ship by a different carrier for each package.

If you have entered dozens or hundreds of products without their weights, you can edit them in a spreadsheet by having your technical pro install the extension Import/Export tool. Otherwise, choose a non-weight based shipping method such as per-item or flat-rate (per order).

For weight-based shipping to work correctly, you must first do these two steps:

1. You must also enter product weights for each product, AND
2. Set a weight class (pounds, kilos etc.) in SYSTEM - Settings - Local tab - WEIGHT CLASS.

Example:

- To weigh your products by ounces, such as a 5 oz. t-shirt, specify "5" in the CATALOG - Products - select the product and click the DATA Tab.
- If you choose pounds as your weight class, the 5 oz. t-shirt is .32 pounds, so enter .32 instead.

NOTE that you can choose to enable this method for local, state, US, and/or all customers. Click the left-column TABS shown below and repeat for each one:

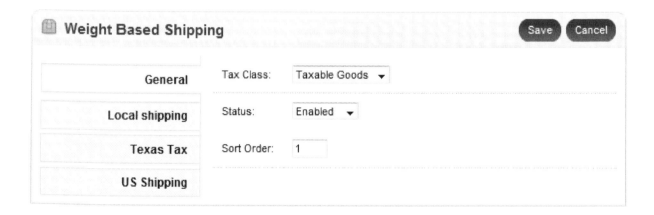

TAX CLASS: Are you required by your taxing authorities to charge tax on shipping costs? If so, select TAXABLE GOODS.

STATUS: MUST be enabled for it to appear to customers. NOTE the left tabs in the above example; the GENERAL tab is selected. I must select ENABLED or DISABLED for each of these groups.

SORT ORDER: If you offer multiple shipping methods, do you want this to appear first, second, etc.? The numbers do not need to be in exact order, the lowest number will appear first. Note that zero is the lowest number you can use.

When you are finished, be sure to click the top right SAVE Button.

Remember to test, test, test! Sign in as a customer and put a product in your cart. Does this shipping method appear in checkout? If not, go back and check the above settings.

EXTENSIONS MENU

Payment

Online Payment Security Summary

Online security has been tightened over the last few years. Strict security standards are now being applied to small online merchants, and this will affect your online store's procedures.

In a nutshell, to easily meet the tight security standards, we recommend:

- Use an off-site, third-party payment processor like PayPal.com or 2CheckOut.com
- Have SSL Security Certificate properly installed and configured on your Admin and checkout pages by your web host.
- NEVER use a payment method that keeps customer credit card information on your website.
- Keep informed of new security developments and requirements.

CAUTION: An SSL security certificate MUST be installed on ALL ecommerce sites before going live. Without SSL to encrypt the data, it could be intercepted by hackers on the way to or from the secure off-site processor. Ask your web host to install SSL and configure your store to use it in your Admin and Checkout pages.

SEE ALSO – APPENDIX B, Online Security, Database & Records Management.

Selecting the Payment Processor Right for You

Getting information from these companies is like pulling teeth. If they want you to be their customer, why do they make it so difficult? Why do they hide the very information you need?

Well, here are the answers. This comparison answers the nitty-gritty questions that YOU care about.

Choosing a Payment Processor Checklist:

1. What countries does it work in - both for the store owner AND for his or her customers?
2. How much does it cost?
3. How long of a commitment is it? and,
4. How easy or difficult is it to set it up?

Please see the detailed information about each company in the sections that follow. Once you have decided on a payment processor, follow the directions to apply for an account with them, and then continue this section.

CAUTION: The OFF-SITE processors are easiest and safest (see last 2 columns below). We recommend ONLY these methods WITH SSL for new online store owners.

Payment Processor Comparison Chart

#	Payment Gateway	US	UK	EUR	FR	CAN	AUS	Other	Initial Fee	Mo. Fee	Trans-action Fee	Term	OFF/ON SITE?	Ease of Set up*
1	AlertPay	•				•			0	0	4.90 % + $0.25 USD	None	OFFSITE	1
2	Authorize.net	•	•	•	•	•	•	•	299	20	2.4% + .10	30 Day	ONSITE	2
3	Bank Wire Transfer	•	•	•	•	•	•	•	0	0	Varies	None	OFFSITE	
4	Check/ Money Order	•	•	•	•	•	•	•	0	0	0	None	OFFSITE	1
5	Cash on Delivery	•	•	•	•	•	•	•	0	0	0	None	OFFSITE	1
6	Free Checkout	•	•	•	•	•	•				0	None	OFFSITE	1
7	LIQpay	•	•	•	•	•	•	•	0	0	$0-1.95 USD + 1%.	None	OFFSITE	1
8	MoneyBookers (Skrill) Quick Checkout	•	•	•	•	•		•			2.90% or less + €0.25	None	OFFSITE	1
9	Nochex		•						0	0	2.9% +20p	None	OFFSITE	3
10	Paymate (Aus and NZ)						•		0	AU$0 to AU$33	1.7 to 2.4%		OFFSITE	3
11	PayPoint Web Shop Pymts		•						£58.75	£10	0.39p to 1.9%	1 Yr	ONSITE	3
12	Perpetual Payments (now cashflows.com)		•	•	•				4*	4*	4*	4*	ONSITE	
13	PayPal Standard	•	•	•	•	•	•	•	0	0	2.9% + .30 3.9% intl	1 Day	OFFSITE	1
14-15	PayPal Certified World Payments Pro	•	•	•	•	•	•	•	0	0	2.9% + .30 3.9% intl	1 Day	ONSITE	2
16	SagePay Form Hosted	•	•	•	•	•	•	•	0	0	£20 mo + 10p over 1000	1 Mo.	OFFSITE	2
17	2CheckOut	•	•	•		•	•	•	49	0	5.5%	1 Day	OFFSITE	2
18	WorldPay Hosted	•	•						£100	£30	£0.50 + 4.5%	1 Yr	OFFSITE	3

*1=easy, 2=medium, 3=more difficult.
4*-will not disclose until after you apply for account.
**These payment contributions must be installed separately.
*a=application fee, b=software fee

Link your store to payments

To begin linking your store to your credit card processor or to activate your manual credit card process, from the main Administration menu, click EXTENSIONS – Payment.

This brings you to Payment Modules. This is a list of third-party credit card processors that can be automatically installed.

Payment List

Payment

Payment Method		Status	Sort Order	Action
AlertPay		Disabled		[Install]
Authorize.Net (AIM)		Disabled		[Install]
Bank Transfer		Disabled		[Install]
Cheque / Money Order		Disabled		[Install]
Cash On Delivery		Enabled	5	[Edit] [Uninstall]
Free Checkout		Enabled	1	[Edit] [Uninstall]
LIQPAY		Disabled		[Install]
Moneybookers		Disabled		[Install]
NOCHEX	Nochex	Disabled		[Install]
Paymate		Disabled		[Install]
PayPoint	PP PayPoint	Disabled		[Install]
Perpetual Payments		Disabled		[Install]
PayPal Website Payment Pro	PayPal	Disabled		[Install]
PayPal Website Payment Pro (UK)	PayPal	Disabled		[Install]
PayPal Standard	PayPal	Disabled		[Install]
SagePay	sagepay	Disabled		[Install]
SagePay Direct		Disabled		[Install]
SagePay (US)		Disabled		[Install]
2Checkout		Disabled		[Install]
WorldPay		Disabled		[Install]

To install any of these payment modules, after opening an account with the merchant, simply click the Install button and enter the account information you received when you opened the account. See the following section for details.

TIP: The third-party credit-card processors use secure servers, so you may not have to. Check with them to be certain.

TIP: Install only ONE payment module at a time, then thoroughly test your site to make sure it is working properly. Only then should you proceed to add another if you wish.

TIP: You can often use this testing credit card number: 4111111111111111 with any expiration date. Try it! No transaction will take place.

EXTENSIONS – PAYMENT
1. AlertPay.com
https://www.alertpay.com/

Off-site transaction processor founded in Canada in 2004 as an alternative to PayPal.

Over six million members in 190+ countries, 22 currencies and localized banking in 46 countries.

English and French only.

Setting up AlertPay is done in three steps:

- **AlertPay Step 1.** Open an account with AlertPay.
- **AlertPay Step 2.** Enter the AlertPay information into your store, and copy the ALERT URL from the form box.
- **AlertPay Step 3.** Go back to AlertPay.com, enter the Alert URL and set IPN Status to ENABLED.

AlertPay setup detail

Step 1. Open an account with AlertPay.

To set up AlertPay, go to http://www.alertpay.com. Select your country name and account type. Enter business and personal information. Choose login email address, password, Transaction PIN and security questions. Check your email box for a Validation email.

After you have validated your account with AlertPay, you will receive a "Welcome Email" with login information including a Merchant ID and Security Code.

Step 2. Enter the AlertPay information into your store, and copy the ALERT URL from the form box.

In your store Admin's top nav bar select EXTENSIONS - Payment. In the ALERTPAY row, click INSTALL if needed, then click EDIT and fill in the form as shown:

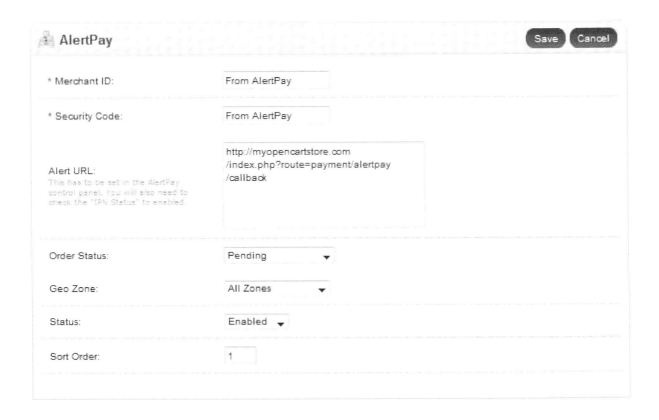

ALERT URL: Copy and paste this into your AlertPay.com account and set IPN Status to ENABLED.

When finished, be sure to click the top right SAVE Button.

Step 3. Go back to AlertPay.com, enter the Alert URL and set IPN Status to ENABLED.

To set up your Alert URL, just follow these steps:

1. Login to your AlertPay account.
2. Click on "Business Tools".
3. Under "Instant Payment Notification - IPN", click on "IPN Setup".
4. Enter your Transaction PIN and click on "Access".
5. Click on the "Edit" icon for the respective business profile. **This is for Business accounts only. Ignore this step if you only have one business profile on your account**
6. Enter the information:
    1. For **IPN Status**, select "Enabled".
    2. For Alert URL, enter the URL that you copied in Step 2.
7. Click on "Update" button.

Remember to test, test, test! Set the price of a product to a very low price such as $0.25, then put the product in your cart and check out. Does this payment method work in checkout? If not, go back and check the above settings.

EXTENSIONS – PAYMENT
2 Authorize.Net

Authorize.net is one of the most respected US credit card processors. Their system is easy to set up and install. You can get an account with them through one of their resellers in 24-48 hours. Their Resellers will answer any questions you have and walk you through installation. See http://www.authorizenet.com/reseller/directory.php

Setting up Authorize.net is done in three steps:

Authorize.net Step 1. Open an account with a Third-Party Authorize.net reseller (Authorize.net does not sell direct to the public) and find the "Welcome email" sent to you by the merchant.
Authorize.net Step 2. Fill in the OpenCart EXTENSIONS - PAYMENTS - Authorize.net

form, as shown below.
Authorize.net Step 3. Test, test, test!

Authorize.net setup detail

In your store Admin's top nav bar select EXTENSIONS - Payment. In the AUTHORIZE.NET (AIM) row, click INSTALL if needed, then click EDIT and fill in the form as shown below:

Authorize.Net (AIM)		Save Cancel
* Login ID:	From Authorize.net	
* Transaction Key:	From Authorize.net	
MD5 Hash:	From Authorize.net	
Transaction Server:	Live	
Transaction Mode:	Live	
Transaction Method:	Capture	
Order Status:	Pending	
Geo Zone:	All Zones	
Status:	Enabled	
Sort Order:	2	

LOGIN ID: The merchant processor will send this to you.
TRANSACTION KEY: The merchant processor will send this to you.
MD5 HASH: The merchant processor will send this to you.
TRANSACTION SERVER: Use TEST while you are testing the store; change to LIVE when you are ready to process sales.
TRANSACTION MODE: Use AUTHORIZE to get a pre-authorization only, such as for a hotel stay; use CAPTURE to actually withdraw the funds from the client's credit card.
ORDER STATUS: Apply this payment method to orders that have this order status.
GEO ZONE: Select a zone if you want it only available to a certain zone, otherwise leave at ALL ZONES.
STATUS: Select ENABLED to allow customers to select this method; or DISABLED to hide it from customers but keep it available to you in your private Admin.
SORT ORDER: If you are offering customers multiple payment methods from which to choose, and wish this method to be displayed first, enter a 1. To display second, enter a 2, and so forth.

Click the SAVE Button when you are finished.

Remember to test, test, test! Set the price of a product to a very low price such as $0.25, then put the product in your cart and check out. Does this payment method work in checkout? If not, go back and check the above settings.

EXTENSIONS – PAYMENT
3. Bank Wire Transfer

Bank transfer is a payment method best for large purchases or as an additional payment method. After checking out, customers must manually go to their bank (or go to their online banking website) to complete the wire transfer.

Call your bank for exact instructions. Note the order status is set to PENDING until after you receive the wire; then return to the customer's order to manually change the order status.

In your store Admin's top nav bar select EXTENSIONS - Payment. In the BANK TRANSFER row, click INSTALL if needed, then click EDIT and fill in the form as shown:

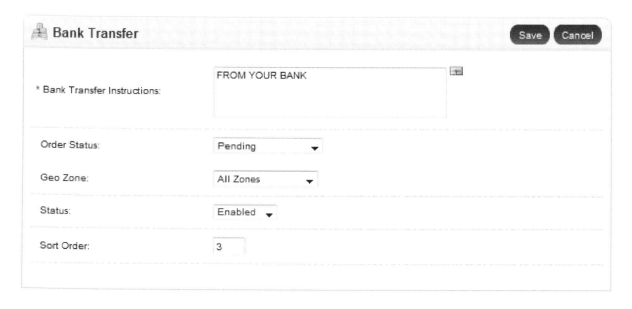

Remember to test, test, test! Put a test product in your cart and check out. Does this payment method work in checkout? If not, go back and check the above settings.

EXTENSIONS – PAYMENT
4. Check/Money Order

You can accept checks or money orders from customers. Be sure to write a policy for delaying shipment until a check has cleared, or for receiving certified checks or money orders only. Be sure to specify in your policy whether you will accept foreign checks, etc.

In your store Admin's top nav bar select EXTENSIONS - Payment. In the CHEQUE/MONEY ORDER row, click INSTALL if needed, then click EDIT and fill in the form as shown:

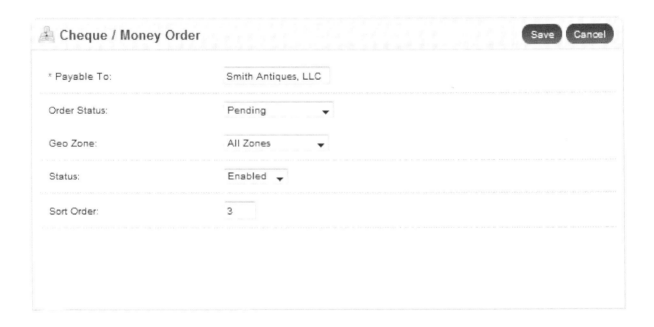

Remember to test, test, test! Put the product in your cart and check out. Does this payment method work in checkout? If not, go back and check the above settings.

EXTENSIONS – PAYMENT
5. Cash on Delivery (COD)

Select Cash on Delivery if you are willing to send merchandise and have the postal service collect the funds for you.

OR use it temporarily during store setup, to test purchasing before you have a real payment method set up.

In your store Admin's top nav bar select EXTENSIONS - Payment. In the CASH ON DELIVERY (COD) row, click INSTALL if needed, then click EDIT and fill in the form as shown:

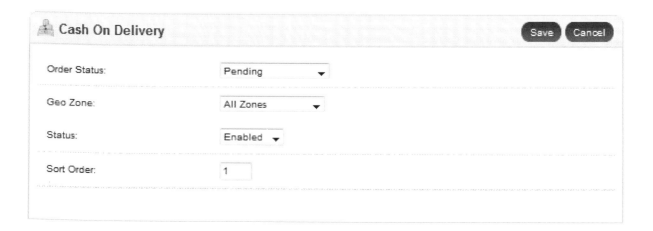

Remember to test, test, test! Set the price of a product to a very low price such as $0.25, then put the product in your cart and check out. Does this payment method work in checkout? If not, go back and check the above settings.

EXTENSIONS – PAYMENT

6. Free Checkout

If you want to give away your merchandise for free, but have the transaction recorded in your store, OR have an easy way to test your store without testing the payment system, simply use this method. There is actually no charge card involved. :-)

In your store Admin's top nav bar select EXTENSIONS - Payment. In the FREE CHECKOUT row, click INSTALL if needed, then click EDIT and fill in the form as shown:

Remember to test, test, test! Put a product in your cart and check out. Does this payment method work in checkout? If not, go back and check the above settings.

EXTENSIONS – PAYMENT

7. LIQpay mobile phone payments

https://www.liqpay.com

LIQpay is a global open, secure payment system that lets anyone easily send money using mobile phones, Internet and payment cards worldwide, and designed by the largest commercial bank in the Ukraine, PrivatBank. Users need only a mobile phone and internet. Every transaction is authenticated by a dynamic one-time password, which comes in the form of an SMS text to your mobile phone number.

Fees are low, from zero to 1.95 USD + 1%.
LIQpay fees: https://www.liqpay.com/?do=pages&p=fees

Money is credited to the card in 3 to 6 days. If the merchant also uses PrivatBank, money is deposited to the account almost immediately.

To use LIQpay, first register your mobile phone for an account (your account number is the same as your phone number) at https://www.liqpay.com/?do=pages&p=shopgreet

In your store Admin's top nav bar select EXTENSIONS - Payment. In the LIQPAY row, click INSTALL if needed, then click EDIT and fill in the form as shown:

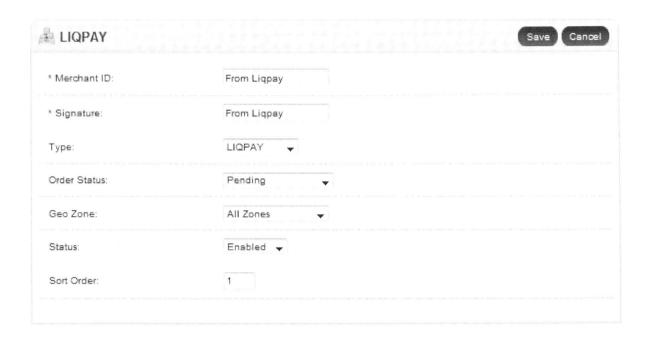

When finished, be sure to click the top right SAVE Button.

Remember to test, test, test! Set the price of a product to a very low price such as $0.25, then put the product in your cart and check out. Does this payment method work in checkout? If not, go back and check the above settings.

EXTENSIONS – PAYMENT
8. Moneybookers – now Skrill Quick Checkout
http://www.moneybookers.com/

Skrill (formerly Moneybookers) is the secure way to pay globally without revealing your financial details. With just your email address, you can send and spend with over 100 payment options, including all major credit and debit cards, in 200 countries. Skrill is one of the world's largest online payment providers currently being used by over 100,000 merchants. More than 100 payment options, with 41 currencies covering 200 countries and territories. With one easy connection you can instantly enter new markets and grow your business. Supported local payment methods in over 30 countries.

- **Pros:** Off-site, secure, highest security standards, anti-fraud check included. Free set-up, no monthly fees, easy to use, immediate access to your funds via a Prepaid ATM Debit Card, no need to wait 2-3 days for your funds to clear.
- **Cons:** Withdrawal fees of 1.80 EUR for bank transfer or ATM, 3.50 EUR for cheque. Debit card must be pre-paid, so you are actually using your money. Check withdrawal available to residents of OECD countries only.

To enable Skrill (formerly Moneybookers) Quick Checkout (off-site credit card processing, after registering for an account from the above website address, get your registration information and log into your store Admin.

Select MODULES – Payment, then select Moneybookers from the payments list.

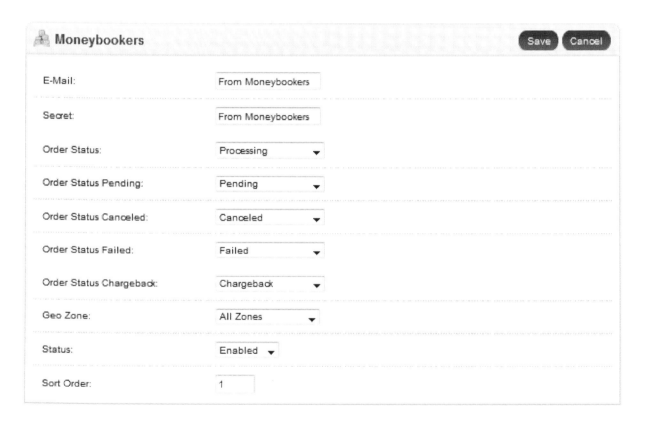

When finished, be sure to click the top right SAVE Button.

Remember to test, test, test! Set the price of a product to a very low price such as $0.25, then put the product in your cart and check out. Does this payment method work in checkout? If not, go back and check the above settings.

SKRILL/MONEYBOOKERS SUPPORT: Email merchantservices@moneybookers.com

EXTENSIONS – PAYMENT

9. Nochex

http://www.nochex.com.

Nochex is the quick and easy way in the UK to collect payments funded by all major credit and debit cards from your website. Suitable for merchants of all sizes, with no monthly fees and instant cash withdrawals - they provide you with the complete real-time online payment package.

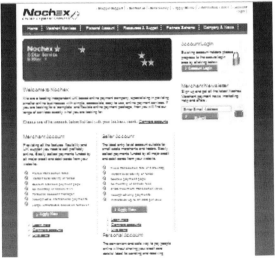

With no setup fees, they charge 2.9% plus 20p for each transaction.

Withdrawals over £50 are free; under £50 are 25p.

Limited UK-only accounts for small companies £100 maximum transaction value 2.9%+20p, or worldwide merchant accounts for larger companies with no monthly or annual fees, daily limit up to £1,000.

To set up Nochex, in your store Admin's top nav bar select EXTENSIONS - Payment. In the NOCHEX row, click INSTALL if needed, then click EDIT and fill in the form as shown:

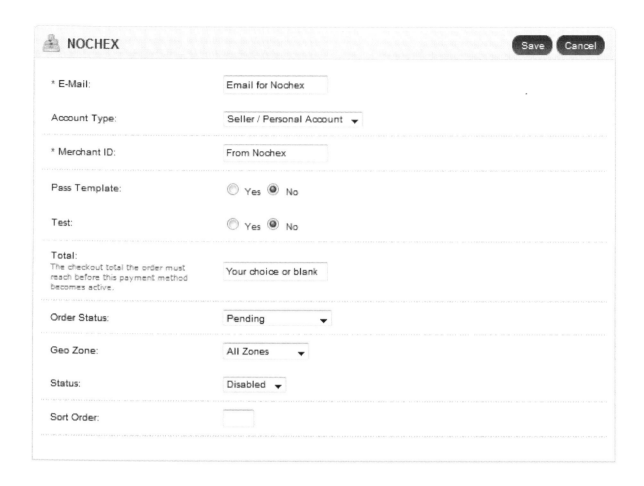

Enter the email address you used to sign up for the NOCHEX service.

You can accept checks or money orders only in certain zones that you have established in the LOCATIONS/TAXES menu, for example, only in your city or state.

Order status can be automatically set to "PENDING, PROCESSING or DELIVERED.

You can enable multiple methods of payment; the sort order is a column on the PAYMENT MODULES screen. Zero will be displayed first, 1 next, etc.

When finished, be sure to click the top right SAVE Button.

Remember to test, test, test! Set the price of a product to a very low price such as $0.25, then put the product in your cart and check out. Does this payment method work in checkout? If not, go back and check the above settings.

EXTENSIONS – PAYMENT

10. Paymate

http://www.paymate.com

Acquired in Dec. 2011 by Flexigroup. One of only three checkouts used by EBay.

- Australia: both buyer and seller fees. Credit card payments charged at 1.7 to 2.4% depending on account type and volume. Limit AUS $10,000.00 per month.
- New Zealand: Standard account 3% + $0.50 per payment, monthly limit NZ $5,000. eBusiness account monthly limit NZ $15,000.
- US: 3% + $0.50 per successful transaction. There is a $5,000 limit on how much you can receive in a month.

To set up Paymate, in your store Admin's top nav bar select EXTENSIONS - Payment. In the Paymate row, click INSTALL if needed, then click EDIT and fill in the form as shown:

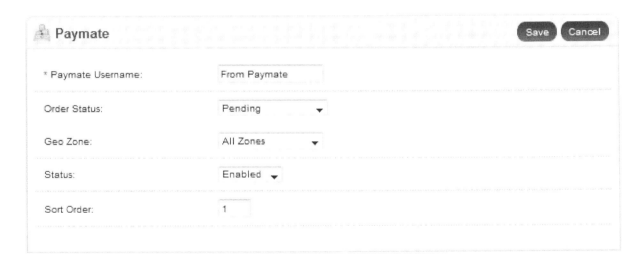

When finished, be sure to click the top right SAVE Button.

Remember to test, test, test! Set the price of a product to a very low price such as $0.25, then put the product in your cart and check out. Does this payment method work in checkout? If not, go back and check the above settings.

EXTENSIONS – PAYMENT
11. PayPoint
http://www.paypoint.net/

UK processor Payment Gateway + Merchant Account.

From £15 / month, 24 hour account setup.

Formerly known as SECPay.

After opening a PayPoint account, in your store Admin's top nav bar menu, select MODULES - Payment, then select PAYPOINT.

This brings you to the PayPoint Form:

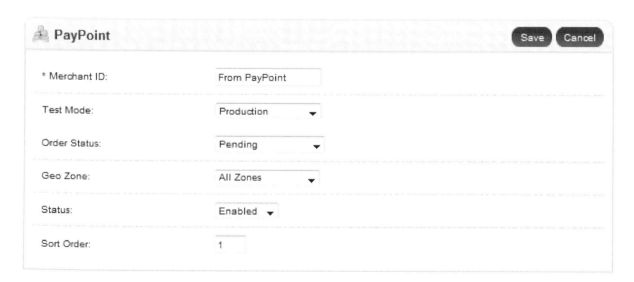

Fill in the form as shown above. When you have finished, be sure to click the SAVE Button.

EXTENSIONS – PAYMENT
12. Perpetual Payments - now Cashflows.com

UK merchant provides merchant accounts and credit card processing services for adult and dating; gaming, gambling, and bingo; European and international; high risk; Internet and ecommerce; mail-order and telephone; offshore and off-shore; and travel, travel agent, travel industry, tourism, and ticket merchant accounts. It was purchased by Voice Commerce Group in 2009. Voice Commerce Group was founded by Nick Ogden, the creator of the WorldPay global Internet payments system, later sold to Royal Bank of Scotland.

PerpetualPayments.com now goes to cashflows.com.

EXTENSIONS – PAYMENT
13. PayPal Standard
http://www.paypal.com

PayPal is the US's number 1 email money service. No setup fees, 2.9% + 30 cents for each transaction, 3.9% for foreign transactions. Customers were formerly required to register, but no more.

Recommended for most small businesses (and larger businesses as an additional payment method).

Setting up PayPal Standard is done in three steps:

> **PayPal Standard Step 1.** Open and set up your PayPal.com account for website payments as shown below.
> **PayPal Standard Step 2.** Fill in the OpenCart EXTENSIONS - PAYMENTS - PayPal Standard form as shown below.
> **PayPal Standard Step 3.** Test, test, test!

PayPal Standard Step 1.

Open and verify your PayPal.com account, set up website payment preferences on the paypal.com website as shown below and copy the "Payment Data Transfer" (PDT) Identity Token from the PayPal website; and

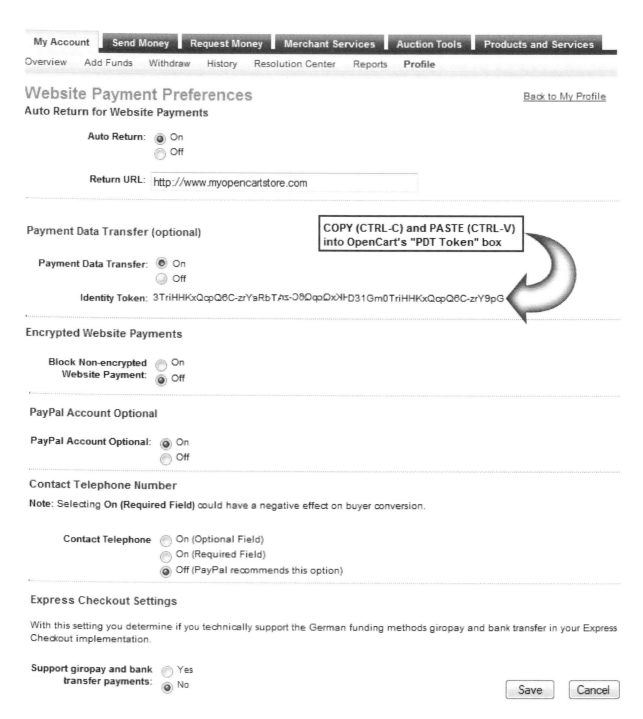

PayPal Standard Step 2.

Fill in the OpenCart EXTENSIONS - PAYMENTS - PayPal Standard form, paste (CTRL-V) the PDT Identity Token from the PayPal website, and fill in each box as shown below:

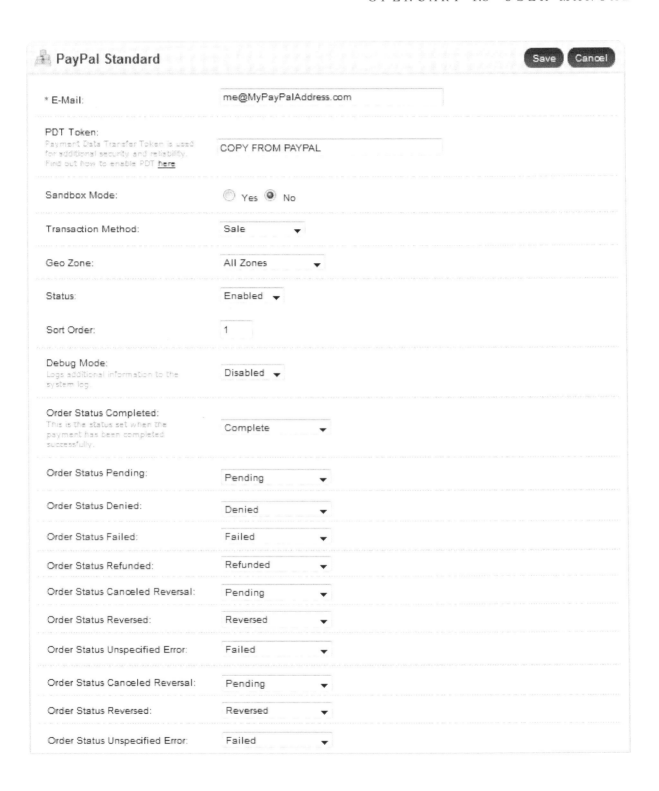

PayPal Standard Step 3.

Register several test accounts in your OpenCart store, and make several test transactions from different locations to be sure everything is set up properly.

TIP: PayPal not showing the correct shipping charges? Login to your Paypal account, and under MY ACCOUNT Tab click on PROFILE link. Under the Hosted payment settings heading, click the "Shipping Calculations" Link and make sure that it is turned OFF. Clear any custom shipping settings and click the SAVE Button.

Remember to test, test, test! Set the price of a product to a very low price such as $0.25, then put the product in your cart and check out. Does this payment method work in checkout? If not, go back and check the above settings.

EXTENSIONS – PAYMENT
14. PayPal Certified Website Payments Pro (US)
http://www.paypal.com

Website Payments Pro enables you to use PayPal as a real-time credit card payment option and keeps your customers on your website -- customers never jump to the PayPal website.

Note that you must meet stricter PCI requirements with this module, and might need your own expensive web server or VPN hosting. We recommend using an off-site transaction method such as PayPal Standard for most small businesses. Move to this when your sales justifies it.

Setting up PayPal WPP is done in two steps:

> **PayPal WPP Step 1.** Set up on PayPal.com website, and
> **PayPal WPP Step 2.** Set up in your Store's Admin.

PayPal WPP Step 1. Set up on PayPal.com website

Log in to your PayPal Business Account and click the Merchant Services tab. Find Website Payments Pro and then click Sign Up Now.
Fill in the form, and click SUBMIT to submit your application. Approval takes between 24 and 48 hours.

When you are approved, you will receive an email. Click the link and accept the Pro billing agreement.

For help getting started, in PayPal.com, go to the main Account Overview page and in the left column click SET UP YOUR ACCOUNT: Getting Started Steps.

To set up WPP API Access on PayPal.com:

In your PayPal account, under My Account click PROFILE. In the left column "Account Information" click "API ACCESS." This brings you to the page "Setting up PayPal API Credentials and Permissions."

Click the link that says, "Request API Credentials to create an API username and password for either your pre-integrated shopping cart or a custom solution that you are developing."

This brings you to the Request API Credentials page.

Click "Request API Signature" and click the AGREE & SUBMIT Button. This brings you to the "View or Remove API Signature" screen which contains the following information:

> **Credential: API Signature**
> **API Username: xxxxxxxxxxx**
> **API Password: xxxxxxxxxx**
> **Signature: xxxxxxxxxxxxxxx**
> **Request Date: xx/xx/xxxx**

Copy, print and save this information. you need this for your OpenCart Admin to configure the Certified PayPal WPP module.

Still on the "Setting up PayPal API Credentials and Permissions" page, in the box "Give Third-Party API Permission" click the link, GRANT API PERMISSION." This brings you to the Give Third-Party API Permission page.

Enter the API Account username as shown above, check the EXPRESS CHECKOUT box and click the SUBMIT Button.

Confirm the API Permission by clicking the GIVE PERMISSION Button.

You're done in PayPal, now move to your OpenCart Admin to finish up.

PayPal WPP Step 2. Set up PayPal WPP in your Store's Admin.

From your Admin's Top Bar Navigation Menu, click MODULES - PAYMENT - PayPal Certified WPP/
Express Payment. This brings you to the PayPal Certified WPP/Express Payment screen.

Fill in the form as shown below:

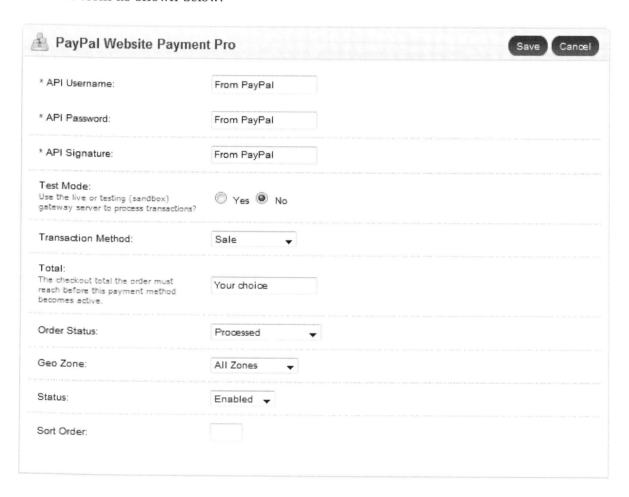

EXTENSIONS – PAYMENT
15. PayPal - Website Payment Pro (UK)
https://www.paypal.co.uk/uk

Identical to Website Payment Pro (US) above, except for merchants operating in the UK, with no "STATE" box. Please follow the above instructions.

EXTENSIONS – PAYMENT
16. SagePay Direct UK and US
http://www.sagepay.com/sage-pay-direct-integration

Now called "Sage Pay Go with Direct integration," this is essentially a white-label payment solution, giving you complete control over the way you process card payments. All processing is done on YOUR website, so you are responsible for security and PCI Compliance. Not recommended for shared hosting accounts.

Transaction processing on the Sagepay.com website, so they take care of data security. Available to merchants in most countries, fees are charged in pounds.

Up to 1,000 transactions per quarter £20 per month; add 10p for each transaction over 1,000 per quarter. 24/7 support.

No application or setup fees, but you must open and be approved for a separate merchant account.

Application:
https://support.sagepay.com/apply/

After opening a SagePay account, in your store Admin's top nav bar menu, select MODULES - Payment, then select SAGEPAY. This brings you to the SagePay Form:

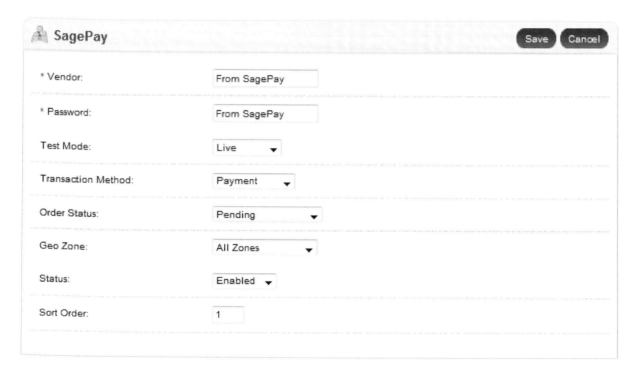

Fill in the form as shown above. When you have finished, be sure to click the SAVE Button.

EXTENSIONS – PAYMENT
17. 2CheckOut
http://www.2checkout.com/home.html

Application: http://www.2checkout.com/home.html

2CheckOut is a fee-based payment processor with over 100,000 stores. $49 one-time application fee, $ 0.45 per Sale and 5.5% of Sale Amount. No monthly fees, statement fees or gateway fees. 96% of applicants are approved.

Services all countries except North Korea, Cuba, Libya, Iraq, Iran, Sudan and UNITA-Controlled Portions of Angola. Based in Ohio, founded in 2000.

Has a high transaction fee, but low initial setup and NO monthly or hidden fees. NOTE: 2CheckOut has a manual fraud detection program which may delay receipt of your payments especially during the first few payment cycles.

They may also delay or refuse to pay any payment that they deem suspicious, and request your customer to fax a copy of their most recent statement and a copy of their driver's license. In my experience with them, one transaction was considered suspicious because the credit card holder's name was not on their voice mail recording. They do not verify by email. Hopefully the company will update their verification methods in the near future so they are not so intrusive.

IMPORTANT: You will be required to add some additional language to your website and/or your checkout pages.

IMPORTANT: 2CO retains a rolling reserve from your account equal to five percent (5%) of gross sales. The Reserve is in addition to the fees and charges that will be assessed against Supplier and each deduction from Purchase Payments to Supplier shall be held for at least ninety (90) days from the date the Purchase Payment was made. In the event 2CO deems it necessary, 2CO may, in its sole discretion, hold a deducted amount for more than 90 days. The funds held by 2CO in the Reserve accrue no interest, or any other earnings After opening a 2CheckOut account, in your store Admin's top nav bar menu, select MODULES - Payment, then select 2CheckOut. This brings you to the 2CheckOut Form:

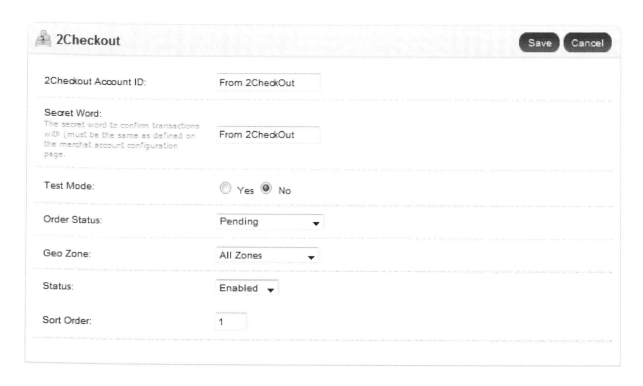

Fill in the form as shown above. When you have finished, be sure to click the SAVE Button.

EXTENSIONS – PAYMENT
18. RBS WorldPay Hosted
https://www.worldpay.com/

Partners with Authorize.net. Processes payments for companies in the UK, Ireland, Germany, US, Singapore, Hong Kong, Australia, New Zealand, and 42 other countries.

RBS WorldPay is part of The Royal Bank of Scotland Group and supports a wide range of payment types: international credit cards, domestic debit cards and cardless systems like Lastschriften (ELV), popular in Europe;

same-currency or multi-currency payment processing; Processes payments in real-time (payments are automatically routed to the appropriate bank for authorization) or deferred (you review your customers' orders and payment details before they are processed). Over 90% of applicants are approved.

Select Junior is one of several methods that you can use to integrate with WorldPay. It uses HTMLforms to pass information between your site and WorldPay. Costs are as follows:

Item	Fee
Setup Fee (payable on application)	100.00 GBP
Annual Fee (payable on application and each anniversary)	160.00 GBP
Credit/charge cards (inc. Visa Debit Cards)	4.5%
Risk Management Transaction Charge	0.06 GBP
Standard Administration Fee Per Chargeback	10.00 GBP
Transfer charge	10.00 GBP
Minimum transfer amount	100.00 GBP
Remittance period	weekly, 4 weeks in arrears

NOTE: Many new users have difficulty implementing WorldPay; the transaction is successfully processed through WorldPay, but the payment is sometimes not recorded in OpenCart.

TIP: WorldPay can also integrate with QuickBooks! See http://www.worldpay.com/quickbooks/settingup.php

After opening a WorldPay account, in your store Admin's top nav bar menu, select MODULES - Payment, then select WorldPay. This brings you to the WorldPay Form:

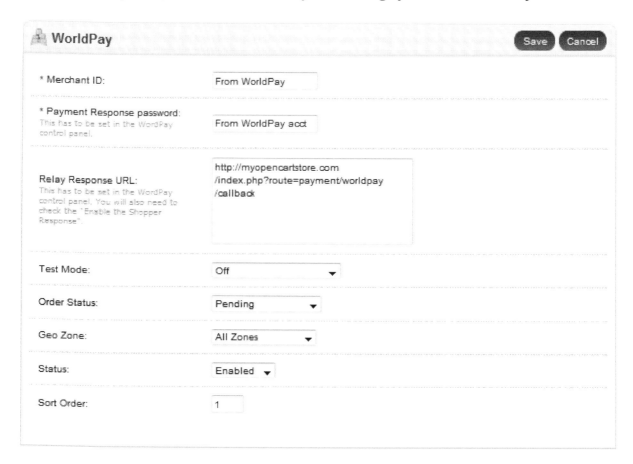

Fill in the form as shown above. When you have finished, be sure to click the SAVE Button.

Remember to test, test, test! Set the price of a product to a very low price such as $0.25, then put the product in your cart and check out. Does this payment method work in checkout? If not, go back and check the above settings.

Extensions menu

Order Totals

These pages allows you to customize what the customer sees as they check out - and rank (or sort) the order in which checkout screens appear.

- Additional setup is required for MANY of the items to display. Instructions or links to the instructions are included below and also on the tour screens below.
- Some items will NOT appear to all customers. For example, Low Order Fee will not appear unless the customer's order is below the minimum amount you have set. This can make it difficult to see and test. However, simply log onto your store as a customer and put an item in your cart that is below the minimum.
- NOTE that the sort order of some items cannot be changed. For example, total must be the last screen; it cannot add the total and later add on a gift certificate.

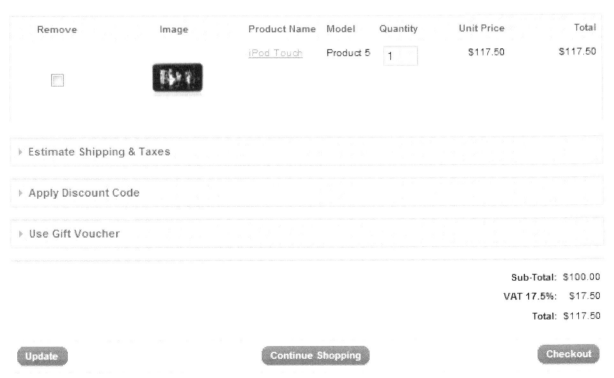

To choose order total screens, from your store Administration's top nav bar, click
EXTENSIONS - Order Totals. This brings you to the Order Totals List:

Order Totals

Order Totals	Status	Sort Order	Action
Coupon	Enabled	4	[Edit] [Uninstall]
Store Credit	Enabled	7	[Edit] [Uninstall]
Handling Fee	Disabled		[Edit] [Uninstall]
Low Order Fee	Disabled		[Edit] [Uninstall]
Reward Points	Enabled	2	[Edit] [Uninstall]
Shipping	Enabled	3	[Edit] [Uninstall]
Sub-Total	Enabled	1	[Edit] [Uninstall]
Taxes	Enabled	5	[Edit] [Uninstall]
Total	Enabled	9	[Edit] [Uninstall]
Gift Voucher	Enabled	8	[Edit] [Uninstall]

REMOVE order total pages from checkout by:

- On the Order Total List, clicking the far right UNINSTALL Link (removes all shipping account data for that method), OR
- By clicking the far right EDIT Link on the screen name row, and then clicking DISABLED.

BE CAREFUL in changing the Sort Order! This is the order the program needs to calculate the purchase price, shipping, taxes, etc. correctly.

 TIP: If two are set to the same sort order, only ONE of them will display. Sort order of ZERO will display FIRST. Sometimes multiple items are on the same screen, see the example above.

 TIP: Give your customers enough information to complete the sale, but NOT so many screens that you overwhelm them with so much information that they get tired of going through the checkout process. Think of each screen as an obstacle in a physical store preventing the customer from buying.

EXTENSIONS – ORDER TOTAL
Discount Coupon in checkout

If the customer has a coupon code, they must enter it during checkout on the **Shopping Cart Order Total page** and then click the APPLY COUPON Button.

 Usually if a customer has difficulty applying a coupon to his or her order, they are either typing the code incorrectly (usually capitalization or spacing), OR failing to click the APPLY COUPON Button.

Coupons are set up in two steps:

- **Coupons Step 1. First set up coupon codes in SALES - Coupons and, of course, give the coupon code to your customers either directly or by email.**
- **Coupons Step 2. Enable coupons in EXTENSIONS - Order Total - Coupons.**

To enable Discount Coupon during checkout, from your store Admin's top nav bar menu, select EXTENSIONS - Order Total and then from the list select Coupon. This brings you to the coupon form:

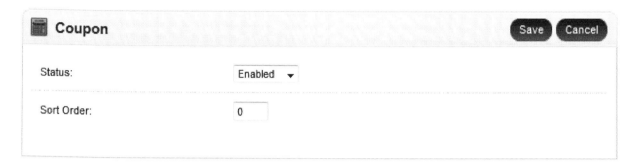

Set STATUS to "Enabled and set sort order to any number as long as box is not blank. Coupon will appear in SHOPPING CART regardless of the Sort Order number.

When you are finished, click the top right SAVE Button.

EXTENSIONS – ORDER TOTAL

Store Credit in checkout

If a customer has a store credit, it can be applied to their order during checkout.

To enable Store Credit during checkout, from your store Admin's top nav bar menu, select EXTENSIONS - Order Total and then from the list select STORE CREDIT. This brings you to the store credit form:

Set STATUS to "Enabled and set sort order to any number as long as box is not blank. Store Credit will appear regardless of the Sort Order number.

When you are finished, click the top right SAVE Button.

EXTENSIONS – ORDER TOTAL
Handling fee in checkout

You may choose to charge a separate HANDLING FEE to all customers. If so, this screen will display the exact cost to the customers.

To enable a handling fee during checkout, from your store Admin's top nav bar menu, select EXTENSIONS - Order Total and then from the list select Handling Fee. This brings you to the handling fee form:

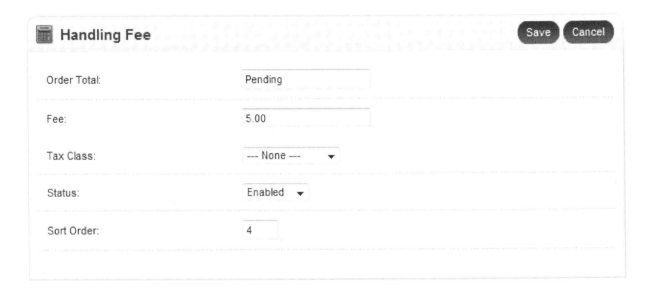

Set up the handling fee as shown and click the top right SAVE Button.

EXTENSIONS – ORDER TOTAL
Low Order Fee in checkout

If the customer orders less than a minimum dollar amount, you can add an extra charge to their order. This will encourage them to either leave or place a larger order.

To enable a low order fee during checkout, from your store Admin's top nav bar menu, select EXTENSIONS - Order Total and then from the list select Low Order Fee. This brings you to the low order fee form:

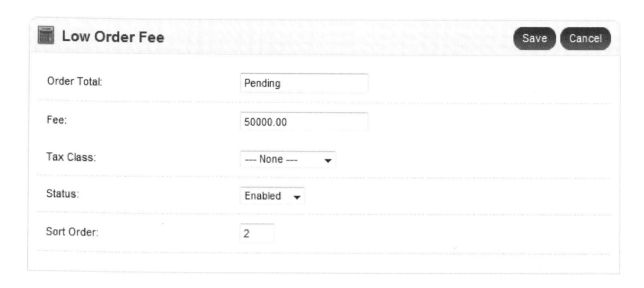

Set up the low order fee as shown and click the top right SAVE Button.

EXTENSIONS – ORDER TOTAL

Reward Points in checkout

Allow customers to redeem their accumulated Reward Points for merchandise during checkout.

To enable reward point redemption during checkout, from your store Admin's top nav bar menu, select EXTENSIONS - Order Total and then from the list select Reward Points. This brings you to the Reward Points form:

Set up the Reward Points fee as shown and click the top right SAVE Button.

EXTENSIONS – ORDER TOTAL

Shipping in checkout

If you offer multiple shipping methods, this page allows the customer to choose the shipping method they wish:

Disable this only if ALL of your products are either DOWNLOADABLE, or you ONLY offer local pickup of goods.

To enable reward point redemption during checkout, from your store Admin's top nav bar menu, select EXTENSIONS - Order Total and then from the list select Reward Points. This brings you to the Reward Points form:

Enable the shipping screen as shown below, and click the top right SAVE Button.

EXTENSIONS – ORDER TOTAL

Sub-Total in checkout

If you want the customer to see a detailed list of all charges in a separate Sub-Total section, add this extra section. It is typically not necessary and just delays the customer.

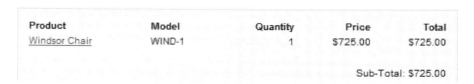

Product	Model	Quantity	Price	Total
Windsor Chair	WIND-1	1	$725.00	$725.00

Sub-Total: $725.00

Set up as shown below and click the top right SAVE Button.

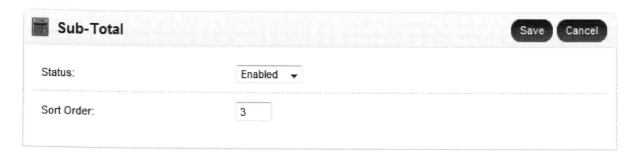

EXTENSIONS – ORDER TOTAL

Taxes in checkout

If you want the customer to see a detailed list of all taxes in a separate Taxes section, add this extra section. It is typically not necessary and just delays the customer.

City tax: $8.72
State tax: $45.44
Total: $781.16

Set up as shown below and click the top right SAVE Button.

EXTENSIONS – ORDER TOTAL

Total in checkout

Do not remove this page. Set up as shown below and click the top right SAVE Button.

Total		Save	Cancel
Status:	Enabled ▼		
Sort Order:	6		

EXTENSIONS – ORDER TOTAL

Gift Voucher in checkout

This screen only turns the gift voucher in checkout ON. Please see **SALES - Gift Vouchers** chapter for full instructions on setting up gift vouchers.

Set up as shown below and click the top right SAVE Button.

Be sure to test, test, test! Set up gift vouchers, open a customer account in your store, and purchase a voucher. Then log onto your Admin and release the voucher to yourself. Finally, purchase an item in your store using the voucher.

Extensions menu

Product Feeds

A product feed is a data file that lists information about your products in a special machine-readable format so other computers to read it so they can include it in search engine results. Some product feeds must be uploaded to another site; others simply need to be available on your own site.

EXTENSIONS –PRODUCT FEEDS
Google Base

Product Feed Google Base uploads a special data file to Google, to help people find your products when they do related searches. Based on your items' "relevance" as determined by Google, users may find their store products in search results on Google Product Search and even the main Google web search.

Added in version 1.5.2 - a behind-the-scenes improvement in the functioning of Google Product uploads, there are no menu changes: If an item is out-of-stock or cannot be purchased, availability "out of stock" is a request to remove the item from Google search. MORE INFO: http://groups.google.com/a/googleproductforums.com/forum/#!category-topic/merchant-center/troubleshooting/oQdRcK8uB7s

 TIP: If you sell merchandise such as apparel, books, consumer electronics, furniture, kitchen appliances, jewelry, music, movies, shoes, toys or video or pc games, you will need to modify your product attribute types to comply with Google's guidelines. See "Attributes for specific item types" info: http://www.google.com/support/merchants/bin/answer.py?answer=160081

More info on Google Base: http://www.google.com/base

Google Base Setup Checklist:

Google Base Step 1: In your store's Admin, install and edit your data feed's settings.
Google Base Step 2: Sign in to Google Base Merchant Center OR create a new account.
Google Base Step 3: Create and schedule the new data feed in Google Base
Google Base Step 4: On Google, check that your feed was received and whether it had any errors.

Google Base Step 1: In your store's Admin, install and edit your data feed's settings.

From your store Admin's top nav bar, select EXTENSIONS - Product Feeds. This brings you to the PRODUCT FEEDS List:

In the row named GOOGLE BASE, at the far right, click the INSTALL Link, then click the EDIT Link. This brings you to the GOOGLE BASE form:

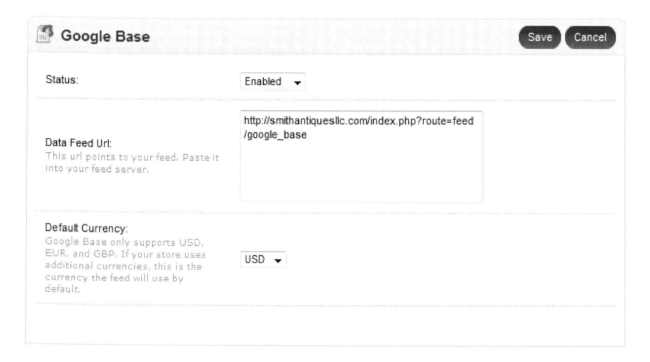

Change the STATUS to ENABLED and if necessary, change the DEFAULT CURRENCY.

Do not edit the DATAFEED URL which is already filled in for you.

When finished, at the top right, click the SAVE Button.

Google Base Step 2: Sign in to Google Base Merchant Center OR create a new Google Account.

To create a new Google Account, go to https://www.google.com/base, select the link "create an account now" and follow the instructions.

Looking for a way to upload products?

We've created a new website, the **Google Merchant Center**, where you can upload your product feeds and make them easy to find on Google Product Search.

If you have been uploading Products through Google Base, your data feeds and account settings have been migrated to the new Merchant Center.

Be sure to bookmark the new Merchant Center page, and see our FAQs for more information.

Sign in to Merchant Center

Don't have a Google Account?
Create a new Google Account

@2009 Google - Google Home - Advertising Programs - Business Solutions - Privacy - About Google

Fill out your new Google Base account settings following the example below:

Google base   **Account settings**

Configure your account

Please configure your account with the following information, which may be displayed publicly. You can change this information later by visiting the Settings page of your account.

Company or organization name (Required) - *Please do not include promotional text.*

Smith Antiques, LLC

Description

Unrestored antiques from the 17th Century.

Website URL

http://www.smithantiquesllc.com

☐ This site contains content that may be unsuitable for minors.

Private contact information

Google will use this information to contact you if needed. This information won't be displayed publicly.

Primary contact name

Robin Smith

Primary contact email

robin@gmail.com   - Verified

Technical contact name

Jerry Watson

Technical contact email

jerry@bestsupport.com   - Verified

We'll send email to this address if there are technical issues such as problems with the content you submitted. If you leave this empty, your primary contact email will be used.

Published contact email

Publicly display the following contact email in my hosted item pages and in the API.

◉ Do not include contact email

When finished, at the bottom left, click the SAVE UPDATES Button. This brings you to Google MY ITEMS Tab.

Google Base Step 3: Create and schedule the new data feed in Google Base

To create the new data feed, still on the Google Base MY ITEMS Tab, at the bottom left, click the NEW DATA FEED Button.

Fill in the New Data Feed form as listed below:

ITEM TYPE:	Select type from the drop-down menu.
CUSTOM ITEM TYPE:	If you cannot find a match in the Item Type list, you can create a custom one.
TARGET COUNTRY:	Where you want your items displayed in Google's Search Results. Currently available only in the US, UK, Germany and Australia; more may be added.
CONTENT LANGUAGE:	Currently only available in English or English U.K.; more may be added.
DATA FEED FILENAME:	Any filename you want for your data feed - it doesn't matter. Choose a name that you can remember, use letters and underscores (_) only, and end it with ".txt".

When finished, at the bottom left click the SAVE CHANGES Button.

This brings you to Google's DATA FEEDS list.

Next, create a schedule in the "Upload schedule" column in the center of the page, click the CREATE MANUAL UPLOAD Link:

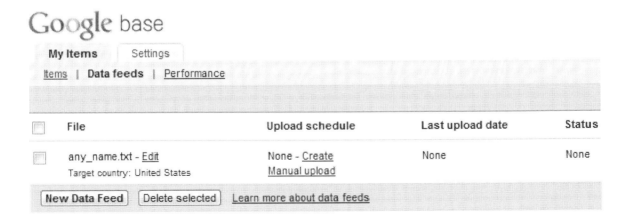

This brings up Google's SCHEDULED UPLOAD BOX. Fill in the form as follows:

UPLOAD: Choose a schedule Daily, Weekly or Monthly depending on how frequently your products are updated. Choose a day and time.

TIMEZONE: Select your time zone so Google knows what day and time you want.

FEED URL: IMPORTANT! Copy and paste from your store Admin's MODULES - Feeds - Google Base - DATA FEED URL Box.

USERNAME: If the Feed URL you just entered starts with "HTTPS" instead of "HTTP" then it is a secure, encrypted file. You will need to enter the username for this area (ask your techie if not sure).

PASSWORD: If the Feed URL you just entered starts with "HTTPS" instead of "HTTP" then it is a secure, encrypted file. You will need to enter the password for this area (ask your techie if not sure).

When you are finished, at the bottom click the SCHEDULE AND FETCH NOW Button.

Google Base Step 4: On Google, check that your feed was received and whether it had any errors.

You will see a message that says "PROCESSING....." Wait a few minutes to see the results. Hopefully you will see the following in the STATUS Column:

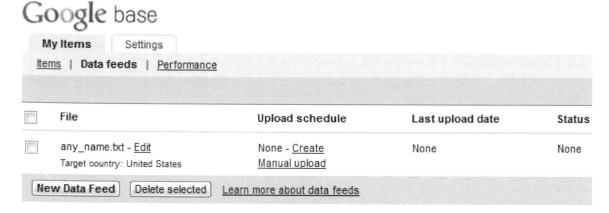

 TIP: If the STATUS column shows an error message, check the OpenCart forum for help or ask your techie.

208 | P a g e

Important! If there is any error your feed file will not be used.

Common problems:

The most common cause of upload errors is using punctuation in your category or product names, especially the ampersand symbol (&).

If you use an ampersand in your category names, such as "Toys & Gifts" in your Admin's top nav bar, select CATALOG - Categories and change the ampersands in any category names from the symbol to the character code & amp ; with no spaces in front of or after the word amp. Many other symbols can cause upload problems, but may be used with their character code, for a list see http://rabbit.eng.miami.edu/info/htmlchars.html

EXTENSIONS –PRODUCT FEEDS
Google Site Map

Product Feed Google Site Map is a data file hidden from users that lists all of your categories and products using a machine readable language called XML. It helps Google and its users to find your products more easily. This is helpful in getting your products listed in Google because search engines cannot always find products that are listed in a database like OpenCart's database.

Create the Google Site Map in two steps:

Google Site Map Step 1. Enable the Site Map in your store Admin
Google Site Map Step 2. Submit the Sitemap to Google.

Google Site Map Step 1. Enable the Site Map in your store Admin

To enable the Google Site Map data feed, from your store Admin's top nav bar, select EXTENSIONS - Product Feeds. This brings you to the Product Feeds List. In the row GOOGLE SITEMAP, in the far right ACTION column, click the INSTALL Link, then click the EDIT Link.

This brings you to the GOOGLE SITEMAP Form:

Product Feeds

Product Feed Name	Status	Action
Google Base	Enabled	[Edit] [Uninstall]
Google Sitemap	Disabled	[Edit] [Uninstall]

The DATA FEED URL is already filled in for you. COPY this box (CTRL-C), as you will need it in the next step on Google.com.

Change the STATUS to ENABLED as shown above, then at the top right click the SAVE Button.

Google Site Map Step 2. Submit the Sitemap to Google.

To submit your Google Sitemap to Google, you must have a Google Webmaster Account AND have added and verified your website with Google.

To open a Google Webmaster Account, go to http://www.google.com/webmasters/ click the button SIGN INTO GOOGLE WEBMASTERS and log in or create an account.

TIP: If you opened a Google account in the GOOGLE BASE section above - or have ever opened an account and logged in to Google, you do not need to create a new Google login. Just use your same Google login name and password, then follow the above instructions for adding the Webmaster account to your Google account.

After you have logged into your Google Webmaster Account, on your Webmaster Tools Home page, in the middle of the page click the ADD A SITE Button. A box pops open below the button. Enter your WEBSITE address (not the link to your Site Map), then click the CONTINUE Button:

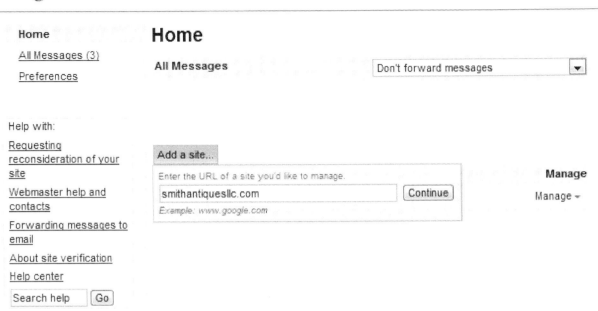

Now you have added your site. To verify your website with Google, the easiest method is to upload a file to your web host. On Google's VERIFY OWNERSHIP page item #1, click the link that says "THIS HTML VERIFICATION FILE" to download it to your personal computer:

Verify ownership

Recommended method	Alternate methods	History

Recommended: Upload an HTML file to your server

You can use this option if you can upload new files to your site.

Instructions:

1. Download this HTML verification file. [google373dfa137.html]

2. Upload the file to http://www.pithypublications.com/

3. Confirm successful upload by visiting http://www.pithypublications.com/google373dfc50d571a137.html in your browser.

4. Click Verify below.

To stay verified, don't remove the HTML file, even after verification succeeds.

[Verify] [Not now]

If you have access to your web host's Control Panel or cPanel, use the File Manager to click the folders on your web host to get to the top level of your website (usually public_html OR www), click the UPLOAD Icon, then click the BROWSE Button to find the file on your computer that you just downloaded.

IF NOT, or if you have any problems, ask your techie or web host to upload the file for you!

After the file is uploaded to the top of your website (you can see the file if you click http://youropencartstorename.com/googlefilenameandnumber.html), then in the VERIFY OWNERSHIP page shown above, click the VERIFY Button.

IF you followed the instructions correctly, you will see a SUCCESS! Message and the site will be added to the SITES column as shown below:

Google webmaster tools

	Home
Home	
All Messages (3)	**All Messages**
Preferences	Don't forward messages

Help with:

Requesting reconsideration of your site

Webmaster help and contacts

Forwarding messages to email

Add a site...

Sites   **Manage**

☐ ◎ smithantiquesllc.com   Manage ▾

Delete

Finally, click the name of the website - in the example above it is "smithantiquesllc.com." This brings you to the Google Webmaster Tools Dashboard for your site, which is mostly blank because it is new. At the bottom right, click the SUBMIT A SITEMAP Link:

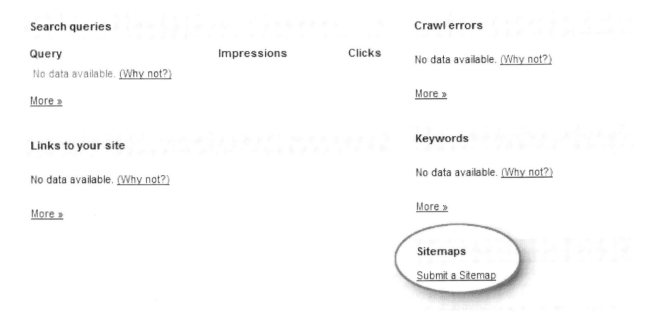

Click Submit a Sitemap and paste the link from Step 1.

« Back to Home

Sitemaps

Submit a Sitemap to tell Google about pages on your site we might not otherwise discover.

CAUTION: Notice that Google already inserted the "smithantiquesllc.com" above... do NOT copy that part of your website address in the box also or you will get an error SITEMAP NOT FOUND.

When you are finished, click the SUBMIT SITEMAP Button.

Google Sitemaps Success

At the top of the page, you will see a happy confirmation message like, " http://smithantiquesllc.com/index.php?route=feed/google_sitemap has been added as a Sitemap." YAY!

6

6. Sales Menu

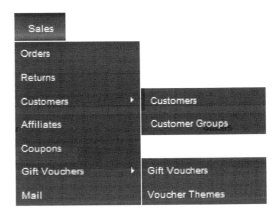

After your store is set up, this is where you will spend most of your time managing your store, managing and processing your orders and counting your money.

Orders

It's easy! You will love managing your store orders with OpenCart. The Order Editing System was updated in Version 1.5.2. To get to the Orders list, from your Admin's top nav bar, click SALES – Orders. This brings you to the ORDERS page. From here you may do the following:

- **Insert or edit an order**
- **Process new orders**

Each item is discussed below.

Insert or edit an order

Starting with version 1.5.2 it is EASY for store administrators to edit an order OR place a new order for the customer. From your Admin's top navigation bar, click SALES – Orders then Insert Order or Edit Order. This brings you to the Order Edit page:

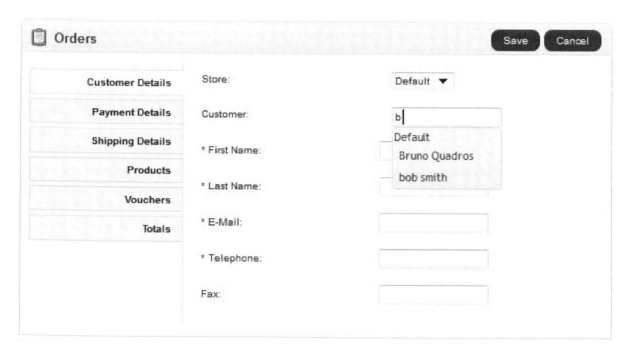

CUSTOMER DETAILS: in Customer box, begin typing the customer's name, then select it from the drop-down list. Type the customer information, then repeat on Payment Details and Shipping Details Tabs.

TIP: If the customer's name does not appear in the Customer box, you can also add them in SALES – Customers – Customers, then return to this drop-down list and continue.

Next click the PRODUCTS Tab:

CHOOSE PRODUCT: Begin typing the name of the product to add, then select it from the drop-down box.

QUANTITY: Type the number desired.

Click the ADD PRODUCT Button when finished.

If the customer wants to purchase a Gift Voucher, click the VOUCHERS Tab and fill in as shown.

NOTE that you can apply an existing gift voucher to the order next on the TOTALS Tab.

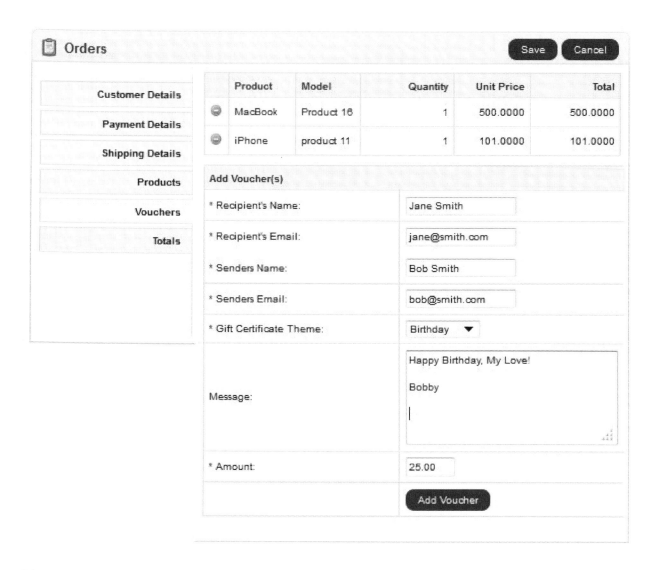

Finally, click the TOTALS Tab:

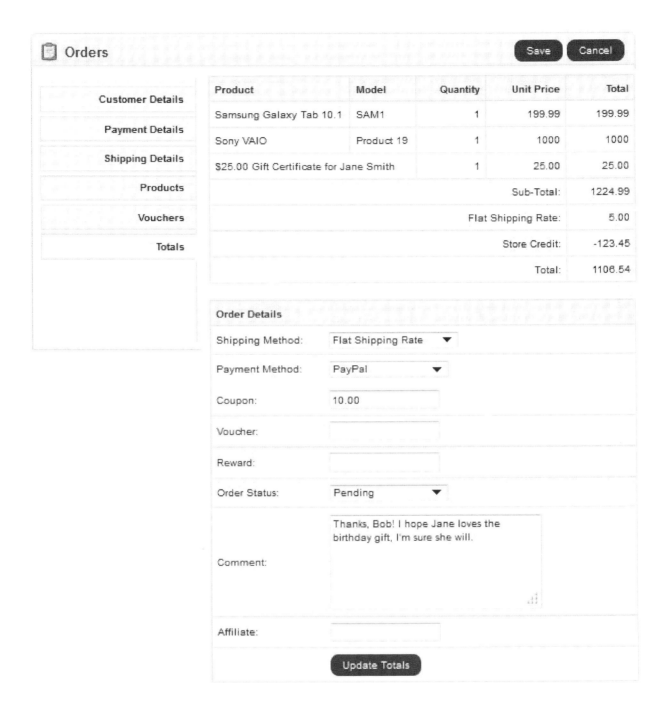

SHIPPING METHOD: Select the shipping method. You must have at least one shipping method properly set up for this box to work.

PAYMENT METHOD: Select the payment method. You must have at least one payment method properly set up for this box to work.

COUPON: If the customer has a coupon code, enter it here.

VOUCHER: If the customer has a gift voucher code, enter it here.

REWARD: If the customer has rewards points to apply to their order, enter the number here.

ORDER STATUS: Manually select the order status you want, usually PENDING.
COMMENT: Insert an optional comment.
AFFILIATE: If the sale was via an affiliate, you can type the affiliate code here for the affiliate to receive a commission for the sale.

When finished, click the UPDATE TOTALS Button, then the top right SAVE Button.

Process new orders

 ## Process new orders checklist:

Process new orders Step 1. Sort pending orders
Process new orders Step 2. For each order, print the invoice, insert an optional comment for you and/or the customer, and notify customer.

To begin managing your orders, from the Top Bar Navigation Menu, click SALES - Orders. This brings you to the Orders List.

Order Processing Step 1. Sort pending orders

To see only pending orders that are ready for you to fill, in your store Admin's Top Navigation Bar, click SALES - ORDERS and in the STATUS Drop-down box select Status of Pending and click the far right FILTER Button:

	Order ID ▼	Customer Name	Status	Date Added	Total	Action
			Pending ▼			Filter
	5	Shanna Smith	Missing Orders Canceled	14/04/2011	$3,302.00	[Edit]
	4	Sally Hershey	Canceled Reversal Chargeback	14/04/2011	$5,052.00	[Edit]
	3	Patrick Kingsley	Complete Denied	14/04/2011	$2,577.00	[Edit]
	2	Joe Starbucks	Failed Pending	14/04/2011	$50,552.00	[Edit]
	1	Ariana Wellington	Processing Refunded Reversed Shipped	14/04/2011	$2,902.00	[Edit]

Orders — Print Invoices — Delete

To PRINT a complete list of pending orders, from your Browser's top navigation bar select FILE-PRINT.

Order Processing Step 2. For each order, print the invoice, change order status, and notify customer

If you are ready to process this order, click the top right PRINT INVOICE Button:

Orders		Print Invoice	Cancel
Order Details	Order ID:	#4	
Products	Invoice ID:	#4	
Shipping Address	Customer:	Sally Hershey	
Payment Address	Customer Group:	Default	
Order History	E-Mail:	sally@hershey.com	
	Telephone:	512 456-1234	
	IP:	174.39.181.57	
	Store Name:	Smith Antiques, LLC	
	Store Url:	http://smithantiquesllc.com	
	Date Added:	14/04/2011	
	Shipping Method:	Flat Shipping Rate	
	Payment Method:	Cash On Delivery	
	Order Total:	$5,052.00	
	Order Status:	Pending	

That brings up the INVOICE Form:

INVOICE

Smith Antiques, LLC
123 45th St.
My City, OH 12345
Telephone 212 555-1212
robin@gmail.com
http://smithantiquesllc.cor

Order Date: 14/04/2011
Invoice No.: INV-2011-002
Invoice Date: 2011-04-19 07:13:57
Order ID: 4

To	Ship To (if different address)
Sally Hershey 938 Chocolate Bar Lane Hershey, Pennsylvania 58949 United States sally@hershey.com 512 456-1234	Sally Hershey 938 Chocolate Bar Lane Hershey, Pennsylvania 58949 United States

Product	Model	Quantity	Unit Price	Total
Wingback Sitting Chair	WING1	2	$2,525.00	$5,050.00
			Sub-Total:	$5,050.00
			Flat Shipping Rate:	$2.00
			Total:	$5,052.00

Comment

Note in the left column there are five pages of information. To process the order, edit the REQUIRED pages and any optional pages, as follows:

ORDER DETAILS:* — Summary of the order, customer's contact information.
If you will ship this order today, click the PRINT INVOICE Button.
OPTIONAL: If needed, edit customer info by clicking the customer name link.

PRODUCTS: — Details of the actual products ordered by customer.
OPTIONAL: If needed, add more products to the customer's order here.

SHIPPING ADDRESS: — Details of customer's shipping address. Copy this info to your shipping label or to another online shipping method such as USPS.com, UPS.com or a private postage company such as Stamps.com.
OPTIONAL: If needed, edit the customer shipping address here.

PAYMENT ADDRESS: — Details of customer's credit card billing address.

OPTIONAL: If needed, edit the customer payment address here.

ORDER HISTORY:*   REQUIRED:
1. Change ORDER STATUS to "SHIPPED"
2. Check the checkbox "NOTIFY CUSTOMER" for a copy of the invoice to be emailed to customer
3. insert any comment in the COMMENT Box such as shipping, tracking, and returns information, and
4. you MUST click the bottom right ADD ORDER HISTORY Button for actions to be saved. SEE IMAGE BELOW.

Order History Tab

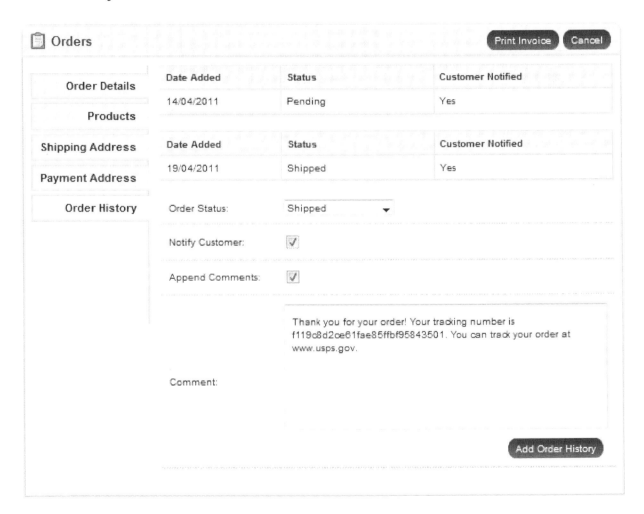

Put the paper invoice form in the package to the customer.

Repeat the above steps for each order. Mail the packages. Now relax!

SALES MENU

Returns

Also known as RMA or Returns Management Authorization. Sometimes a customer wants to return the merchandise for a refund. For example, if the product was faulty, damaged, or you shipped the wrong item.

To process customer returns or RMA's after receiving the item back, do the following:

Customer returns checklist:

Returns Step 1. Record the pending refund and give the customer a Returns or RMA Number.
Returns Step 2. Issue the refund using your payment processor's Virtual Terminal or other payment processing page.
Returns Step 3. Notify customer and mark the return Complete.
Returns Step 4. Optional: If you use the stock tracking module, return item(s) to stock.

Returns Step 1. Record the pending refund and give the customer a Returns or RMA Number.

Record the pending refund in your store Admin's SALES - Returns menu and give the customer the RMA Number.

From your store Admin's top nav bar menu, select SALES Returns. This brings you to the Product Returns List. In the top right corner, click the INSERT Button and fill out the Product Returns Form as follows:

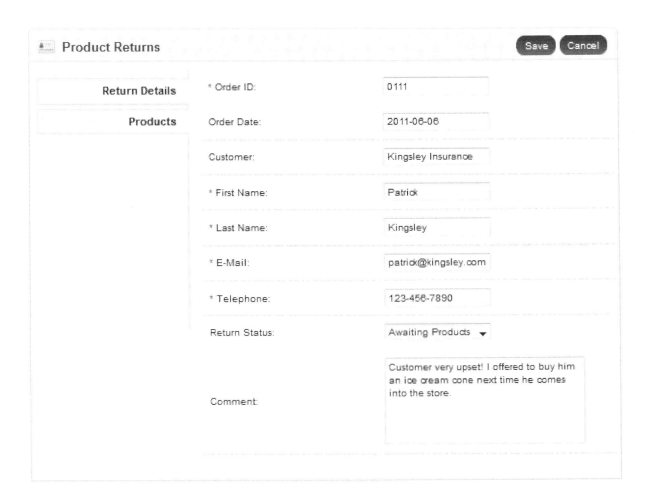

When finished, click the top right SAVE Button. This brings you back to the Returns List, where you can get the RETURN ID to tell the customer. Normally the customer must mark the package with this RETURN ID for the return to be accepted by your store. The Return ID is also often called the RMA Number.

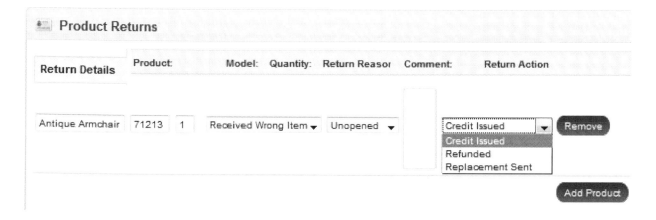

Returns Step 2. Issue the refund.

When you have received the product back from the customer, in your payment processor's Virtual Terminal or other payment processing page, follow their instructions to issue a refund. Instructions are different for each payment processor. Contact their support if you need help.

You may also issue a paper check as a refund.

Returns Step 3. Mark the return Complete and notify the customer.

Return to your store to mark the return Complete. In your store Admin's top nav bar menu, select SALES - Returns. Match the Return ID on the box of the return to the Return ID's in your list, and at the far right click the EDIT Button.

Change the STATUS to Complete and click the top right SAVE Button.

Notify the customer. In your store Admin's Top Navigation Bar click SALES - Orders, find the order at the top of the CUSTOMER NAME column, in the list find the customer's order, check the box at the far left to select it, then at the far right click the EDIT Link.

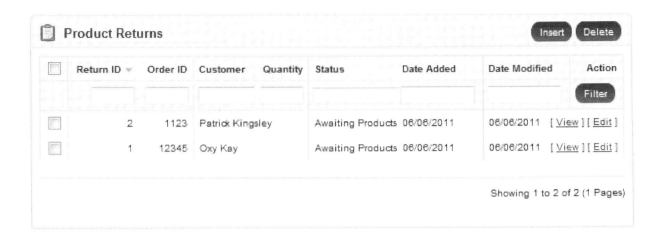

This brings you to the Product Returns – Return Details Tab. Fill in as follows, with an optional Customer Number and Order Date; all other boxes are required:

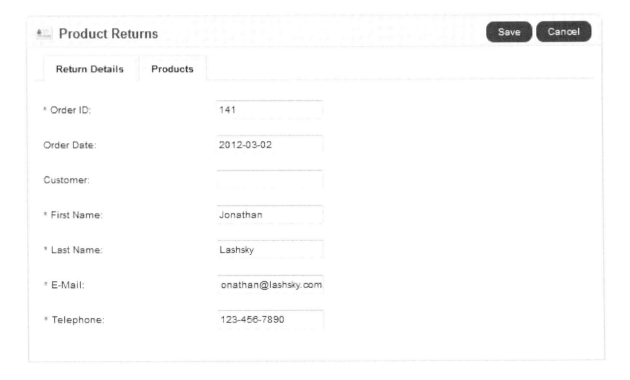

Next click the top Products Tab, select the product and fill in the form as shown:

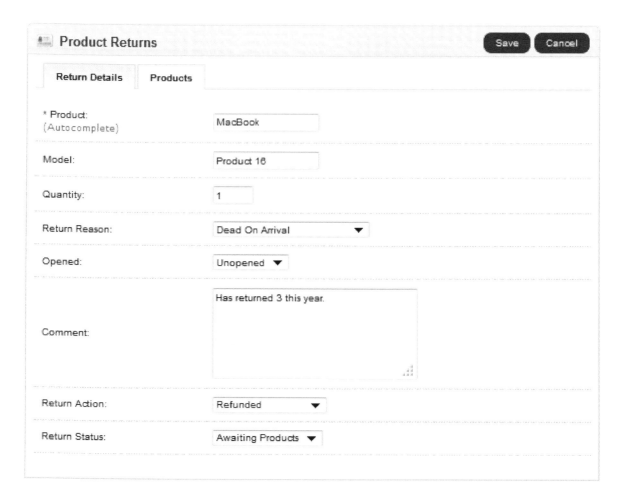

At the top right, click the SAVE Button. The product is returned to stock if you use the stock module.

SALES MENU

Customers

To begin managing your customers, from your Admin's Top Bar Navigation Menu, click SALES - Customers. This brings you to the Customers List:

 # Customers Checklist

From the Customers List you may:

VIEW LIST of customers OR FIND a customer record   In the blank row of the Customer List, select the box you want to view (example wholesale or unapproved customers) OR the last name of the customer, and at the far right click the FILTER Link.

Edit or VIEW a customer record   Click the far right EDIT Link

Delete a customer   Check the far left checkbox, then at the top right click the DELETE Button.

Approve a customer account   Check the far left checkbox next to customer name, then at top right

	click the APPROVE Button.
ADD a new customer account	Click the top right INSERT Button and filling in the below screen
ADD the customer to a customer group such as "Wholesale customers"	After you have created the customer group, select the customer you wish to add, select the group name, and click the top right INSERT Button.

VIEW A LIST of customers OR FIND a customer record

In the blank row of the Customer List, select the box you want to view (example wholesale or unapproved customers, the last name of the customer), and at the far right click the FILTER Link. This gives you the following Customer Results List:

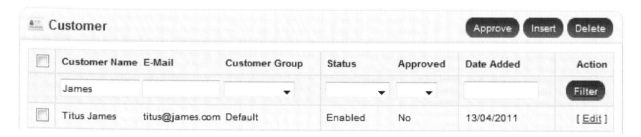

Edit or view a customer record

Edit a customer record if the customer:

- Changed email addresses and can no longer access to the email account they registered with to receive their forgotten password. Simply enter the customer's new email address and they are happy again, they can log in and receive the system emails.
- Cannot remember the name and/or email address they used to register for their account.
- Forgot that they signed up for your newsletter, and sends you a nasty reply that they no longer wish to receive newsletters, so you change their newsletter status to Disabled.
- If you have been defrauded by the customer and wish to ban them from your store using the IP Addresses Tab.

From the Customer List, at the top far right, click the EDIT Button. This brings you to the Customer page:

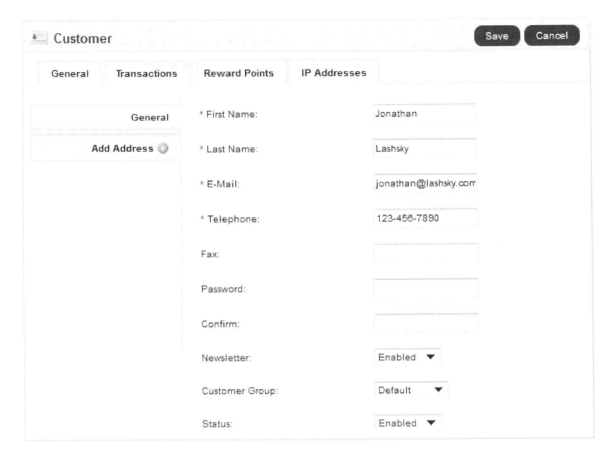

 TIP: Add a customer address in the left column above by clicking the ADD+ Button.

Customer - Transactions Tab

View a list of all the customer's transactions or add a summary transaction. Note if you want to add a full order do that in SALES – Orders.

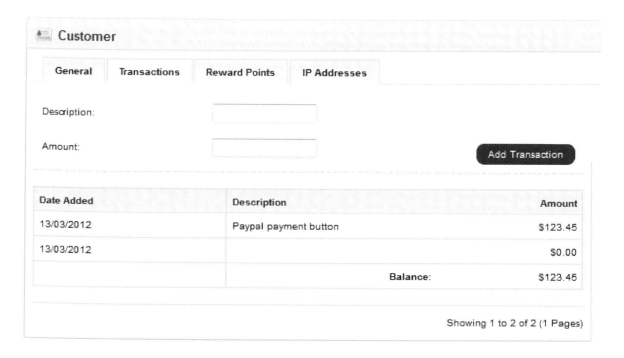

Customer - Reward Points Tab

View a list of all the customer's reward points or add reward points.

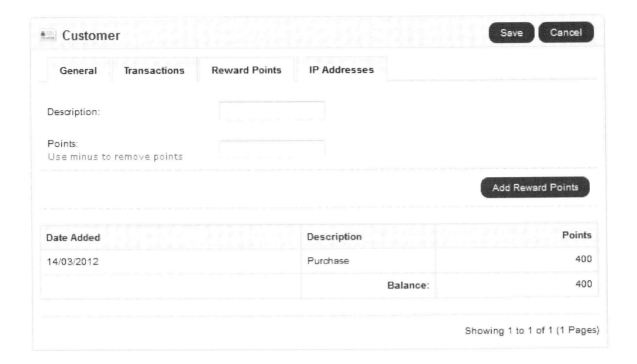

Customer - IP Addresses Tab

Use this tab to look up where a customer is located, see how many accounts that customer has, or to ban a customer who as defrauded you.

From your Admin's top navigation bar, click SALES – Orders – select a customer order – and click the IP Address Tab. This brings you to the Customer IP Address page:

IP Address: Click the IP Address to see where the customer is located via the website http://www.geoiptool.com. SEE screenshot below.

Total Accounts: Click to see which accounts are registered to this IP Address.

Action: Click to add this IP Address to the blacklist.

See where a customer is located:

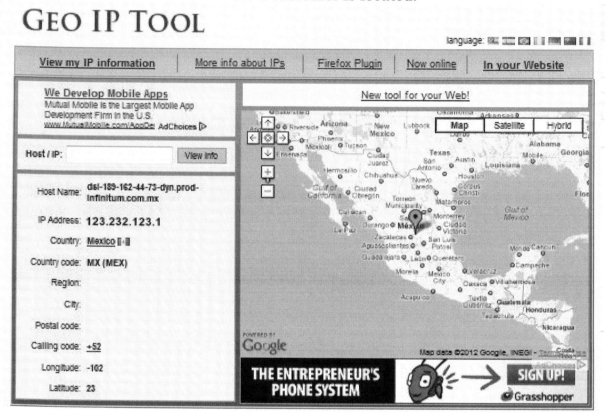

Approve a new customer account

Some companies are required to approve all customers before the customer can buy. For example, wholesale-only sales, or if you sell only to licensed practitioners such as dentists. Do not use this setting unless it is required.

TIP: APPROVE NEW CUSTOMERS must first be set in SYSTEM - Settings - Option. Set Approve New Customers to YES and click the SAVE Button.

TIP: To receive an alert email each time a customer submits a new account, go to SYSTEM - Settings - Mail. Set New Order Alert Mail to YES and click the SAVE Button.

To approve a customer account or a list of customer account, select SALES - Customer. This brings you to the Customer List.

Next FIND the customer record, and on the Customer Results List, put a check in the far left column next to the Customer Name, and click the APPROVE Button.

TIP: To approve a LIST of customers, in the top row check the CUSTOMER NAME Box, then click the APPROVE Button.

CAUTION: After a customer is approved, there is no way to change their APPROVED Status to NO (Unapproved). Instead, you must change their STATUS to DISABLED.

SALES MENU - CUSTOMERS

Customer Groups

Your store can display different prices to customers if they are part of a group like wholesale customers, employees, or any other custom group you want to create.

Customer Group Checklist:

- **Customer Group Step 1. Create the group name** in SALES - Customers - Customer Groups, THEN add the customers to the group in SALES - Customers.
- **Customer Group Step 2. Specify the special pricing for EACH product** in CATALOG - Products - Product name.
- **Customer Group Step 3. Approve the membership** of a new customer who belong to a group when they register, before they will see the special pricing. NOTE: The customer must be logged in to see and receive the special pricing.

Customer Group Step 1. Create the group name.

To begin creating a new customer group, from your store Admin's top nav bar menu, select SALES - Customers - Customer Groups. This brings you to the Customer Groups List:

To edit the name of a Customer Group, click the far right EDIT Link.

To add a new Customer Group, click the top right INSERT Button. This brings you to the Insert Customer Group form:

Simply enter the name of the new group, then click the SAVE Button.

Next, add customers to the new Customer Group. From your store Admin's top nav bar menu, select SALES - Customers and select the customer you wish to add to the group. This brings you to the Customer Record:

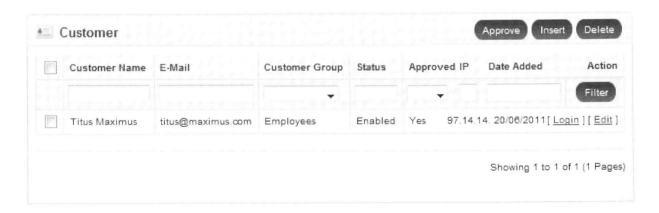

At the near bottom, in the Customer Group box, select the name of the group you want to add this customer to, then at the top right click the SAVE Button.

Customer Group Step 2. Specify the special pricing for EACH product.

Next, specify the discount the Customer Group will receive on EACH product. You may offer it for one or all products, but each product must be specified individually. From your store Admin's top nav bar menu, select CATALOG - Products - Product Name, then click the DISCOUNT Tab. This brings you to the Discount form:

For each discount you wish to offer, fill in the form as follows:

CUSTOMER GROUP: Select the group you want to receive this discount.

QUANTITY: Specify a minimum number of items for members of this group to receive the discount.

PRIORITY: If you offer multiple discounts, specify 1 for this discount to be applied first, 2 to be applied second, etc.

PRICE: Specify the discount price for this group.

DATE START: To limit the discount, specify a start date for the discount to appear.

DATE END: To limit the discount, specify an end date for the discount to disappear.

When finished, click the top right SAVE Button.

 TIP: You can also specify SPECIALS (short-term discounts) for customer groups on the SPECIALS Tab, in exactly the same way as listed above.

 TIP: You can also specify REWARD POINTS for customer groups on the REWARD POINTS Tab.

 TECH TIP: Your Technical Pro can change product pricing quickly by doing it directly to each record in the database, OR by using the Import/Export Extension available for purchase on OpenCart.com.

Customer Group Step 3. Approve memberships as customers register.

Approve the membership of a new customer who belong to a group when they register, before they will see the special pricing, in SALES – Customers – find the customer name in the list, select the ADD TO GROUP drop-down and click the SAVE Button.

SALES MENU

Affiliates

The OpenCart Affiliate Program lets other companies refer business to your store or to a particular product, and if the referral produces an actual sale, the affiliate automatically earns a referral fee. Some businesses pay a $50 or more for each verified referral that purchases!

NOTE that affiliate program setup is spread across several menus. See description below.

Affiliate Program Summary

1. **SET UP YOUR AFFILIATE PROGRAM:**

   - Create or edit your Affiliate Terms & Conditions in CATALOG – Information – Affiliate Terms & Conditions. Google "Affiliate terms & conditions" for examples.
   - Turn ON the Affiliate Module in EXTENSIONS – Modules – Affiliate.

2. **MARKET YOUR AFFILIATE PROGRAM:**

   - Tell people to sign up as affiliates on your affiliate page (linked from all pages in your store's footer), by making a new page in Information Pages, or they find it on their own.
   - Potential affiliates fill out the simple affiliate application and specify whether they want you to deposit by check, PayPal, or bank transfer. They must also agree to your Affiliate Terms & Conditions. They see the Affiliate Success page, but cannot do anything further until you approve the application.

3. **ADMINISTER YOUR AFFILIATE PROGRAM:**

   - You approve (or deny) their affiliate application
   - After you approve the affiliate account, the new affiliate can see the "tracking code" that they must place on their website. When a visitor to their site clicks on the link, it saves a "cookie" in their browser. If they return to your site to make a purchase, the cookie gives the referrer credit for the purchase.
   - Periodically check your Affiliate Report in REPORTS – Affiliate and manually release checks to affiliates who have met your Terms & Conditions. Mark the affiliates PAID in Sales – Affiliates.

Affiliate Step 1: Set up your Affiliate Program

Create or edit your Affiliate Terms & Conditions in CATALOG – Information – Affiliate Terms & Conditions. Google "Affiliate terms & conditions" for examples.

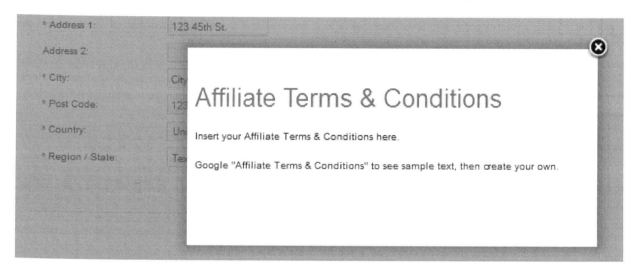

Turn ON the Affiliate Module in EXTENSIONS – Modules – Affiliate. SEE CHAPTER 6 EXTENSIONS for detailed instructions.

Affiliate Step 2: Market your Affiliate Program

Tell people to sign up as affiliates on your affiliate page (linked from all pages in your store's footer), by making a new page in Information Pages. SEE CHAPTER 5 CATALOG – Information Pages for detailed instructions.

Advertise your affiliate program as you wish using traditional and online marketing: newspaper ads, online ads, search engine AdWords, on websites such as Facebook.

Affiliate Step 3: Administer your Affiliate Program

To begin managing your store's Affiliate Program, from your Admin's top nav bar menu, select SALES - Affiliates. This brings you to the Affiliate List:

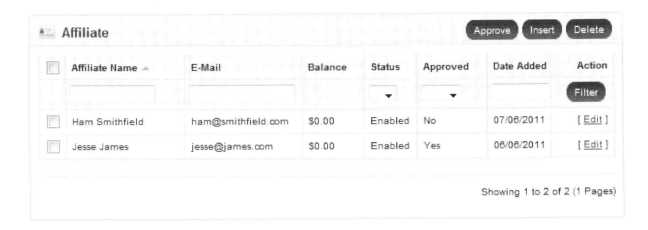

	Affiliate Name ▲	E-Mail	Balance	Status	Approved	Date Added	Action
☐				▼	▼		Filter
☐	Ham Smithfield	ham@smithfield.com	$0.00	Enabled	No	07/06/2011	[Edit]
☐	Jesse James	jesse@james.com	$0.00	Enabled	Yes	06/06/2011	[Edit]

Showing 1 to 2 of 2 (1 Pages)

AFFILIATE ACTIONS:	DESCRIPTION
APPROVE NEW AFFILIATES	Put a check in the left-column box, then click the top right APPROVE Button.
ADD (INSERT) AN AFFILIATE	Click the top right INSERT Button, see next screen for details.
DELETE AN AFFILIATE	Put a check in the left-column box, the click the top right DELETE Button. A warning box comes up "DELETE CANNOT BE UNDONE! Are you sure?" Answer Yes to delete or No to cancel.
FIND AN AFFILIATE	In the top empty row, type any piece of information - last name, email address, status, whether approved or not, then click the top right FILTER Button.
EDIT AN AFFILIATE:	Find the affiliate's name, put a check in the left-column checkbox, then in the far right column click the EDIT Link. This brings you to the AFFILIATE RECORD (see below).
PAY AN AFFILIATE:	Open the affiliate's record, click the top PAYMENT DETAILS Tab, and see which payment method they have chosen. Mail the check OR send the PayPal transaction OR send the bank wire, then record the transaction on the next tab, TRANSACTIONS.
SEE AN AFFILIATE'S TRANSACTIONS:	After paying the affiliate, record the transaction and a payment description i.e. "PayPal payment" and click the top right SAVE Button. The payment will be deducted from the affiliate's balance and they will see the transaction in their affiliate account.

SALES MENU

Coupons

Many people get confused between coupons and gift vouchers. Here are the differences:

- A coupon is issued by YOU, the store owner, often in an email to all customers. Anyone who has the coupon code can use it.
- A gift voucher is actually a PRODUCT, like a paper gift certificate, that customers can buy. You then create a single-use gift voucher code and email it to the one recipient specified by the purchaser.

- Both lead to a discount in your store during checkout.

To add a new coupon, from your store Admin's top nav bar menu, select SALES - Coupons. This brings you to the COUPON LIST:

Coupon List

	Coupon Name	Code	Discount	Date Start	Date End	Status	Action
☐ Coupon						Insert	Delete
☐	-10% Discount	2222	10.0000	01/01/2011	01/01/2012	Enabled	[Edit]
☐	-10.00 Discount	1111	10.0000	01/11/1970	01/11/2020	Enabled	[Edit]
☐	Free Shipping	3333	0.0000	01/03/2009	31/08/2009	Enabled	[Edit]

Showing 1 to 3 of 3 (1 Pages)

At the top right of the Coupons List, click the INSERT Button. This brings you to the Add Coupon Form:

 TIP: As you type the product name below, the drop-down list of products will appear in the window.

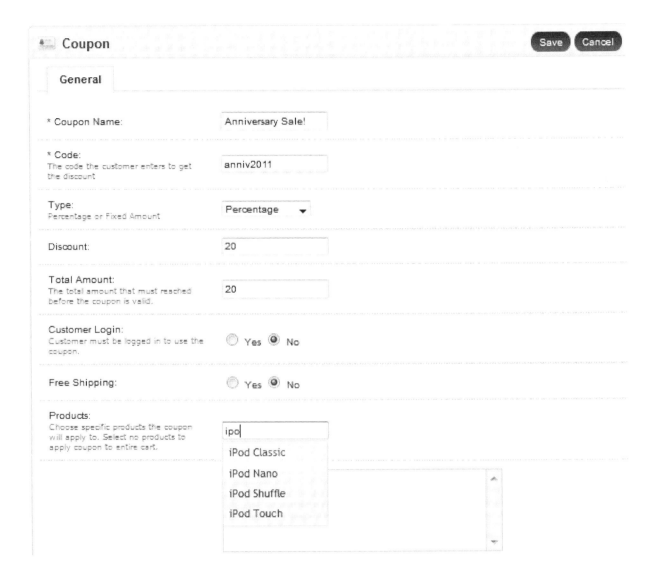

Date Start:	2011-06-08
Date End:	2011-06-08
Uses Per Coupon: The maximum number of times the coupon can be used by any customer. Leave blank for unlimited	100
Uses Per Customer: The maximum number of times the coupon can be used by a single customer. Leave blank for unlimited	1
Status:	Enabled ▾

COUPON NAME: Give the coupon a unique name so you can identify it later in your Admin.

CODE: Give a unique code that cannot be guessed easily. Customers must type this code exactly into the Coupon box as they check out.

TYPE: Select percentage or fixed amount from the drop-down box. This will apply to the next box.

DISCOUNT: The amount of the discount in numbers. EXAMPLE: 20 with "Percent" selected as TYPE above gives a 20% discount. 20 and "Fixed Amount" selected as TYPE above will give $20 off the order.

TOTAL AMOUNT: Do you want to specify a minimum purchase to qualify for the discount?

CUSTOMER LOGIN: Do you want to require customers to log in to receive the purchase, or will you allow it for those who choose "Guest checkout"? Since customers who log in are more likely to be long-term customers, store owners often choose yes.

FREE SHIPPING: YES means the customer will not be charged shipping if they use the coupon and meet all other requirements (such as minimum purchase and login).

PRODUCTS: Leave blank if you want the coupon to apply to ALL products. OR start typing product name(s) and select the products from the drop-down list that appears.

DATE START: Most coupons have a time limit. Set a start date here.

DATE END: Most coupons have a time limit. Set an expiration date here.

USES PER COUPON: If you enter a number, the discount will no longer apply after that many customers have used it. Leave blank for unlimited. In the example above, the coupon is limited to the first 100 customers.

USES PER CUSTOMER: If you enter a number, the discount will no longer apply after EACH customer has used it. Leave blank for unlimited. In the example above, each customer can only use it one time. Note this is limited by customer account, so a customer could open more than one account to receive the coupon multiple times.

STATUS: Enabled to turn ON or disabled to turn OFF.

When you have finished, be sure to click the SAVE Button.

SALES MENU

Gift Vouchers

Customers can purchase a non-refundable gift voucher of any amount between $1.00 and $1,000.00 (OR your units of currency) by clicking the footer link "Gift Vouchers":

This brings the customer to the Gift Certificate form for them to fill out and purchase:

Purchase a Gift Certificate

This gift certificate will be emailed to the recipient after your order has been paid for.

* Recipient's Name: `Dover Cashel`

* Recipient's Email: `dover@cashel.com`

* Your Name: `Customer/Giver Nam`

* Your Email: `Customer/Giver Emai`

Message:
(Optional)

```
Happy birthday, Dover! I hope you enjoy
selecting something for yourself from
this terrific store.

Love,
Mom
```

* Amount:
(Value must be between
$1.00 and $1,000.00)

`25.00`

* Gift Certificate Theme:
- ⦿ Birthday
- ○ Christmas
- ○ General

I understand that gift certificates are non-refundable. ☑ [Continue]

Note that to help prevent fraud, the voucher is NOT released until you manually release it from the customer's Order page.

About Gift Vouchers

- Gift vouchers, like paper gift certificates, are virtual products that can be purchased by a customer by clicking the "Gift Certificate link in any footer.
- After verifying that you have received the full payment from the purchaser, you release the email to the recipient telling them about their gift. The email contains a gift voucher code.
- The recipient enters the code in the Gift Voucher box during checkout.
- If the recipient's purchase is larger than the gift voucher amount, the recipient sees the normal credit card payment screens during checkout. EXAMPLE: Gift voucher for $25, the total purchase is $47. The recipient will charge the remaining $22 on their own credit card.
- If the recipient's purchase is smaller than the gift voucher amount, the recipient will not see the credit card payment screens during checkout. The remaining balance stays in their store account and can be applied to future orders. EXAMPLE:

The gift voucher is for $25, but they purchase only $15 worth of merchandise with the gift voucher. The recipient's store account will show a balance of $10 which can be used on their next purchase.

EACH TIME you see an order for a Gift Voucher in SALES - Orders, first verify that the payment went through (i.e. if you use Paypal.com check to see that the payment is complete), THEN manually release the gift voucher to the recipient as shown below.

Gift Vouchers Checklist

Setting up Gift Vouchers is done in three steps:

Gift Vouchers Step 1. (Optional) First set up gift voucher themes.
Gift Vouchers Step 2. Then set up gift vouchers.
Gift Vouchers Step 3. Turn Gift Vouchers in checkout ON.

You must turn on Gift Certificates during checkout in EXTENSIONS - Order Totals, or the customer will not be able to use the voucher during check out - there will not be a box for them to enter the voucher code.

Gift Vouchers Step 1. (Optional) First set up gift voucher themes.

Gift Voucher Themes

You can upload images that will be included in the gift voucher emails. After you have uploaded the images, then you can select them as you create each gift voucher. Birthday, Christmas and General theme images are included in your store BUT the images are just placeholders.

You can buy royalty-free stock images at very reasonable prices from iStockPhoto.com. Be careful if you search for free images; they may not be licensed and free sites can contain viruses.

Start by saving the voucher theme images you want to use to your computer.

To create new gift voucher themes, from your store Admin's top nav bar menu, select SALES - Gift Vouchers - Voucher Themes. This brings you to the Voucher Themes List:

Insert the new voucher image by clicking the top right INSERT Button. This brings you to the Voucher Themes Form:

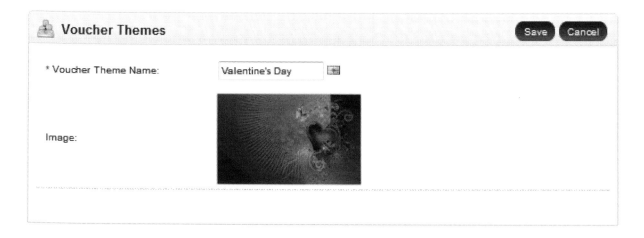

Give your new voucher a name, click the image and the image uploader will appear. Select your image from your computer, and click the top right SAVE Button. Now the theme will be available for customers to select.

Gift Vouchers Step 2. Then set up gift vouchers.

In your store Admin, from the top nav bar select SALES - Gift Vouchers. This brings you to the Gift Voucher List:

248 | P a g e

In the top right, click the INSERT Button. This brings you to the Gift Voucher form. Fill in the information as detailed below:

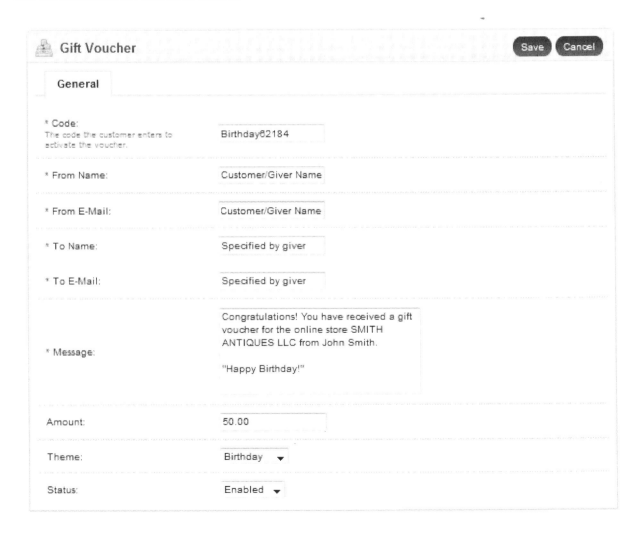

GIFT VOUCHER CODE: Give a unique code that cannot be guessed easily. The gift voucher recipient must type this code exactly into the Coupon box as they check out.

FROM NAME: Name of the customer who purchased this gift voucher, as shown in SALES - Orders.

FROM EMAIL: Email address of the customer who purchased this gift voucher, as shown in SALES - Orders.

TO NAME: Name of the recipient specified by the purchaser, as shown in SALES - Orders. If the customer did not specify in the COMMENTS box, you may need to email the customer.

TO EMAIL: Email address of the recipient specified by the purchaser. Voucher will be sent to this address.

MESSAGE: A message to the recipient.

AMOUNT: Amount purchased by the customer, as shown in SALES - Orders.

THEME: Select a template or theme for the look of the gift voucher. Default choices are BIRTHDAY, CHRISTMAS or GENERAL.

STATUS: Enabled to turn ON or disabled to turn OFF (for example, if a customer stopped payment, turn off the gift voucher until payment issue is resolved).

When you are finished, be sure to click the top right SAVE Button.

Gift Vouchers Step 3. Turn Gift Vouchers in checkout ON.

Go to EXTENSIONS – Order Totals and select GIFT ORDERS IN CHECKOUT. Be sure to click the top right SAVE Button.

SALES MENU

Mail

Send emails or newsletters to customers. With OpenCart you can send rich emails using special fonts, colors, images, that look just like a web page. NEW IN 1.5.2: OpenCart no longer limits the number of emails sent (though your web host may have a limit in the Terms & Conditions you agreed to; check with them to be sure).

Your email messages can be sent to any the following groups:

- All Newsletter Subscribers
- All Customers
- A specific CUSTOMER GROUP
- A specific customer(s) that you can SEARCH on and select,
- All affiliate program members, OR
- Only customers who have ordered a certain product or products.

To send an email, from your store Admin's top nav bar, select SALES - Mail to get to the MAIL Page. Fill in the boxes as shown:

The email system does not store a copy of the message in your store. It is best to compose the email in your own email program, save, and paste into OpenCart to send.

TIP: Be sure to send any message first as a TEST. Sign up for your store as a customer before sending an email, then in MAIL select your own name as a test. It can look very different than you expect, especially spacing and codes.

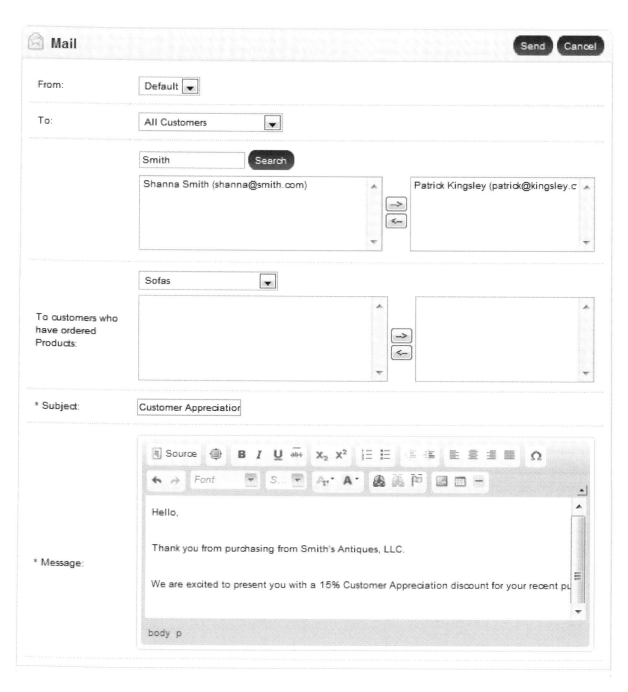

FROM: If you manage multiple stores select the store name you want to display. Otherwise, leave at "Default."

TO: From the drop-down box, select ALL NEWSLETTER SUBSCRIBERS or ALL CUSTOMERS.
OR from the SEARCH box, type the name of customer you want to email. THEN click their name to select it, and click the RIGHT ARROW to add the customer to this mailing list.
To remove a customer from the mailing list, highlight his or her name and click the LEFT ARROW.

TO CUSTOMERS WHO OR select a category name, then a product name. TIP: the product name will appear in the box

HAVE ORDERED PRODUCTS: ONLY IF at least one customer has purchased it.
THEN click the product name to select it, and click the RIGHT ARROW to add the customers of this product to this mailing list.
To remove a customer from the mailing list, highlight the product name and click the LEFT ARROW.

SUBJECT: Enter the subject name you want to appear in the email.

MESSAGE: Enter your message here, OR copy and paste from your email program.
When you have finished, at the top right click the SEND Button.

TIP: Be very careful emailing to all customers! The USA's CAN-SPAM Act requires, among other things, that you unsubscribe recipients who request it. Fines can reach $10,000 for each infraction. This is why most SPAM is sent from other countries. YOU ARE RESPONSIBLE for compliance with the laws of your area. Check with your attorney for the laws that apply to you.

*The add-on extension **MAILCHIMP INTEGRATION** sends and saves information TO your Mailchimp account. Use MailChimp's powerful and easy website to send your emails!*
http://www.opencart.com/index.php?route=extension/extension/info&extension_id=1707&filter_search=mail&sort=e.name&order=ASC

7. System Menu

These are the global, system-wide settings that will customize your store.

You will spend a lot of time here when your store is new. Over time you will return less and less.

SYSTEM MENU

Settings

Everything relating to your store begins here. Look at each of the tabs when your store is first installed.

To look at your store's system settings, from the Admin's top nav bar menu, select System Settings. This brings you to a list of all the stores you can administer when you have multiple stores. Of course you have only one store now, so click the EDIT Link:

This brings you to SETTINGS with information organized into seven tabs. Click a tab below to jump directly to detailed information on that tab:

SYSTEM MENU - SETTINGS

General Tab

The general information on this page is used throughout your store and in emails that the program sends to you and your customers.

Filling in this information is required for all stores, or your potential customers will see the placeholder information on pages such as the Contact Us page:

Contact Us page

To edit your general store settings, in your store Admin's Top Navigation Bar, click SYSTEMS - Settings, then click the EDIT Link next to your store name.

This brings you to the SYSTEM SETTINGS page. The top left GENERAL tab is already selected:

IMPORTANT: THE FIRST TWO BOXES BELOW APPEAR ONLY THE FIRST TIME THIS PAGE IS OPENED.

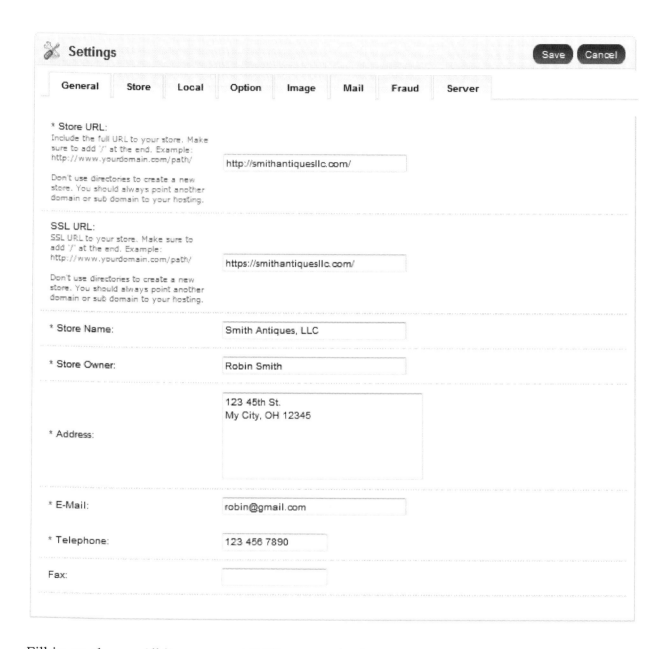

Fill in as shown. All items except FAX are required:

*STORE URL: The address you want customers to type in to get to you. NOTE: you must have purchased this URL (or DOMAIN NAME), and it must be pointed to your website. DO NOT CHANGE THIS if your technical pro has already inserted the address here. Ask your web host for help.

*SSL URL: **The secure, encrypted address for when customers are checking out. NOTE: you must purchase a SECURITY CERTIFICATE and have your web host set it up for your website. DO NOT CHANGE THIS if your technical pro has already inserted the address here.**

STORE NAME: The name you want to appear on the Contact Us page, and in emails sent to your customers.

STORE OWNER: The name of the person you want customers to see is the owner of your store. This will be visible in emails sent from the store in the FROM: line of all emails.

ADDRESS: The address you want to appear on the Contact Us page, and will likely be used to return products to you. Many payment processors require this to be a street address.

E-MAIL: The email address of the person you want customers to see is the owner of your store. This will be visible in emails sent from the store in the FROM: line of all emails.

TELEPHONE: The phone number you want to appear on the Contact Us page, and will likely be used by customers to call you. Many payment processors will check this phone number.

FAX: An old outdated machine that was used before email. If you enter a fax telephone number here, it will automatically appear on your Contact Us page.

Be sure to click the top right SAVE Button when you finish.

SYSTEM MENU - SETTINGS

Store Tab

Name and description of your store, select a template if you have installed one separately.

To edit your store settings, in your store Admin's Top Navigation Bar, click SYSTEMS - Settings.

This brings you to the SETTINGS page. At the top left, click the STORE Tab:

STORE URL: The address you want customers to type in to get to you. NOTE: you must have purchased this URL (or DOMAIN NAME), and it must be pointed to your website. DO NOT CHANGE THIS if your technical pro has already inserted the name here.

*TITLE: The title you want to appear in the top bar of your customers browser, and also appears as the title in Search Engine results when people search for you.

META TAG DESCRIPTION: Appears as the store description in Search Engine results when people search for you.

TEMPLATE: If you have had multiple templates installed, select which one you want customers to see.

NOTE: Installing templates is a subject for advanced users. See the TEMPLATES Chapter for more information about installing templates.

DEFAULT LAYOUT: Leave at default unless your template requires a different layout.

Be sure to click the top right SAVE Button when you finish.

TIP: Older versions of OpenCart (1.4.9 and earlier) edited the Welcome Message on this screen. In 1.5 the Welcome Message was moved to EXTENSIONS - Modules - Welcome.

SYSTEM MENU - SETTINGS

Local Tab

These local settings are important for payment and shipping to be calculated correctly, and for your store to operate properly.

To edit your local settings, in your store Admin's Top Navigation Bar, click SYSTEMS - Settings.

This brings you to the SETTINGS page. At the top left, click the LOCAL Tab:

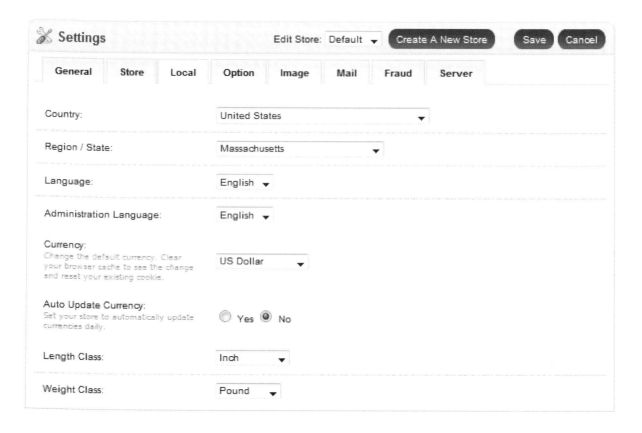

COUNTRY: In what country is your store - your "ship from" address.

REGION/STATE: In what state or region is your store - your "ship from" address. The items in the drop-down box will be different according to the country you select.

LANGUAGE: if you have installed additional "Language Packs," in what language do you wish buttons and messages to appear in your store? SEE ALSO SYSTEM – Localization - Languages for detailed information on installing additional languages.

ADMINISTRATION LANGUAGE: if you have installed additional "Language Packs, in what language do you want your store's Admin to appear? SEE ALSO SYSTEM – Localization - Languages for detailed information on installing additional languages.

CURRENCY: If you have specified multiple currencies for your store, what do you want to be the main currency?

NOTE: You may continue to see the old currency for some time unless you clear your browser's cache after changing this setting. After saving, in your browser, hit your F5 button until the window flashes white for a fraction of a second to indicate that it has been refreshed.

AUTO UPDATE CURRENCY: The currency rate for other currencies can be automatically checked and updated by your store program. The program gets and inserts the daily rate from Yahoo Finance, http://finance.yahoo.com/currency-converter.

LENGTH CLASS: Select a default measurement length class (inches, or centimeters or millimeters) which you will use to describe product sizes and weights. EXAMPLE: in a product description, if you enter "2" in the weight box, choose here whether the "2" means pounds, kilos, ounces.

SEE ALSO BELOW: SETTINGS - LOCALIZATION - LENGTH CLASS AND WEIGHT CLASS to add new units of measure.

WEIGHT CLASS: Select a default weight class (Kilos, grams, pounds or ounces) which you will use to describe product sizes and weights. EXAMPLE: in a product description, if you enter "2" in the weight box, choose here whether the "2" means pounds, kilos, ounces.

SEE ALSO BELOW: SETTINGS - LOCALIZATION - LENGTH CLASS AND WEIGHT CLASS to add new units of weight.

Be sure to click the top right SAVE Button when you finish.

SYSTEM MENU - SETTINGS

Option Tab

Allows you to fine-tune the display of many, many items in your store. The word "Options" in this case does not mean product options.

To edit your option settings, in your store Admin's Top Navigation Bar, click SYSTEMS - Settings.

This brings you to the SETTINGS page. At the top left, click the OPTION Tab:

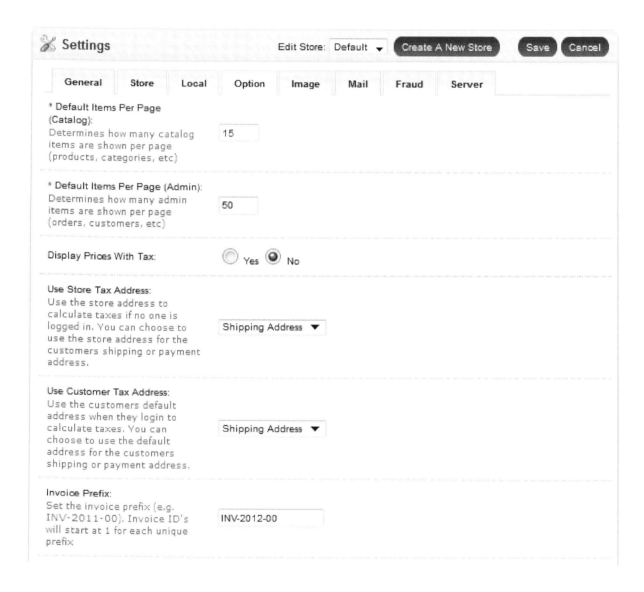

Order Editing:
Number of days allowed to edit
an order. This is required
because prices and discounts
may change over time
corrupting the order if its
edited.

`100`

Customer Group:
Default customer group.

Default ▼

Login Display Prices:
Only show prices when a
customer is logged in.

○ Yes ◉ No

Approve New Customers:
Don't allow new customer to
login until their account has
been approved.

○ Yes ◉ No

Guest Checkout:
Allow customers to checkout
without creating an account.
This will not be available when a
downloadable product is in the
shopping cart.

◉ Yes ○ No

Account Terms:
Forces people to agree to terms
before an account can be
created.

Privacy Policy ▼

Checkout Terms:
Forces people to agree to terms
before an a customer can
checkout.

Terms & Conditions ▼

Affiliate Terms:
Forces people to agree to terms
before an affiliate account can
be created.

About Us ▼

Affiliate Commission (%):
The default affiliate commission
percentage.

`10`

Display Stock:
Display stock quantity on the
product page.

○ Yes ◉ No

Show Out Of Stock Warning:
Display out of stock message on the shopping cart page if a product is out of stock but stock checkout is yes. (Warning always shows if stock checkout is no)

◯ Yes ⦿ No

Stock Checkout:
Allow customers to still checkout if the products they are ordering are not in stock.

⦿ Yes ◯ No

Out of Stock Status:
Set the default out of stock status selected in product edit.

Pre-Order ▼

Order Status:
Set the default order status when an order is processed.

Pending ▼

Complete Order Status:
Set the order status the customers order must reach before they are allowed to access their downloadable products and gift vouchers.

Complete ▼

Return Status:
Set the default return status when an returns request is submitted.

Awaiting Products ▼

Allow Reviews:
Enable/Disable new review entry and display of existing reviews

⦿ Yes ◯ No

Allow Downloads:

⦿ Yes ◯ No

Allowed Upload File Extensions:
Add which file extensions are allowed to be uploaded. Use comma separated values.

jpg, JPG, jpeg, gif, png, txt, pdf

Display Weight on Cart Page:
Show the cart weight on the cart page

◯ Yes ⦿ No

DEFAULT ITEMS PER PAGE (ADMIN):

How many items do you want to appear on a list in the Admin? I like to set it to a very big number to avoid scrolling, 50 or 100 or more, even though it may make the page load more slowly.

DEFAULT ITEMS PER PAGE (CATALOG):

How many items do you want customers to see on a list in your store? Consider slower page load times vs. customers having to click less. Leave at default unless you have a good reason.

DISPLAY PRICES WITH TAX: Some localities are required to display the full price including tax; others are required to display tax separately. If you are required to display with tax, select yes.

INVOICE PREFIX: If you would like customer invoices to have a prefix for your own bookkeeping purposes, add it here.

CUSTOMER GROUP: IF YOU HAVE ADDED Customer Groups such as "Wholesale" or "Employees" in SALES - Customer Groups, you may select the default group here (all customers who register will automatically be included in this group - for example, if you accept wholesale orders only). NOTE: You may wish to approve all customers in this group manually before allowing them to place their first order. See APPROVE NEW CUSTOMERS below.

LOGIN DISPLAY PRICES: Do you want to hide prices until after you have approved a customer AND they have logged in?

APPROVE NEW CUSTOMERS: Do you want to manually approve all new customers before they can place their first order? If you choose YES, you will receive an email each time a customer registers, and need to log onto your store, go to SALES - Customers and approve each new customer.

GUEST CHECKOUT: Allow customers to check out without creating an account? If so, customers who need to check on the status of their order will need to call you, they cannot log on and see.

ACCOUNT TERMS: If you want to require customers to accept terms and conditions before you will accept their new CUSTOMER ACCOUNT, check yes. NOTE: You must also edit the TERMS & CONDITIONS page in CATALOG - Information.

CHECKOUT TERMS: If you want to require customers to accept terms and conditions before you will accept their new ORDER, check yes. NOTE: You must also edit the TERMS & CONDITIONS page in CATALOG - Information

DISPLAY STOCK: If you wish to track stock levels AND enter the quantity on each product information page, do you want the product page to actually display the stock level remaining?

SHOW OUT OF STOCK WARNING: If a product is out of stock but you have selected YES to STOCK CHECKOUT (next item below), do you want the customer to see a message that the product is out of stock?

STOCK CHECKOUT: If you want customers to be able to order a product and check out even when the product is out of stock, select YES. To hide products when their inventory level becomes zero, select NO.

ORDER STATUS: After customers have placed and order and go to check on their account, what do you want to display in the "ORDER STATUS" box? Leave at default unless you have a specific reason for changing it; some payment methods require a specific order status to be triggered.

OUT OF STOCK STATUS: What message do you want to display when an item is out of stock? Select from IN STOCK, 2-3 days, Pre-Order, and Out of Stock.

ALLOW REVIEWS: Allow customers to write reviews and display reviews in your store? Disable by selecting NO.

ALLOW DOWNLOADS: Allow customers to download products such as music, ebooks or other digital products? Must be set to YES to let customers download. Set to NO if you will manually deliver the products (such as by sending an email link or the digital file).

DOWNLOAD ORDER STATUS: After customers have purchased a downloadable product, status what do you want to display so they can download? Set to COMPLETE to allow customer to download. NOTE: Product weight MUST BE ZERO or shipping will be charged and download will not be triggered.

DISPLAY WEIGHT ON Do you want the product weight to be displayed on the shopping cart page? NOTE: You

CART PAGE: must have entered product weights into product information pages for the weight to display.

USE SHIPPING SESSION: If you use a shipping method that connects to the shipper for a custom quote, saves the shipping quote to session to avoid re-quoting unnecessarily. Quotes will only be re-quoted if cart or address is changed.

Be sure to click the top right SAVE Button when you finish.

SYSTEM MENU - SETTINGS

Image Tab

One of the great things about OpenCart is that you can upload one image, and the program will resize it for the various needs of your store without changing the original. The resizing is done to the specifications you set here.

 TIP: Sizes are expressed in "PIXELS" or 1/100's of an inch. So 500 pixels on the web will generally appear as 5.00 inches.

EXAMPLE: When you upload ONE product image, the same image will be resized on the different pages on which it displays. ALL IMAGE BELOW ARE ACTUAL SIZE:

Product page
main image
Resized to 250x250

Category page image
Resized to 120x120

Additional
product images
150x150

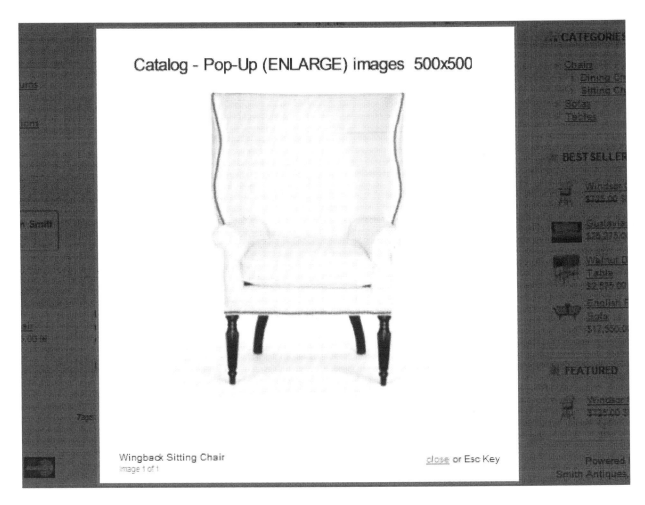

**Product image in cart
75x75**

Home › Shopping Cart

Shopping Cart

Image	Product Name	Model	Quantity	Unit Price	Total
	Wingback Sitting Chair	WING1	1 ↻ ✖	$2,713.11	$2,713.11

TIP: For best image quality, upload an image LARGER THAN the pop-up size you want. Recommended size is approximately 500x500 since that is the largest size needed.

 TIP: If images look stretched in width or height, then you have not loaded images that are the same proportion of height and width. Play with the numbers until the images look right to you.

In this menu you can UPLOAD or SELECT YOUR STORE LOGO, and insert images and "favicon" that will be displayed in your store. Everything except a store logo is optional.

The Icon or FAVICON (the shopping cart image shown below) is a very tiny OPTIONAL image that appears in both the address bar (http://smithantiques.com) and in the Favorites or Bookmark tab when a customer bookmarks it (the cart next to Smith Antiques LLC below).

 TIP: You can generate your own favicon with free tools such as http://www.favicongenerator.com/

Favicon cart image shown in address bar and in browser tab

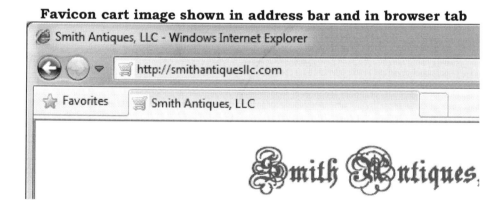

To edit your image settings, in your store Admin's Top Navigation Bar, click SYSTEMS - Settings.

This brings you to the SETTINGS page. At the top left, click the IMAGE Tab:

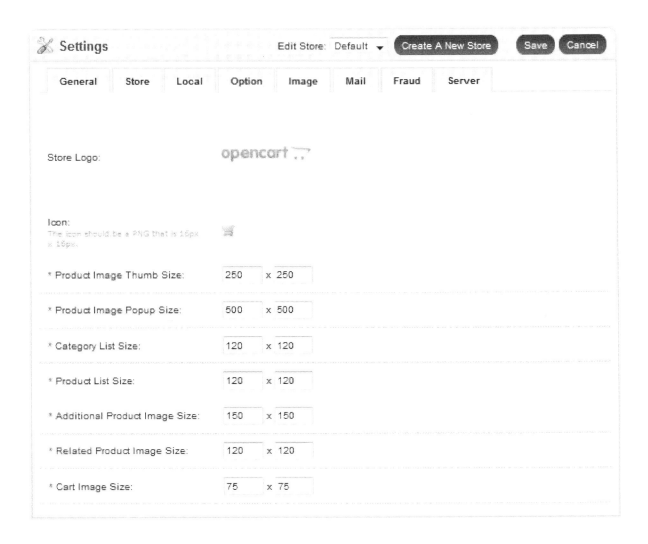

See next page for description:

STORE LOGO:	Click the OpenCart "Your Store" logo to bring up IMAGE MANAGER and select the new logo for your store; original is 210 pixels wide by 43 pixels high.
ICON:	Leave at default, or, upload a "Favicon" that will be remembered in bookmarks or "favorites" in browsers.
PRODUCT IMAGE THUMB SIZE:	The size you want product to appear on product information page. See example above.
PRODUCT IMAGE POPUP SIZE:	The size you want product pop-up to appear on product information page. See example above.
CATEGORY LIST SIZE:	The size you want images to appear on category page, see example above.
PRODUCT LIST SIZE:	The size you want product to appear on category product information page. See example above.
ADDITIONAL PRODUCT IMAGE SIZE:	If you choose to upload additional product images (side, top or rear views), the size you want them to appear.
CART IMAGE SIZE:	The size you want product to appear on the shopping cart page.

SYSTEM MENU - SETTINGS

Mail Tab

Except for "Additional Alert Emails" do not change these settings unless you have trouble sending messages from your store. If your web host uses non-standard mail settings, get the correct settings from your web host's support department and enter them here.

Additional Alert Emails allow you to receive an alert email each time an order is placed or an account is opened, and enter additional email addresses of employees who need these alert emails.

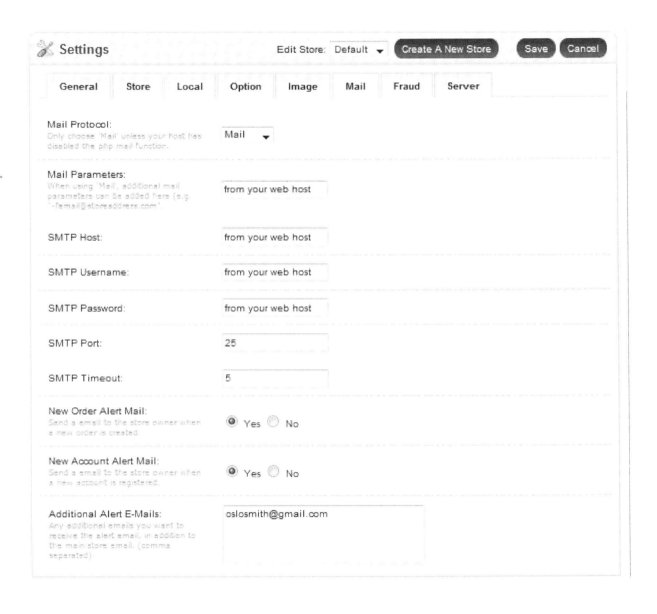

SYSTEM MENU - SETTINGS

Fraud Tab – MaxMind

Added in Version 1.5.2 - for more information see maxmind.com. Rejects orders based on a Risk Score assigned by IP address, country/billing address mismatch, and many other factors. A Risk Score can be any number from 0 to 100.

According to the company, a score of 20 means there is a 20% likelihood that the order is fraudulent. Setting the Risk Score is a decision you must make for yourself. Remember that the lower the number, the more likely your store will automatically reject GOOD orders. The MaxMind company has a formula to help mathematically-inclined shop owners to decide based on your profit margin. See the MaxMind Fraud Detection Manual for full details: http://www.maxmind.com/app/fraud-detection-manual

- Sign up for 1,000 free enquiries with a free trial account at http://www.maxmind.com/app/ccv2r_signup.
- If you like the trial, additional queries are half a penny each (US $0.005 per query) payable monthly. See details: http://www.maxmind.com/app/ccv_buynow

After setting up an account on MaxMind.com, in your Admin, from the top navigation bar click SYSTEM - Settings select your store and click EDIT – then click the new Fraud Tab. This brings you to the MaxMind page. Fill in as shown and discussed above.

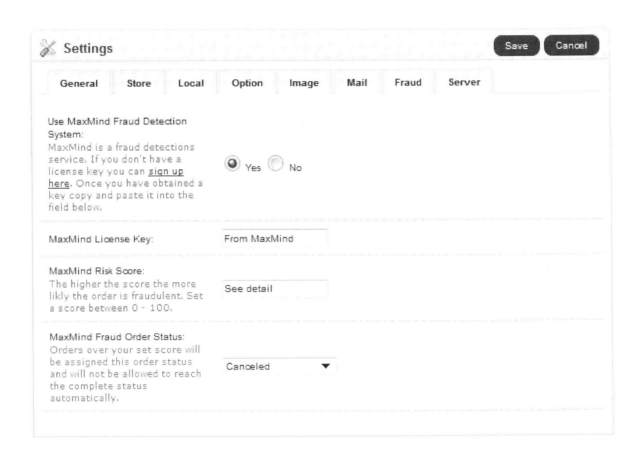

When finished, be sure to click the top right SAVE Button.

SYSTEM MENU - SETTINGS

Server Tab

These settings affect the computer that stores the files of your web site. Except for Maintenance Mode, and Google Analytics, do not change these settings unless you are having trouble with your store.

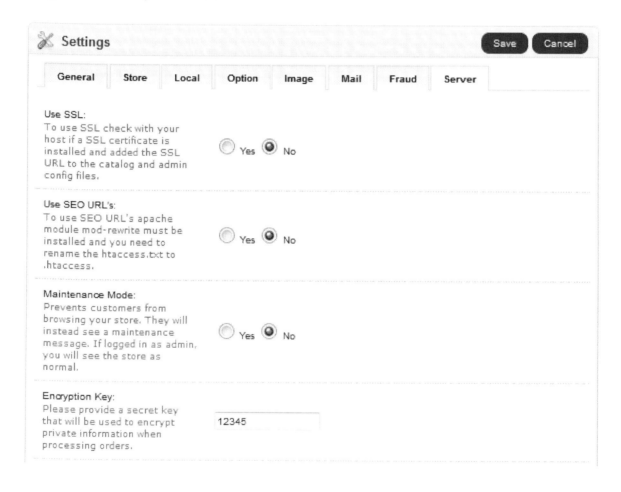

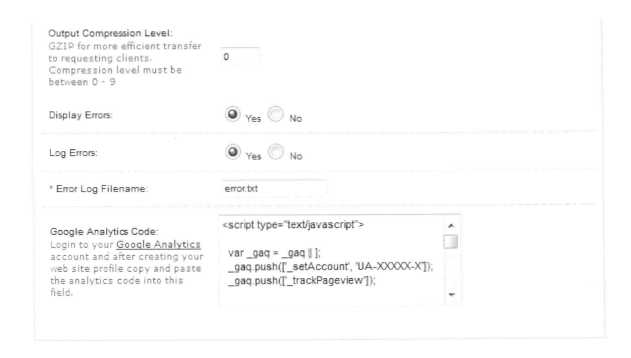

USE SSL:	AFTER YOUR WEB HOST INSTALLS YOUR SSL OR "SECURE SOCKET LAYER CERTIFICATE" encryption, SELECT YES for secure order processing. This changes the configuration to accept the new configuration.
USE SEO URL'S:	Select YES on USE SEO URLs to change page addresses from numbers and punctuation TO plain-English addresses (FIRST Ask your web host if they allow Apache module "mod-rewrite" and you must also rename a file named htaccess.txt TO .htaccess, OR ask your web host or techie to do it for you.
MAINTENANCE MODE:	Temporarily take your store off-line while you are working on it by selecting YES on Maintenance Mode.
ENCRYPTION KEY:	Any letters or numbers to be used as part of the algorithm for encrypting the order id during the PayPal processing.
OUTPUT COMPRESSION LEVEL:	Speeds page download times on heavily used servers. Higher number means more compression, faster download times.
DISPLAY ERRORS:	Choose DISPLAY ERRORS while debugging, set to NO for normal customer use.
LOG ERRORS:	Yes for debugging, no for normal use.
ERROR LOG FILENAME:	Specify a filename for error logging so you can find it later.
GOOGLE ANALYTICS CODE:	SEE FULL DETAIL BELOW.

Google Analytics

Google Analytics is a free service that generates detailed statistics about the visitors to a website. It is the most widely used website statistics service, used by more than 50% of the 10,000 most popular websites in the world.

Google Analytics can help you figure out if marketing campaigns are working, by comparing traffic before and after a marketing campaign. Below is a screenshot of the Google Analytics "Dashboard":

To use Google Analytics, you must have a Google Account. Go to http://google.com and at the top right, click the "SIGN IN" link. Click on the "Don't Have an Account?" and follow the instructions.

Next, still logged into your Google account, go to http://www.google.com/analytics and then click on "Access Analytics". This brings you to your dashboard, which will look like the example above after you have been using it for a while.

In the middle your dashboard, click on the link, "Add Website Profile". This brings you to the Create New Website page:

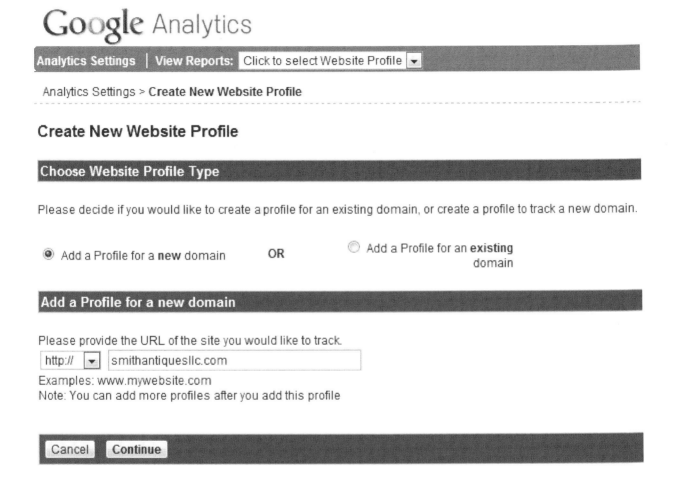

To set up your new Google Analytics account:

- Click the "Add a profile for a new domain" Button
- Enter your domain name – For example, mywebsite.com.
- When you have finished, click the CONTINUE Button.

This brings you to Google's TRACKING CODE PAGE where you can copy the snippet of tracking code to paste into your OpenCart page:

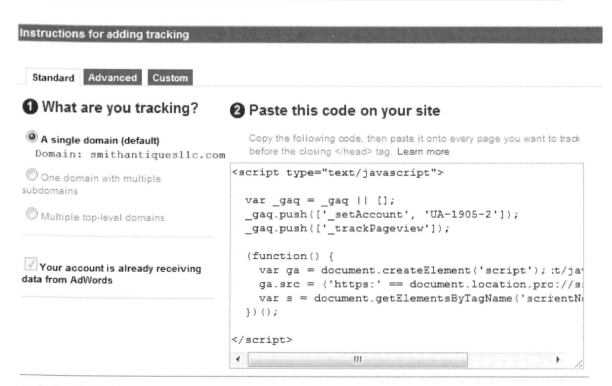

In the box labeled "Paste this code on your site" copy everything in the box by highlighting it, then RIGHT-CLICK and from the menu that pops up, select COPY.

Now in your OpenCart store Admin, select SYSTEM – Settings – select your store name and click the Edit Link. From the top tabs, select the Server Tab, scroll down to the Google Analytics box, and paste the code into the box. At the top right click the SAVE Button.

 Go back to Google Analytics TRACKING CODE page in about an hour to be sure the TRACKING STATUS link has changed to a happy green check mark. Check Google Help for help with any problems.

SYSTEM MENU - SETTINGS

Multi-store setup

Setting up two stores is, well, more than twice as complex as setting up one. We really, really recommend that you use a technical pro. Very little of it is done in your Admin - the majority is domain and web host work. If you must do it, here is how.

1. First install and set up Store #1. You will need to purchase a "Wildcard" or multi-domain security certificate to cover multiple stores. We recommend that you purchase the Wildcard SSL Certificate from your web host to make it as easy as possible! Ask your web host if you need help. We will call this Domain1.
2. Buy another domain name (We'll call this Domain2) and set the name server to go to the same name server as your existing OpenCart store. Again, we recommend that you purchase your domain name from your web host to make it as easy as possible. Ask your web host if you need help.

   In your web host's cPanel or other control panel, Domains - Add-On Domains section, add Domain2 and point it to the same folder as Domain1, example, public_html/store (substitute your own path for the path shown here). Ask your web host if you need help.
3. Install a different template for the second store so it will be easy to tell the two stores apart.
4. Ask your web host to install domain2's wildcard certificate.
5. NOW you are ready to add this to your store's Admin! In your store Admin's SYSTEM - Settings list, click the top right INSERT Button. Follow the instructions

above for the SYSTEM - Settings - General, using Domain2 instead of Domain1. Be sure to click the SAVE Button.

TIP: Instead of two different domains, you can use two different "sub-domains" like horses.petpalace.com and dogs.petpalace.com, or austin.mystore.com and atlanta.mystore.com. This is just a domain record setting at your domain registrar. Contact your domain registrar for help.

SYSTEM MENU

Design

Layouts and Banners

Select special sub-templates for specific pages, manage ad banners and slideshows. Note the sub-templates (layouts), ad banners and slideshows must first be made separately using a graphics program, then uploaded to your store. Using graphics programs is an advanced topic not covered in this manual.

SYSTEM MENU - DESIGN

Layouts

Layouts just tells your store how you want individual pages to look, and where to find the template for that page. Non-technical users should not need to use this menu.

If your template includes them, you can select special sub-templates for the following pages:

Account   **Default**
Affiliate   **Home**
Category   **Information**
Checkout   **Manufacturer**

Contact   **Product**
                           Sitemap

From your store Admin's top nav bar menu, select SYSTEM - Design - Layouts. This brings you to the Layouts List:

Select the layout you wish to edit and click the far right EDIT Link:

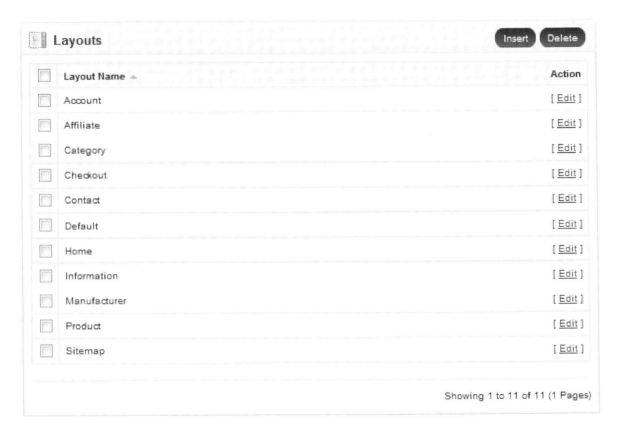

Click the top right INSERT Button. This brings you to the Layout Form:

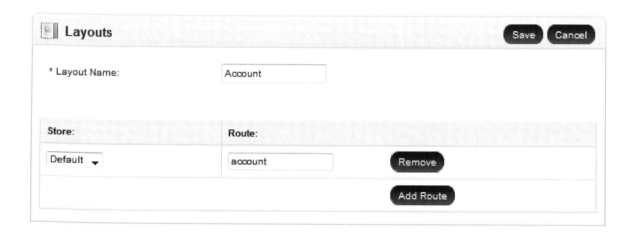

Click the bottom right ADD ROUTE Button, then select **Store Name** or leave blank for Default, specify the route or URL in the ROUTE field and click the Save button.

LAYOUT NAME: Give the new layout a name.
STORE: If you administer multiple stores from the same Admin, select the store name here.
ROUTE: The path to the layout as measured from the template folder. Your technical pro should help you with this item.

When finished, in the top right, click the SAVE Button.

SYSTEM MENU - DESIGN

Banners

Manage ad banners and slideshows. Banner helps you upload the banner images, shows you a thumbnail-sized copy of the image, and tells what pages to link if a customer clicks on that image.

Uploaded ad banners must be previously created in a graphics program like Photoshop.

Note that advertisers who wish to advertise in your store will generally supply that advertisement. After you have saved that ad to your computer, continue with this screen.

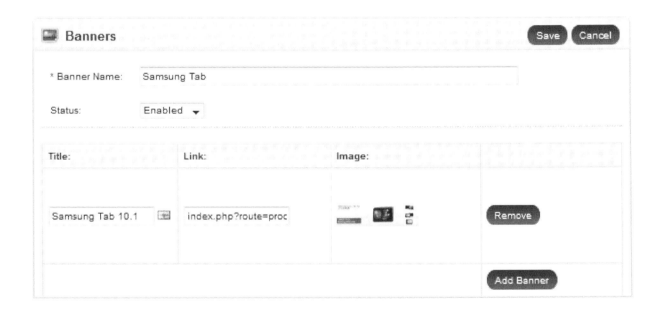

Status	Select Enabled to allow ad to display or Disabled to hide.
Title	Give the ad a name that is easy to remember when you view it in the Admin.
Link	The exact URL where you want the customer to go when they click the ad banner.
Image	Click the photo to bring up Image Manager, then select the ad banner from your computer.

Click the Save button to upload and save the image.

TIP: You must also turn ON the banners and specify where to display them in EXTENSIONS - Modules - Banner.

SYSTEM MENU

Users

Users

Add or edit Administration users to process orders or assist with technical work in your store. If you have created user groups in SYSTEM - Users - User Groups, the user can be restricted to certain portions of the administration.

TIP: You can use an email address as the username.

Restrict Administrators to certain areas of your Admin by FIRST creating a User Group, and then assigning them to the group.

To give a new login to a new administrator with ALL PRIVILEGES (they can see and edit all parts of your store's Admin), from the Admin's top nav bar menu, select SYSTEM - Users - Users. This brings you to the User List:

To insert the new user name, in the top right corner of the User List click the INSERT Button. This brings you to the INSERT USER page:

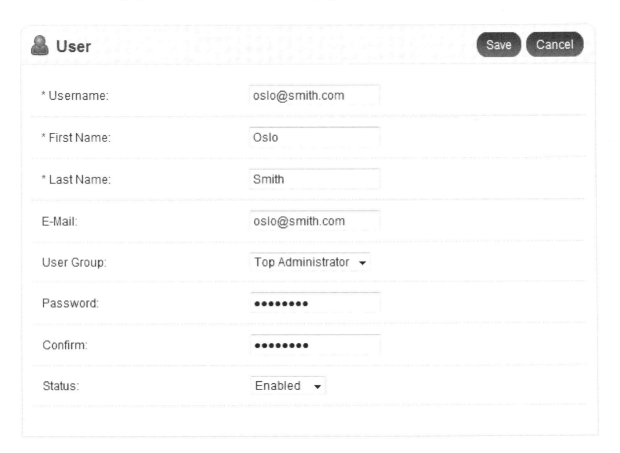

Fill out the form as shown above and at the top right, click the SAVE Button.

SYSTEM MENU - USERS

User Groups

Restrict Administrator access to certain parts of the admin. You can allow users to SEE certain parts or MODIFY others.

Give permission to access and/or edit your store Admin by role. For example, create a User Group named "Fulfillment" for your company's order fulfillment employees that allows them to edit only customer and order information, then create user logins for each employee and assign them to the group.

To create a new user group, from the Admin's top nav bar menu, select SYSTEM - Users - User Groups. This brings you to the User Group List.

To ADD a new user group, at the top right click the INSERT Button.

To edit an existing group, in the right column click the EDIT Button.

This brings you to the EDIT USER GROUP page:

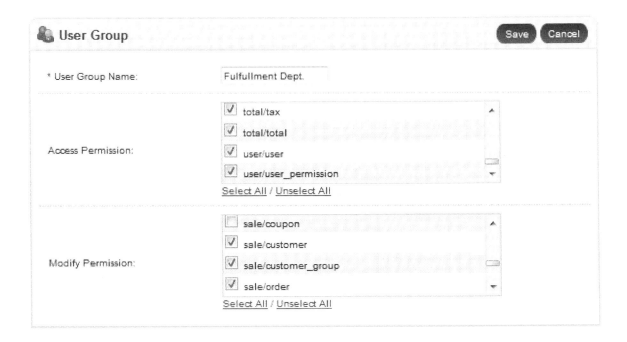

Fill in the information as shown above, then in the top right click the SAVE Button.

SYSTEM MENU

Localization

Languages

ADVANCED USERS ONLY. You must be familiar with downloading files and uploading to your web host before you can select the language in your store's Admin.

Install a language pack for languages other than English by first finding the most recent version, then downloading a language pack from OpenCart.com as shown below:

 CAUTION: Be sure to download a language pack ONLY for your version of OpenCart - in your Admin, check the footer to see your version number.

After downloading the correct file, use cPanel's File Manager to extract the zip file and upload the two folders to

> admin/languages/languagename and
> languages/languagename.

Then in your store's Admin, from the top nav bar select SYSTEM - LOCALIZATION - Languages. This brings you to the LANGUAGES List.

Click the INSERT Button, and enter the Language information from the README file contained in the zip file as shown below.

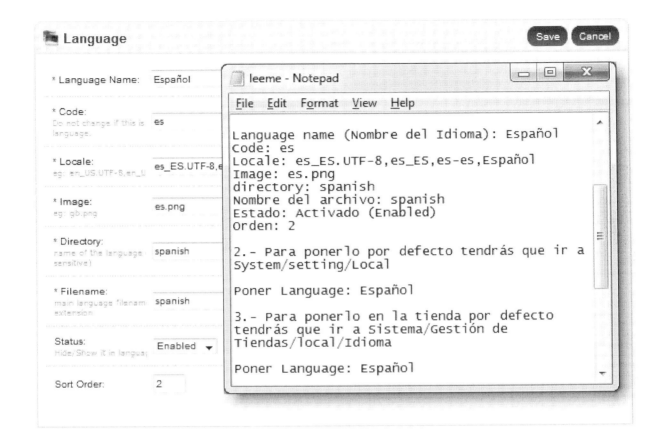

SYSTEM MENU

Localization - Currencies

Display store prices in other currencies that you specify.

Default is British Pounds (CHANGE DEFAULT IN SYSTEM - SETTINGS - LOCAL).

To add a new currency, click the top right INSERT Button:

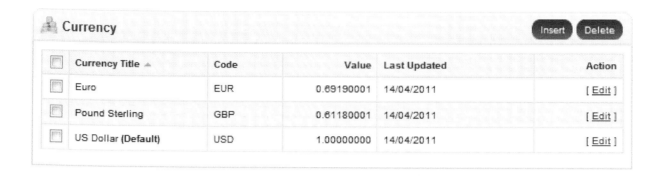

This brings you to the EDIT CURRENCY page as shown below:

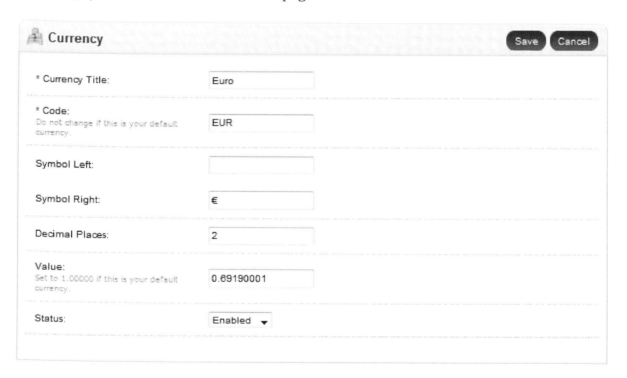

CURRENCY TITLE: Insert the new currency name you want to display in your store.

CODE: Insert the standard 3-letter international currency code. SEE http://www.currencysystem.com/codes/

SYMBOL LEFT: Insert the Currency Symbol or letters you want to display to the left of the price. SEE http://www.xe.com/symbols.php

SYMBOL RIGHT: Insert the Currency Symbol or letters you want to display to the right of the price. SEE http://www.xe.com/symbols.php

DECIMAL PLACES: Specify the number of decimal places that is standard for this currency.

VALUE: Specify today's currency exchange rate for this currency (set to 1.00000 for default). SEE http://www.xe.com/

STATUSES: Select ENABLED or DISABLED to display or hide.

Click the SAVE Button to save.

To automatically update exchange rate each day, go to SYSTEM - SETTINGS - LOCAL - AUTO-UPDATE CURRENCY.

SYSTEM MENU

Localization - Stock Statuses

OPTIONAL: IF YOU CHOOSE to use the stock module, create or edit various stock messages relating to a product's stock level.

Default statuses are 2-3 days, In Stock, Out of Stock (DEFAULT WHEN USING STOCK MODULE), and Pre-Order.

Note that ONLY the message wording is set on this menu; enable and tweak stock settings in SYSTEM - SETTINGS - OPTIONS beginning with "Display Stock."

To add or edit stock status wording, from your store Admin's top nav bar, select SYSTEM - Localization - Stock Statuses. This brings you to the STOCK STATUSES LIST:

Insert a new status by clicking the top right INSERT Button or edit an existing status by clicking the right column EDIT Link. Either way brings you to the STOCK STATUS Page:

Insert or edit the stock message you want, then in the top right click the SAVE Button.

SYSTEM MENU

Localization - Order Statuses

OPTIONAL: Set wording for the various statuses that an order may hold as it is processed through your store. This allows you to sort orders by status (i.e. PENDING to see orders you need to fill today), and change the status to allow the customer to see their order has been processed, shipped, etc.

Default statuses are Canceled; Canceled Reversal; Chargeback; Complete; Denied; Failed; Pending (THE DEFAULT); Processing; Refunded; Reversed; and Shipped.

You may edit any messages for language, spelling or even use different words. To review or edit, from the top nav bar, click SYSTEM – Localization – Order Statuses. This brings you to the Order Status List:

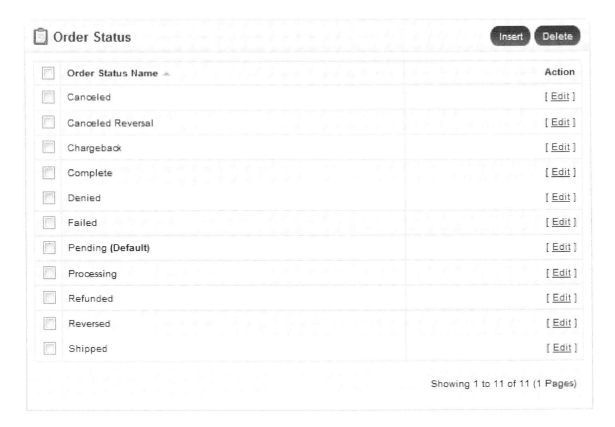

ADD new statuses if these are not enough by clicking the top right INSERT Button, typing the new status and clicking the SAVE Button.

SYSTEM MENU

Localization - Countries

There are 240 countries listed in OpenCart, and any customer who visits your store can place an order from these countries unless you restrict them from registering or specifying a shipping address in these countries.

To refuse orders from certain countries OR add new countries that are not listed. Removes or adds country names on the drop-down list when customers register or place an order.

Also customizes the address fields that appear to customers in that country, and whether or not to require a postal code or zip code.

To customize your store's list of countries, from your Admin's top nav bar menu, select SYSTEM - Localization - Countries. This brings you to the Country List:

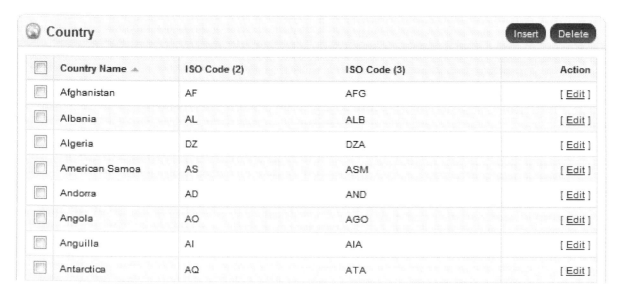

	Country Name ▲	ISO Code (2)	ISO Code (3)	Action
☐	Afghanistan	AF	AFG	[Edit]
☐	Albania	AL	ALB	[Edit]
☐	Algeria	DZ	DZA	[Edit]
☐	American Samoa	AS	ASM	[Edit]
☐	Andorra	AD	AND	[Edit]
☐	Angola	AO	AGO	[Edit]
☐	Anguilla	AI	AIA	[Edit]
☐	Antarctica	AQ	ATA	[Edit]

To DELETE countries from your store's drop-down country lists, in the left column put a check in the checkbox of the countries you wish to delete, then at the top right click the DELETE Button.

To EDIT the address format displayed to customers from a specific country, find the country name and then in the right column click the EDIT Button.

To INSERT a new country in your store's drop-down country lists, at the top right click the INSERT Button. This brings you to the Edit Country page:

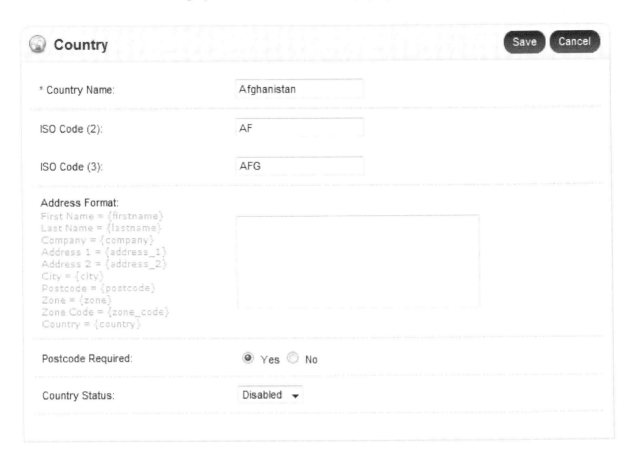

At the bottom, in the COUNTRY STATUS box, select DISABLED, then click the top right SAVE Button.

 TIP: to remove dozens or hundreds of countries at one time, ask your techie to do this with phpMyAdmin.

 TIP: For easy two-rate shipping (domestic + international) buy the extension named "All Other Countries" for $19 + optional $20 installation by the extension developer.

SYSTEM MENU

Localization - Zones

In the US, Zones are the same as States; in Canada or UK, Zones are the same as provinces. For shipping and tax purposes, pre-defined PARTS of a country.

You may refuse to ship or sell to a state/province/zone by removing it from the list.

There are 3,940 world zones listed in OpenCart.

To edit the states or provinces that appear in your customer registration drop-down box, and in the shipping address drop-down box, from your Admin's top nav bar menu select SYSTEM - Localization - Zones. This brings you to the Zones List:

TIP: Change your administrative settings so ALL zones display on the same Admin page! From your store Admin's top nav bar, select SYSTEM - Settings. At the top left select the OPTION Tab. Change Default Items per Page (Admin) to a number greater than 3940. You can change it anytime you want to see more or less on a page.
NOTE: This changes the number of ALL Admin lists, so you will also see long lists of customers, orders, etc.

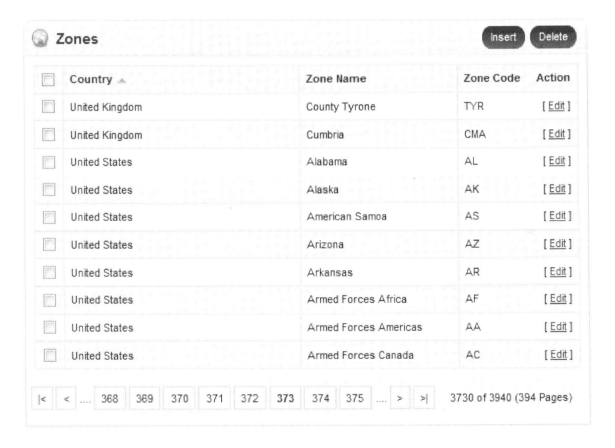

To DELETE states/provinces/zones from your store's drop-down country lists, in the left column put a check in the checkbox of the countries you wish to delete, then at the top right click the DELETE Button.

To INSERT a new state in your store's drop-down state lists, at the top right click the INSERT Button. This brings you to the Edit Zones page:

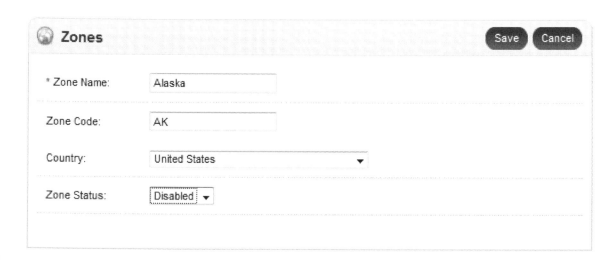

Insert the new state name and postal codes. From the drop-down boxes, select the country name and whether enabled or disabled. When finished, click the top right SAVE Button.

SYSTEM MENU

Localization - Geo Zones

OPTIONAL: For shipping and tax purposes, groups or portions of a country that you custom-select according to your needs.

- EXAMPLE: You want to ship to customers only if they live in your state AND the states around you. Similar to a UPS Zone.
- EXAMPLE: You want to allow customers to pick up orders from your store only if they live in your county and the counties around you.
- EXAMPLE: You are required to charge city or county tax, in addition to state tax.

To create a new custom Geo Zone, from your store Admin's top nav bar, select SYSTEM - Localization - Geo Zones. This brings you to the Geo Zones List:

At the top right click the INSERT Button. This brings you to the Insert or Edit Zones page:

Give the Geo Zone a name and description, THEN Click ADD GEO ZONE Button. Select your country name and state or province where this geo zone is located.

To make a geo zone that includes several states or provinces, continue clicking the ADD GEO ZONE Button until you have added all states or provinces.

When finished, be sure to click the top right SAVE Button.

SYSTEM MENU

Localization - Tax Classes

Links together the WHERE, WHAT and HOW MUCH for all taxes.

TIP: Be sure you have first created a Geo Zone for each tax.

To set or edit tax classes, from your store Admin's top nav bar menu, select SYSTEM -
Localization - Tax Classes. This brings you to the Tax Class List:

To add an additional tax class, at the top right click the INSERT Button. This brings you to
the Edit Tax Class page.

To edit a tax class, on the TAXABLE GOODS line, click the EDIT Link. This brings you to
the Edit Tax Class page:

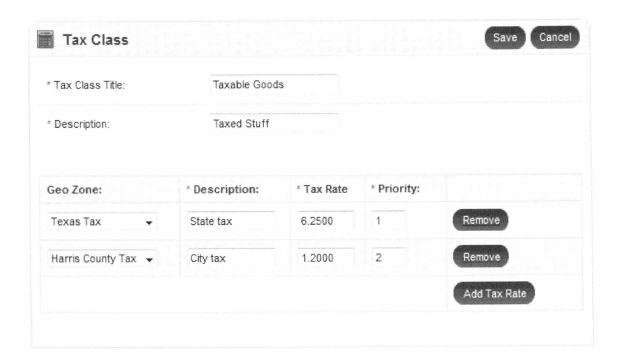

Select the Geo Zone, enter a description and specify the exact Tax Rate you are required to charge.

Enter the priority number (1 for first, 2 for 2nd etc.).

Click ADD TAX RATE Button for each tax you must charge, then in top right click the SAVE Button.

Be sure to make test purchases with a fake customer account from each Geo Zone to be sure tax is set up correctly!! A minimum of two test purchases is required: sign up as a customer who lives IN your state or province, and as a customer who lives in a different state or province. Repeat for each zone and geo zone.

TIP: If your store does not display a tax on a product when checking out, you may have simply forgotten to select "Taxable Goods" on that product's information page! You must tell your store that this product is a taxable item.

SYSTEM MENU

Localization - Length Classes

Choose units of measure to use in product options and shipping by product dimensions OR add additional lengths.

- EXAMPLE: In your industry, goods are sold by the YARD or METER. If a customer orders "5" of an item, that will mean 5 yards or meters.
- EXAMPLE: Your industry sells goods by the INCH or CENTIMETER. If a customer orders "5" of an item, that will mean 5 inches or centimeters.

 You must also set your store's DEFAULT LENGTH in SYSTEM - Settings, Local Tab, scroll to bottom to select LENGTH CLASS from the drop-down box.

To set the length classes for your store, from your store Admin's top nav bar menu, select SYSTEM - Localization - Length Classes. This brings you to the LENGTH CLASS List:

	Length Title ▲	Length Unit	Value	Action
☐	Feet	ft.	12.00000000	[Edit]
☐	Inch (Default)	in	1.00000000	[Edit]
☐	Yard	yd	36.00000000	[Edit]

Showing 1 to 3 of 3 (1 Pages)

To DELETE unneeded length classes, put a check in the left column checkbox, then click the top right DELETE Button.

To EDIT a length class, in the far right Action column, click the EDIT Link.

To INSERT new length classes, click the top right INSERT Button. This brings you to the Length Class Edit page:

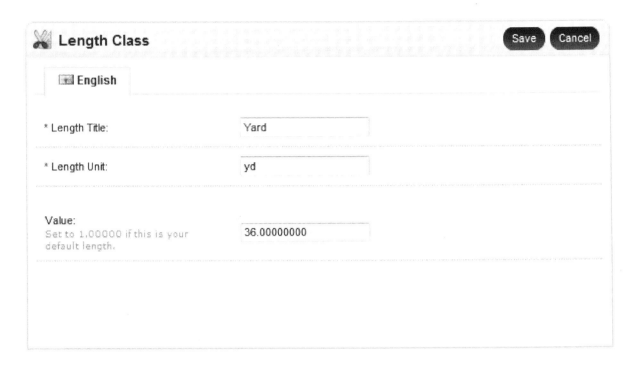

Enter a title, abbreviation, and value for the length class. When finished, click the top right SAVE Button.

SYSTEM MENU

Localization - Weight Classes

Choose units of weight to use in product options and shipping by weight OR add new weights.

SET DEFAULT in SYSTEM - SETTINGS - LOCAL.

Choose units of weight to use in product options and shipping by product weight.

- EXAMPLE: In your industry, goods are sold by the POUND or KILO. If a customer orders "5" of an item, that will mean 5 pounds or kilos.
- EXAMPLE: Your industry sells goods by the GRAM or OUNCE. If a customer orders "5" of an item, that will mean 5 grams or ounces.

 You must also set your store's DEFAULT WEIGHT CLASS in SYSTEM - Settings, Local Tab, scroll to bottom to select WEIGHT CLASS from the drop-down box.

To set the weight classes for your store, from your store Admin's top nav bar menu, select SYSTEM - Localization - Weight Classes. This brings you to the WEIGHT CLASS List:

	Weight Title ▲	Weight Unit	Value	Action
☐	Ounce	oz	35.27400000	[Edit]
☐	Pound (Default)	lb	2.20460000	[Edit]

Showing 1 to 2 of 2 (1 Pages)

To DELETE unneeded length classes, put a check in the left column checkbox, then click the top right DELETE Button.

To EDIT a length class, in the far right Action column, click the EDIT Link.

To INSERT new length classes, click the top right INSERT Button. This brings you to the Weight Class Edit page:

Enter a title, abbreviation, and value for the weight class. When finished, click the top right SAVE Button.

SYSTEM MENU

Error Logs

A full log of every error message your store experiences. Your technical pro will need this in case of any problems. It will help them sort out whether the problem is your web host, the server, the cache, the program, etc. You can copy and paste the log into an email to your techie.

Note that not every error message is a problem.

To view your error logs, from your store Admin's top nav bar menu, select SYSTEM - Error Logs. This brings you to the Error Logs page:

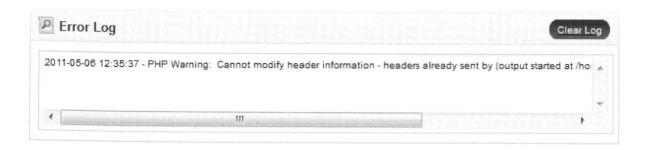

To COPY your error log into an email to your techie, click inside the Error Log text box, then click CTRL-A to Select All (selects everything in the box). Now copy all that text with CTRL-C. Open an email, click in the message body, and paste with CTRL-V.

To CLEAR your error log, click the top right CLEAR LOG Button.

 CAUTION- there is no warning or "Are you sure?" message when you click the CLEAR LOG Button!

SYSTEM MENU

Backup/Restore

BACKUP your database before AND after making any changes to your store. Backup, backup, backup! You cannot back up too often. This saves a copy to your personal computer. Give the file a new name each time -- do not overwrite the same file, that defeats the purpose of a backup!

Here you can:

- **Save a full or partial copy of your store's database to your personal computer in SQL database format.**
- **Restore a full or partial copy of your store's database to your personal computer in SQL database format.**

This does not save a copy of your store files like your templates or CSS files; your technical pro can schedule a regular backup of your full database AND store files, called a "Chron Job" (for chronological job) using your web host's control panel. Ask your web host for assistance if you want to set up a Chron Job yourself.

 The backup file is always named backup.sql. You MUST CHANGE THE NAME immediately or your next backup will -- you guessed it! -- overwrite the previous copy. Add today's date to the name or any random letters or numbers to prevent this.

 RESTORING YOUR STORE'S DATABASE IS DIFFICULT OR IMPOSSIBLE TO FIX IF YOU MESS UP. You must have backups of the backups and of the original. If you do not have time to rebuild your entire store from scratch again, get your techie to do this for you.

To backup or restore your store's database, from your store Admin's top nav bar menu, select SYSTEM - Backup/Restore. This brings you to the Backup/Restore page:

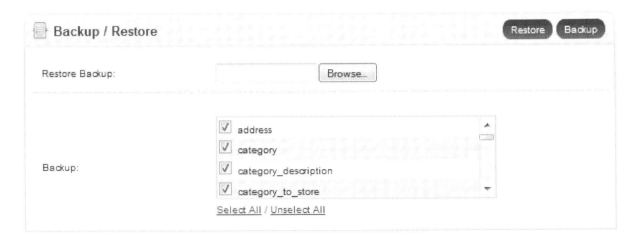

- Backup your full store database by clicking the bottom left SELECT ALL Link, then in the top right click the BACKUP Button.
- Backup part of your store database by checking the boxes you want to backup, then in the top right click the BACKUP Button.
- Restore a backup by clicking the top middle BROWSE Button, browse to the file on your computer, then in the top right click the RESTORE Button.

8. Reports Menu

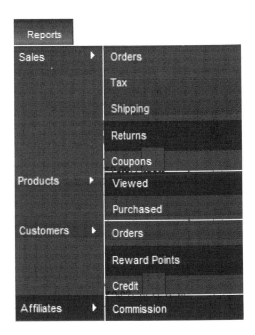

These are strategic, top-level management reports that the store owner or manager will enjoy seeing, and which will give you the advantage of being able to respond quickly to trends in your store.

I recommend a weekly scan of these reports, and more often when your store is new.

TIP: If you are looking for daily operations reports (i.e. orders pending, received, processed, etc.), go to the SALES Chapter.

Sales Reports

Orders Report

Sales report is an incredibly customizable report that can tell you:

- How many orders did we receive on a day, week, month, or other period of time? What was the total dollar amount?
- How many orders did we ship? What was the total dollar amount?
- How many orders were processed, refunded, cancelled? What was the total dollar amount?

To view the Sales Orders Report, from your store Admin top nav bar, select REPORTS - Sales Report. This brings you to the SALES REPORT Page:

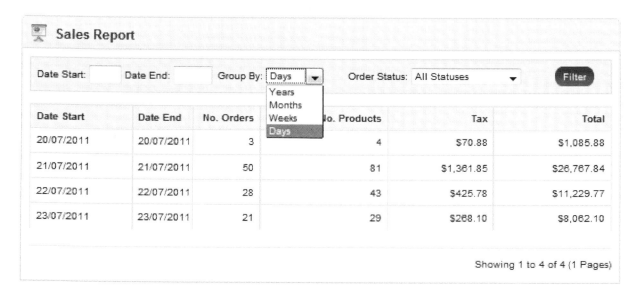

Select a start date and end date, whether you wish to see results by days, weeks, months, and select an order status or leave at "All Statuses."

When finished, at the top right click the FILTER Button.

REPORTS - SALES

Sales Tax Report

Sales Tax Report is a customizable report that can tell you how much tax did we collect on a day, week, month, or other period of time.

You MUST have set up taxes correctly in SYSTEM - Localization - Taxes for this report to work.

To view the Sales Tax Report, from your store Admin top nav bar, select REPORTS - Sales - Tax Report. This brings you to the SALES TAX REPORT Page:

Select a start date and end date, whether you wish to see results by days, weeks, months, and select an order status or leave at "All Statuses."

When finished, at the top right click the FILTER Button.

REPORTS - SALES

Shipping

How many orders were shipped by day/week/month/year. Helps you track shipping trends and order processing trends.

From your Admin's top nav bar, select REPORTS - Sales - Shipping. This brings you to the Shipping Report:

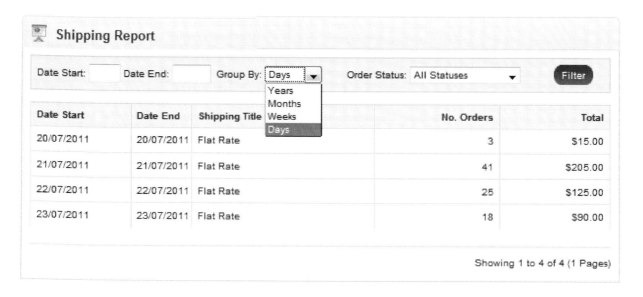

Select a start date and end date, whether you wish to see results by days, weeks, months, and select an order status or leave at "All Statuses."

When finished, at the top right click the FILTER Button.

REPORTS - SALES

Returns

How many orders have had return authorizations requested, pending or complete. Helps you track trends, notice unusual numbers of returns.

From your Admin's top nav bar, select REPORTS - Sales - Returns. This brings you to the Returns Report:

Select a start date and end date, whether you wish to see results by days, weeks, months, and select a return status or leave at "All Statuses."

When finished, at the top right click the FILTER Button.

REPORTS - SALES

Coupons

How many times a coupon has been used in your store. Helps you track coupon usage trends.

From your Admin's top nav bar, select REPORTS - Sales - Coupons. This brings you to the Coupon Report:

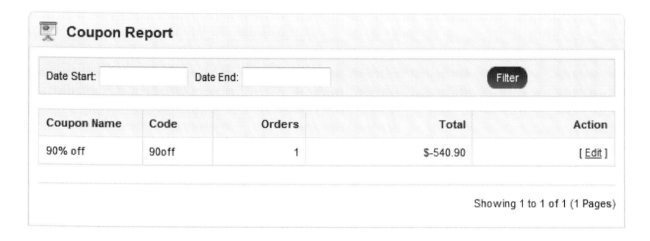

Select an optional start date and end date, then click the top right FILTER Button.

This displays a list of all coupons redeemed in your store, sorted by coupon name.

If you wish to EDIT a coupon, you can click the EDIT Link. This brings you to the SALES - Coupons menu. See that chapter for editing instructions.

Products Reports

Products Viewed

Most popularly viewed products, from most to least viewed. Helps you track expected product popularity.

From your Admin's top nav bar, select REPORTS - Products Viewed. This brings you to the Products Viewed report:

Products Viewed Report

Reset

Product Name	Model	Viewed	Percent
English Regency Sofa	SOFAREG	12	50%
Wingback Sitting Chair	WING1	4	16.67%
Walnut Drop-Leaf Table	TABLEDL	3	12.5%
Gustavian Sofa	GUST-1	3	12.5%
Windsor Chair	WIND-1	2	8.33%
Wingback Sitting Chair*	WING1	0	0%

Showing 1 to 6 of 6 (1 Pages)

Compare the results of this report to the products purchased report:

- If many people are looking at an item but not purchasing, there may be a problem with that product's description, images, pricing, etc.
- If people are not viewing a product at all, it may not be in the right category, the photo may be poor, or some other issue.

REPORTS - PRODUCTS

Products Purchased Report

Lists products actually purchased, ranked by total sales revenue, not number of items sold. Helps you track sales trends.

From your Admin's top nav bar, select REPORTS - Products Purchased. This brings you to the Products Purchased report:

Products Purchased Report

Product Name	Model	Quantity	Total
Gustavian Sofa	GUST-1	2	$50,550.00
Walnut Drop-Leaf Table	TABLEDL	2	$5,150.00
Windsor Chair	WIND-1	5	$3,625.00
			$59,3250.00

Showing 1 to 4 of 4 (1 Pages)

Customers Reports

Orders

Orders by individual customer name, sorted from biggest to smallest spender. Helps you see which customers order the most merchandise.

From your Admin's top nav bar, select REPORTS - Customers - Orders. This brings you to the Customer Orders Report:

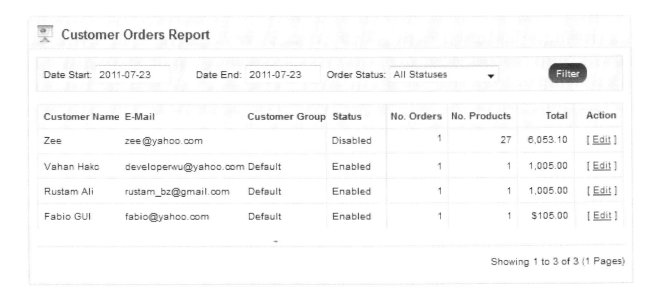

Customer Orders Report

Customer Name	E-Mail	Customer Group	Status	No. Orders	No. Products	Total	Action
Zee	zee@yahoo.com		Disabled	1	27	6,053.10	[Edit]
Vahan Hako	developerwu@yahoo.com	Default	Enabled	1	1	1,005.00	[Edit]
Rustam Ali	rustam_bz@gmail.com	Default	Enabled	1	1	1,005.00	[Edit]
Fabio GUI	fabio@yahoo.com	Default	Enabled	1	1	$105.00	[Edit]

Showing 1 to 3 of 3 (1 Pages)

Select a start date and end date, and select an order status or leave at "All Statuses."

When finished, at the top right click the FILTER Button. You can EDIT any individual customer record by clicking the far right EDIT Link. This brings you to the SALES - Customer menu. See that chapter for editing instructions.

REPORTS - CUSTOMERS

Customers Reward Points Report

A list of customers who have accumulated Reward Points. Helps you track customers that may redeem their points for merchandise.

IMPORTANT: You MUST have awarded Reward Points to at least one customer for this report to show any results. To award Reward Points, go to SALES - Orders, select an order and click the far right EDIT Link. Then on the ORDER DETAILS Tab, find REWARD POINTS and click the (+) Button. Repeat as you process each order.

From your Admin's top nav bar, select REPORTS - Customers - Reward Points. This brings you to the Customer Reward Points Report:

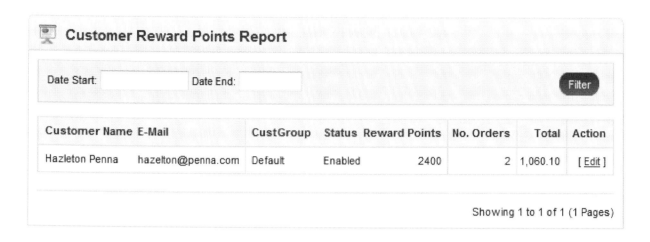

If you have a long list of customers, select a start date and end date, and at the top right click the FILTER Button.

If you wish, you can edit the customer record from this report and/or give that customer additional Reward Points. Select the customer you wish to edit, then at the far right, click the EDIT Link. This brings you to the SALES - Customer menu. See that chapter for editing instructions.

REPORTS - CUSTOMERS

Customer Credit Report

Customers who have a credit balance in your store, for example from a product return.

From your Admin's top nav bar, select REPORTS - Customer - Credit. This brings you to the Customer Credit Report:

Customer Credit Report

Customer Name	E-Mail	Customer Group	Status	Total	Action
Hazleton Penna	hazelton@penna.com	Default	Enabled	$1,000.00	[Edit]

Showing 1 to 1 of 1 (1 Pages)

If you wish, you can edit the customer record from this report. Select the customer you wish to edit, then click the EDIT Link. This brings you to the SALES - Customer menu. See that chapter for editing instructions.

Affiliates Reports

Affiliates Commission

This tracks ONLY affiliates who have referred customers to your store and who are due a commission.

To see a list of ALL Affiliates and their registration information, see SALES - Affiliates.

From your Admin's top nav bar, select REPORTS - Affiliates. This brings you to the Affiliates Commission Report of commissions due:

Select a start date and end date, and at the top right click the FILTER Button.

After you sent a payment via PayPal or the affiliate's other preferred payment method, record the transaction. Find the affiant name and click the far right EDIT Link.

This brings you to the SALES - Affiliate form. See that chapter for editing instructions.

9. OpenCart Themes

OpenCart's look and feel comes from a theme, which consists of images, buttons and coding changes. You can change the look or create a totally custom theme just by finding the theme closest to what you want, and getting a web pro to modify that theme. We have a list of companies that offer themes, some even have free installation. For Super-Users only, we have a bonus section on installing and customizing a theme.

What is a Theme?

A theme (also known as a template or skin), is a professionally-designed store "kit" that includes the images, buttons, and the coding changes (such as changing column widths) that you need to make your store look very rich. Rather than manually making changes on every page in the site, hundreds or even thousands of pages, the changes are made to the theme ONCE and the changes are immediately reflected throughout your store. Wow!

Rather than re-invent the wheel with each store, browse the web for a theme close to what you want, then have a web professional modify that theme to make it uniquely yours. There are many sources for themes, and more are uploaded each day.

One plain theme named the "Default theme" is pre-installed in OpenCart for you to get you started.

If you like the plain, clean look of Default theme, you can simply have that modified.

You can also have a custom theme designed for you completely from scratch, but the designer will still likely choose a similar theme to what you want and then modify it. You can also have an existing design made into an OpenCart theme for you by a theme designer.

If you already have an existing Ecommerce store and you like the look of your current store, it can likely be made into an OpenCart theme by a theme designer.

Similarities among themes

If you open a theme file and take a look, you will find that all themes have the following elements:

- HEADER: or the top of the page that contains your logo and some type of navigation. There may also be a Search box, and other text information such as your store phone number.
- BODY: that contains the main part of the text and photos, and optionally a left and/or right column.
- FOOTER: or the bottom of the page with utility information such as copyrights, additional navigation, often a site map or search to help customers find things in your store.
- BUTTONS: graphical or style elements that visitors click when they want to do something.
- STYLE SHEET: or a specially coded page that specifies the exact look and feel of every element on the site.

Differences between themes

While all themes contain very similar elements, it is possible to make small changes and have a dramatically different look. ANY of these items can be easily changed by a theme designer, regardless of what theme you use. Here are the five main differences in themes.

- NUMBER OF COLUMNS: One, two, or three columns. The left and right columns normally hold the InfoBoxes, with the middle column the body of the page with the products or page content.
- INFOBOXES: Position of InfoBoxes, whether they are used or hidden, all in left or right column. It is possible to use NO InfoBoxes at all, if all functions are moved to the header and footer.
- COLORS: Background color and font color.
- BACKGROUND IMAGE: An image can be made to repeat (or "tile" like floor tiles) so it fills up the entire background of the page. Select a different background image for a very different look.
- FONTS AND FONT SIZE: The type used such as Arial, Helvetica, Times New Roman.

Notice that a "home page photo" is not included in the above list! A dramatic photograph on the home page, often called "Eye Candy" is often the most significant design element in a theme that you think you like, but it is technically not part of the theme itself, it is part of the Home Page Banner Slideshow. Make yourself look past the dramatic home page photos that you may not be able to use. Concentrate on the theme design itself.

TIP: Find dramatic photos that are inexpensive and licensed for website use at http://istockphoto.com.

How to get a good OpenCart theme

Themes can sometimes be missing a piece if the program is updated or if you use a custom module. A reputable theme company will help you with this kind of issue after the sale.

- If you are using a designer to modify the theme, write a list of themes you like and ask them to recommend which one is best for you.
- Ask your questions BEFORE buying! Don't assume that anything except the theme is included after you pay.

- Get your theme from a reputable company that will give you good support for your purchase after the sale.
- Talk to the company on the phone and/or via Live Chat if it is offered. Is Live Chat always offline during business hours? Buyer beware!
- Many template websites are individual resellers who sell on commission, so you may see the same themes offered at more than one site. It's better to buy from the original source if you can.
- To see if a theme is being sold by many resellers, write down the exact name of the theme such as "ThemeOC123" and Google it.
- Some theme sites do not include any technical support or training after the sale; they expect you to be an experienced programmer or designer.
- Some theme sites include written support materials and/or videos for you to read, but no support for your specific questions.
- Find out what kind of support is included, and be sure that is adequate for you.

BONUS: How to install your own theme for super-users

If you're the kind of person who likes playing with this kind of stuff, and your store is not live yet, feel free to try this out. Generally, if you installed your own store and enjoyed it, you can install a theme with confidence.

If you don't like technical stuff, and you are paying someone to install your theme for you, this section can give you an idea of what your theme installer will do for you.

Theme Installation Action Summary:	Method or Admin Menu:
Theme Step 1. Purchase or download the free theme file, and unzip the theme.	Use WinZip or Windows
Theme Step 2. Upload the new files to your website's theme directory	Use your web host's cPanel's File Manager.
Theme Step 3. Select the new theme in your store Admin.	In the Admin SYSTEM - Settings - Store - select theme name.

Theme Step 1. Purchase or download the free theme file, and unzip the theme.

- Select a theme that is specifically made for your version of OpenCart, purchase it, and save to your desktop or another place you can remember.
- Unzip the theme. If using Windows, open Windows Explorer and double-click the zip file name to unzip.

Theme Step 2. Upload the new theme to your website's theme folder.

Open your web host's control panel or cPanel following their login instructions, find the FILE MANAGER icon and double-click it to open:

In cPanel's File Manager, navigate to your store's /catalog/view/theme folder. You can either click the + signs in the left column, OR type the folder name in the box circled below, OR type the folder name "theme" in the search box (you may get too many results with search).

In this example below, the exact folder name is /public_html/catalog/view/theme/, and I can see the "default" theme folder in the body of the page. Now that I know I am in the theme folder, I can click the UPLOAD icon (above the circle) and upload my theme named "LILAC" so the two themes now look like this:

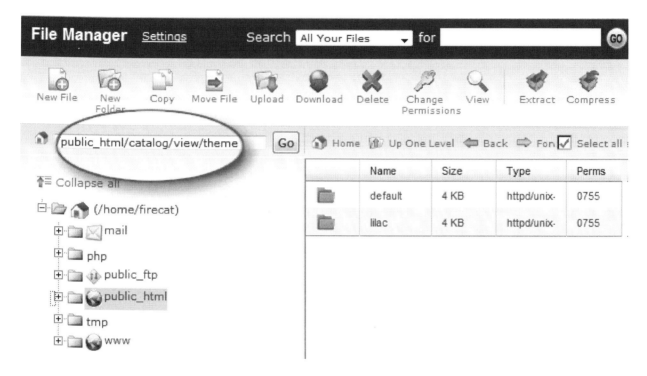

Theme Step 3. SELECT the new theme in your store's Admin.

In a new browser window, log onto your store's Admin.

From your Admin's Top Bar Navigation Menu, select SYSTEM - Settings - Store. If you uploaded the theme to the correct folder, you will now suddenly see the photo and the name of your new theme in the drop-down list. In this example, the new theme is named LILAC:

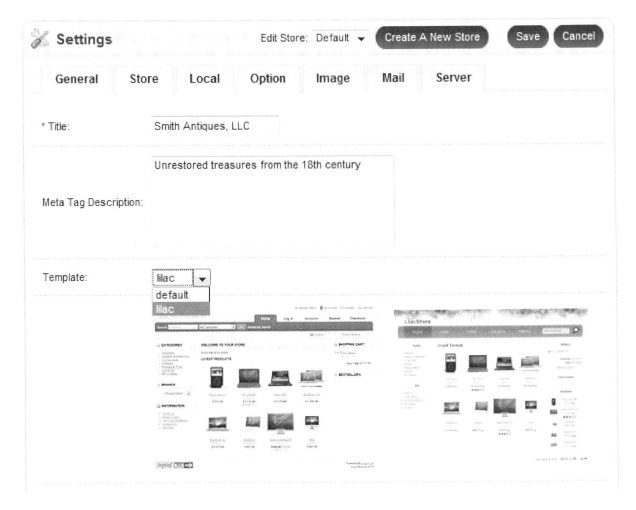

After you select the new theme name, in the top right click the SAVE Button.

Finally, look at your new theme in a new browser window by navigating to your store at http://www.mystorename.com. Woo hoo!

BONUS: 10 theme customizations for super-users

For super-users who find technical stuff FUN, modify your own store by doing the following:

Fonts can look different on all computers! Choose web-safe fonts that will look good on all computers here: http://www.ampsoft.net/webdesign-l/WindowsMacFonts.html

Colors can look different on different computers, too! Choose pleasing web-safe color palettes here: http://www.colourlovers.com/

ALWAYS REMEMBER TO MAKE A BACKUP FIRST. NEVER, EVER WRITE OVER THE ORIGINAL file!

1. HEADER: Change the logo to your company logo by uploading in Admin SYSTEM - Settings - Image and select your new logo.
2. HEADER: Change the top bar from blue to another color by editing these images in public_html/catalog/view/theme/themename/image: header_1_left.png, header_1_center.png, header_1_right.png.
3. BODY: Change background color from white to another color in public_html/catalog/view/theme/themename/stylesheet/stylesheet.css: find #content .middle { background: #FFFFFF;
4. BODY: Add background image in public_html/catalog/view/theme/themename/stylesheet/stylesheet.css: find body { and add "background: url('../themename/imagename.jpg') repeat-x;"
5. FOOTER: Remove the credit card images from footer by deleting the code on line 2 <div class="div1"></div>

6. FOOTER: Remove "Powered by OpenCart" by deleting the words from this page: public_html/language/english/common/home.php. Note, it is common courtesy to give a donation to the OpenCart project if you remove this link.
7. BUTTONS: Change the top bar from blue to another color by editing these images in /view/theme/default/image: button_left.png, button_right.png and button_right.gif AND change this button background style in public_html/catalog/view/theme/themename/stylesheet/stylesheet.css: find .buttons { background: #F8F8F8;
8. STYLE SHEET: change font size in public_html/catalog/view/theme/themename/stylesheet/stylesheet.css: find body, td, th, input, textarea, select, a { font-size: 12px;
9. STYLE SHEET: change font style in public_html/catalog/view/theme/themename/stylesheet/stylesheet.css: find { font-family: Arial, Helvetica, sans-serif;
10. STYLE SHEET: change font color in public_html/catalog/view/theme/themename/stylesheet/stylesheet.css: find { font-family: Arial, Helvetica, sans-serif; and add " color:#FF0000; " inserting your own color number.

APPENDIX A
OpenCart Web Hosts,
Themes & Technical Pros

Recommended Web Hosts with FREE OpenCart Installation

Arvixe Web Hosting – RECOMMENDED
http://www.arvixe.com/3326.html

Arvixe is the official OpenCart web host. They've got to be good! They are specifically set up for easy OpenCart hosting. Arvixe web hosting offers everything an OpenCart store needs: 24/7 great tech support, unlimited space, free domain name, free SSL security certificate install, only $6.00 per month for secure ecommerce hosting ($4.00 per month for hosting and $1 per month for a "dedicated IP address" required for your SSL security certificate.

TIP: To also get FREE security certificate installation from Arvixe, FIRST register for an OpenCart hosting account, THEN send an email to ssl@arvixe.com and they will take care of you. Please tell them Kerry Watson sent you!

TMD Hosting – RECOMMENDED
http://www.tmdhosting.com/opencart-hosting.html

TMDHosting has proven to me to be a great and reliable OpenCart Hosting Provider. Extensive experience and thousands of customers, very responsive and personable. Their feature-rich OpenCart hosting package offers you numerous resources, fast and secure servers, high reliability and great **24/7** OpenCart support.

Strike Hawk Hosting - RECOMMENDED
PCI ready eCommerce hosting for Open Source eCommerce software.
http://www.strikehawk.com/Open-Source-eCommerce-Hosting

Our hosting clients enjoy levels of performance and security higher than anyone else in the business. Our years of experience delivering Open Source eCommerce services using OpenCart led us to believe that eCommerce clients needed a few important features that just were not delivered by the average hosting environments. Features that we were told were "too difficult for the customer" or "only needed for military grade security". After years of promoting these security measures we started our own company and made it happen! All StrikeHawk eCommerce hosting solutions include secure email services, Secure File Transfers, Superior Encryption Security and 24 Hour Service Monitoring.

HostingBeast
http://www.hostingbeast.com/opencart-hosting/
They install OpenCart for you for free, AND install any extensions you want. This is unusual in the ecommerce world! Check them out if you are interested in adding on extensions.

Recommended OpenCart Themes

Some themes available for free, contributed by their author on the OpenCart.com website. Most professionally-designed themes from theme companies are sold in limited quantities and then retired, though sometimes the designer will make some changes and resell them as a new theme. Web hosts that cater to OpenCart owners often will sell themes, as will professional theme companies and individual theme designers.

Algozone – RECOMMENDED
http://www.algozone.com/opencart-templates.php

I've known the owner of AlgoZone, Pavel Rojkov, for at least six years. I have used many AlgoZone OpenCart templates. I have always been impressed with the professionalism and support of the entire AlgoZone team.
Enhance your OpenCart store appearance with professional graphics. Unique high quality OpenCart templates with multilingual support will automatically work with any OpenCart language pack. All templates come ready to install with no need for customization, graphic editing or any extra development, or they will install for you. They also do custom designed templates, Flash, content development/proofreading/editing.
Many of my books are sold on Algozone.com.

TemplateMonster.com – RECOMMENDED
http://www.templatemonster.com/opencart-templates.php

TemplateMonster has been in business for over 10 years. I have used their themes and found them to be very good quality. I have found their support to be excellent.

TemplateMonster also resells my books on their website.

Other sources for OpenCart templates
100+ Free templates on OpenCart.com
http://www.opencart.com/index.php?route=extension/extension&path=1&filter_lice

nse=0&sort=e.name&order=ASC
These are often simple templates made by designers while they are learning OpenCart, or as a way for you to get to know their names and their work. The variety can be surprising, though. I have downloaded and tested several of these templates. NO support is included. Best for simple sites.

Free OpenCart Themes + Free Theme Installation
http://www.tmdhosting.com/templates/free-opencart-templates.html
TMD Hosting is a reputable Ecommerce web host, and I have personally hosted with them. This free template installation does not include customization, and you need to locate your own designer to customize it. In addition to free OpenCart installation and free template installation, they also offer free module installations, free upgrades and 24/7 professional assistance.

Free OpenCart Themes + Free Theme Installation and Customization:
http://hostandwin.com/free-opencart-templates.html
According to the company's website, the promotion is valid for customers who sign up for the one or two year annual plans. Free template customization is minimal, and is only for the templates designed by HostAndWin design team. I do not have personal experience with this web hosting company.
The customization includes a background template color change; your own logo; change of text and font color; template layout structure change; theme module position change. HostAndWin design team starts working on the required theme customization only after you confirm all the details through e-mail correspondence with our designers. The above mentioned changes would be performed for free one time only and for one theme only. Additional theme customization is $50 per hour development/ designers work.

Recommended OpenCart "Technical Pro" Freelancers

Hire a freelance technical pro to help you through any difficult tasks rated in this book as three or more clocks. Much like buying products on EBay, on these freelance sites, each vendor gets a quality reputation rating of one to ten "stars." Funds are generally escrowed at the start of any flat-rate project, and released after you have tested the work to your satisfaction. BOTH PARTIES rate each other after completion!

To get the best work from OpenCart freelancers:

Describe the job as fully and clearly as you can. It's like taking your car to a mechanic: if you say "change the battery" they will change the battery and the job is done, even if you didn't need a battery. If you say "it's not starting" then they will keep troubleshooting until they solve the problem; it may be the battery or it may be that you didn't turn the key all the way.
Offer in your project description to answer questions on the Message Board that is

attached to each project. If you don't know the answer, tell them you do not know.

Test communications with anyone you are considering by sending them a message or two clarifying the task.

Carefully read all the reviews of anyone you want to hire. Make sure they say great communications, fast service, and highly skilled programmer, and that they will definitely hire the freelancer again. If any of those elements are missing, there could be something wrong.

Before awarding any project, confirm in writing via the message board that they are ready to start the job and when they will deliver.

HIRE BY REVIEW RATINGS AND EXPERIENCE, NOT BY PRICE.

Avoid new, unrated programmers! They have nothing to lose if they wreck your store or deliver it late. The more ratings a programmer has, the more carefully and fanatically they will guard their reputation.

For best success as an OpenCart services buyer:

Guard your own reputation as a buyer so you get the best ratings. You will get bids from better programmers, the bids will be lower, the delivery will be sooner because you will generate confidence that you know what you are doing.

Write project descriptions as clearly as you can. A numbered checklist is best.

Post more, smaller projects that you can easily manage.

NEVER expand projects beyond their original scope. Instead, post a separate project. This protects you and also helps you get more good reviews for being a good manager.

On the project description, say they are required to check in daily; disappearing programmers is the #1 problem.

Respond to communications as quickly and clearly as you can. Use the official Project Message Board so you have a record of all communications.

Pad deadlines: if you need it on Friday, in the project description say you need it by Wednesday. This gives you enough time to hire a replacement if the project goes bad.

If you don't know an answer, say so and ask for clarification. Feel free to ask the programmer to recommend a best course of action. This can save you money and time.

When you are new, hire speakers of your native language to minimize your own communication errors. As you gain experience you can branch out.

Have a list of passwords, domain names, etc. ready to send (from your web host "Welcome email") when a programmer accepts a project.

In your first contact with a newly-hired programmer, include your time zone, normal hours that you can be reached, and best ways to contact you (email, instant messenger, phone, text etc.). Ask them to do the same.

Escrow funds quickly so the project can get started without delay.

Contact the programmer at least once a day to see if there is anything they need.

If you don't hear from a programmer for 3 days, most sites allow you to file a dispute. That is an eternity in programming days.

When the contractor delivers, go back to the numbered checklist you posted in #1, and check off each item.

Release escrow the minute you check off all items. Get a reputation for fast payment and great reviews. This will make contractors fight to get jobs from you.

oDesk
https://www.odesk.com/contractors/opencart/look/1

1,095 OpenCart contractors listed. Can hire by the hour or fixed price by the project if you can describe the project accurately. oDesk takes 10% of the price you pay, they take screenshots approximately every 10 minutes while the contractor is working so you can see what they are doing.

Elance
https://www.elance.com/r/contractors/q-opencart/cat-10183/

490 OpenCart contractors listed. Can hire by the hour or fixed price by the project if you can describe the project accurately. Elance takes 6.75% to 8.75% of the project price.

Scriptlance
http://www.scriptlance.com/tag/opencart

39 OpenCart contractors listed. A smaller, scrappier site with cutthroat competition between bidders. Typically smaller, faster projects than on the other sites. If you need something done now for a fixed price, this is the place. Accurate list of exactly what you want is more critical on this competitive site. Scriptlance gets a $5.00 posting fee for flat rate projects, flat $40 for an hourly worker. Additional fees such as "Mark as Urgent" $5.00, Private project (only the freelancers you specify can see it) $1.00, Featured Project $19.00.

APPENDIX B:
Security, Database &
Records Management

What would you do if a hurricane hit, a virus or hacker attacked your website, or you suddenly could not get to your store for a few days, or even forever? This chapter should help you plan for the worst, and hopefully prevent it.

About online security

A lot has been written about online security, but when it comes to security breaches most people still think it happens to other people. It can happen to you! Your job as a store owner is to prevent security breaches, and if the worst happens anyway, to minimize the effects.

Online Security Checklist:

Here is a summary of what you must do about the security of your credit card information and website:

1. INSTALL SECURITY UPDATES. Watch for security updates for OpenCart and any other programs you use on your website. Hackers do, and as soon as a vulnerability is known they work around the clock to figure out how to exploit it. Hire a programmer to install your updates for you - they will follow industry practices by first making a backup of the existing site and database. If your site is large and constantly active, they will set up a mirror copy of your website to install the updates on in a controlled manner, then copy it to your live site after they know the update works.

2. REQUIRE GOOD PROGRAMMING PRACTICES. Your store program is written so that updating is as easy as possible. Poor programming practices by your installer or programmer can make upgrades a costly burden. In any contract with a programmer, require them to adhere to industry best practices, make backups before starting, and specify whether or not they should set up a mirror site.

3. NEVER RETAIN ANY CUSTOMER CREDIT CARD INFORMATION. Make sure that any payment method you use in your store does not store any credit card information. This means do not store the information for manual processing later. See the next item for better solutions.

4. USE SSL IN YOUR STORE EVEN THOUGH YOU DO NOT RETAIN CUSTOMER CREDIT CARD INFORMATION. SSL means your Admin and checkout pages are encrypted, making it more difficult for hackers to mess with your store.

4. USE THIRD-PARTY PAYMENT TRANSACTION PROCESSING. This means payment methods like PayPal IPN and 2CheckOut.com where the customer temporarily leaves your website to pay, types ALL credit card information on the other site, then returns to your site after the transaction is complete. Be careful which of their accounts you select - most third-party vendors offer a dizzying array of accounts where the customer might be required to type their credit card information on YOUR website.

5. LEARN AS MUCH AS YOU CAN ABOUT PCI SECURITY REQUIREMENTS. Even if you strictly follow all of the above items, you still might not meet all PCI security requirements. For example, if you take an order over the phone, jot down the customer's credit card information, and save the note. Currently you are required to burn, shred, or pulp that note, and can face stiff fines if you do not.

About Records Management

Unless you have led a charmed life, you have probably had to deal with a computer crash or virus and loss of some data at least once. If so, you are probably aware of how difficult it can be to reconstruct your records.

Operating your store on the Internet adds *another level of vulnerability.* Not only could your own computer go out, but a connection along the way - your ISP, your telephone company, your web host - could go out, leaving you stranded and unable to operate your store. This is in addition to the possibility that your database simply becomes corrupt, for whatever reason.

This is not intended to scare you, but you must be aware of the risks in order to guard against them. If you have a regular records and database management program in place, you can rest easy.

Creating a Disaster Policy

How do you create a "disaster policy" unique for your store - a policy to cover most disaster scenarios? You stage your own disaster, and see what you need to be able to respond to it properly.

NOTE: This is not intended to be an all-inclusive list of disasters. You must gauge your own situation and your own risk.

Pretend that each of these disasters has happened to you. How could you prevent it? How can you respond?

Possible disaster scenarios:*

1. Your computer crashes, never to work again. You will spend a month reconstructing it.
2. Your computer works, but the hard disk has failed. It may be recoverable.
3. The electricity goes out for a minute. a day. 4 days. It's Hurricane _____ (fill in the name of the latest hurricane, tornado, or other disaster).
4. You forget to pay your dial-up or broadband ISP carrier, and they temporarily turn off your service. Whoops!
5. Your OpenCart installer or programmer (or you) has a bad day, fails to make a backup copy before making just one little edit to the site, and now all you can see is PARSE ERROR on your website-nothing more.
6. Your OpenCart web host has a server die, and they were not following their own backup policy. Their most recent copy, however, is several weeks old. You have lost a week's worth of orders.
7. Your OpenCart web host, who was always so nice and charming before, goes insane, makes a personal vendetta against you, and threatens to turn off your website.
8. Your OpenCart web host had to fire an employee who left with passwords. The ex-employee messes with your store and several others, corrupting your database.
9. Your OpenCart web host uses the same password naming scheme for all websites, and doesn't tell you how to change it. A client or employee with a grudge gets in and messes up your store.
10. Your OpenCart web host goes out of business, simply disappearing without a trace. No word; they simply are gone. Vanished!

*Believe it or not, I've had most or all of these things happen to me - hence the saying at the beginning of this chapter. I have scars. Thankfully I have almost always followed my own disaster policy, so the hassle has been kept to a minimum.

Disaster Prevention Checklist:

Make regular backups of your personal computer AND your web host site. This can be totally automated for you with weekly full backups and daily backups of files that were changed. The backups should go on a SEPARATE read-only hard disk or other storage unit, not on the same one you use every day.

Get an Uninterruptible Power Supply (UPS) and have it set up properly and tested for you. This gives you approximately 3-5 minutes to shut down your computer in an orderly manner in case of a power outage, so you can save all your work.

Put your dialup or broadband ISP carrier on an automatic payment so you can't forget to pay them.

If you work on your own site, get in the habit of always making a duplicate and working on the duplicate file. If you use an installer or programmer, make sure you trust them. At the VERY first sign of sloppiness - like forgetting to make a backup before they work, look for a backup person who will not make that kind of mistake. Don't wait for two signs of sloppiness.

Do your homework, make sure you have a reliable OpenCart web host. They should have a stated "up-time" policy of 99% or more, and LIVE BY IT. If they have an outage, they should report it to you; you should NEVER discover it by yourself. If they make a mistake, they should admit it. If they blame you, it's time to move on.

Use careful password management. Use unhackable random passwords and change them frequently.

Follow your own disaster policy! This is the most important step!

Daily Backups

Print a copy of EACH order as it comes in OR save them to a USB thumb drive. This is the basis of your disaster plan; in case of a fire, flood, or other local emergency, grab your order binder or thumb drive, and run.

An alternative is copying and pasting your orders into a backup directory of your computer, stored on an external USB backup drive. Grab the USB drive, hug it to your body and run!

To print a copy of each orders, from your store Admin's top nav bar, select SALES - Orders. In the DATE ADDED column enter today's date and click the FILTER Button.

In the far right column of each new order, click the EDIT Link to see the order, then from your browser's top nav bar select FILE - PRINT.

Keep the daily orders in a 3 ring binder, and keep the binder in a safe place. A fireproof vault off-site would be even better. You should get in the habit of moving the older records - say 8 week old orders that you know have been shipped, received, and not returned - to permanent storage off-site.

Your personal computer should be backed up daily with an "incremental" backup. This means only the files that have been changed are backed up. There are many back-up programs out there, even free ones, that can totally automate this process for you. Try MOZY.com or Carbonite.com for easy backup over the web.

NOTE this does not backup your website directly; it backs up anything you copy to your computer from your website. So you must first copy your website files and database to your personal computer.

DOUBLE-CHECK regularly to make sure your daily backups are actually happening! You may think that they are scheduled and occurring, but a power outage, expired credit card or other event could cause it to change. Make sure you SEE your backups with your own eyes.

Weekly backups

You need a full digital backup of the database, AND your personal computer each week. You will need to do this in two steps:

Step 1. Copy the database to your personal computer using your Admin's SYSTEM - Backup/Restore. Click SELECT All, then in the top right click the BACKUP Button.

Step 2. Now BACKUP your whole personal computer, which gives you a total of three copies of your database: the live one, the one on your pc, and the one on your backup drive.

It is extremely easy to make backups, and takes only a minute or two.

Your techie or web host should set up a regular "CHRON JOB" that backs up your WEBSITE FILES in addition to your database. Contact them for help.

Regular Testing of Disaster Systems

Once you get these systems working, it is critical that you periodically test them. These tests should be performed at least monthly, AFTER your site is stable. If you have any sign that it is not, and during the implementation phase when you are starting these disaster prevention steps, these tests should be performed even more frequently.

Disaster Testing Checklist:

1. Is your Uninterruptible Power Supply working? Do you see the power light on?
2. Do your automatic daily and weekly backups exist? Do you actually see the files written to your external backup drive?
3. Does your ISP have the new expiration date on your credit card?
4. Are you satisfied with the reliability of your web host? Have they given you any signs that you should be concerned?
5. Have you followed your password policy and kept unhackable random passwords in a safe place?
6. Have you and your programmer followed your own backup policy and always worked on a copy of a file?
7. Have you run through the Possible Disaster Scenarios and developed your own?

INDEX

FREE EBOOK OFFER

Like the paperback?
Get your free ebook!

Get this ebook for FREE when you buy the same paperback from Amazon.com:

Just purchase the paperback from AMAZON.COM and post about it: Write an Amazon review, LIKE "OSC Manuals" on Facebook, Tweet about it, DIGG us, etc. You'll receive a coupon for one free download of this book! If you paid for the ebook, we will refund your purchase price.

The rules: One free ebook of the same title for each retail paperback purchase. We verify your purchase and your "Tell the World" link before we can give you a free ebook. Your refund is limited to the amount you actually paid. Discount or free ebooks good on OSCmanuals.com website only. Send requests with copy of Amazon receipt and your Tell the World link to FREE@oscmanuals.com.

2267630R00186

Printed in Great Britain
by Amazon.co.uk, Ltd.,
Marston Gate.